Legal Queeries

Legal Queeries

Lesbian, Gay and Transgender Legal Studies

Edited by Leslie J. Moran, Daniel Monk and Sarah Beresford

CASSELL

London and New York

Cassell
Wellington House
125 Strand
London WC2R 0BB

370 Lexington Avenue
New York
NY 10017-6550

First published 1998

British Library Cataloguing-in-Publication Data
A catalogue record for this book is available from the British Library.
ISBN 0-304-33863-X (hardback)
0-304-33864-8 (paperback)

Library of Congress Cataloging-in-Publication Data
Legal queeries: lesbian, gay, and transgender legal studies/edited by Leslie J. Moran, Daniel Monk, and Sarah Beresford.
p. cm.
Includes bibliographical references and index.
ISBN 0-304-33863-X (hardback). – ISBN 0-304-33864-8 (pbk.)
1. Gays—Legal status, laws, etc. I. Moran, Leslie J., 1955–
II. Monk, Daniel. III. Beresford, Sarah.
K3242.3.Z9L448 1998
346.01'3–dc21 97-52265
CIP

Typeset by York House Typographic Ltd, London
Printed and bound in Great Britain by CPD, Ebbw Vale, Wales

Contents

Notes on Contributors

LARRY CATA BACKER is currently Professor of Law and Co-Director, Comparative and International Law Center, University of Tulsa College of Law, Tulsa, Oklahoma, USA. While studying for his JD at Columbia University Law School he was an editor of the *Columbia Law Review*. His research is in the areas of sociological jurisprudence, queer theory and studies, comparative and European Union law. He has published widely in the United States.

SARAH BERESFORD has been lecturing in law at the University of Lancaster for five years. She teaches lesbian and gay legal studies, family law, gender and law and employment law and has published on lesbianism and law. Her current research on law focuses upon sexuality, gender and the construction of identity within the family.

BRIAN DEMPSEY has been active in gay politics and is currently studying for an LLB at the University of Edinburgh.

CRAIG LIND is a lecturer in law at Sussex University. His main areas of teaching are constitutional law, family law and child law. His research and publications are primarily in the area of children, the family, sexuality and the law.

ELENA LOIZIDOU studied law and politics at the University of Keele and then at Lancaster University. Her master's dissertation was about the psychoanalysis of common law. She gained her PhD on the legal regulation of insanity in nineteenth-century England. She teaches in public law, criminal law and jurisprudence. Her current research interests are in psychoanalysis and law and film and law.

RONALD LOUW has an LLM from the University of Cape Town, was the founding convenor of the KwaZulu–Natal Coalition for Gay and Lesbian

Equality, and is a member of the executive committee of the National Coalition for Gay and Lesbian Equality.

DANIEL MONK is a lecturer in law at Keele University. He has published a number of articles on sex education; his current research is in the areas of child law and education law and is concerned with the relationship between law and the constructions of childhood.

LESLIE J. MORAN is reader in law at Birkbeck College, University of London. He has published extensively on male sexuality and law. In 1996 his major monograph *The Homosexual(ity) of Law* was published by Routledge. He has edited special editions of journals dealing with 'HIV/AIDS and the law' (*Liverpool Law Review*, 1990) and 'Legal Perversions' (*Social and Legal Studies*, 1997). His current legal research, funded by the ESRC, is concerned with safety and homophobic violence. He is also doing research on law, sexuality and popular culture.

DR MARTIN MOERINGS is a lecturer at the W. Pompe Institute for criminal law and criminology at the University of Utrecht, where he also lectures on homosexuality and the law. He also stands in as a member of the Equal Treatment Commission, which is charged with monitoring compliance with the General Equal Treatment Act.

JUDITH RAUHOFER studied law at Augsburg University (Germany) from 1987 to 1992, undertook the First State exam (academic stage) in January 1992 and the Vocational training (Referendariat) from 1992 to 1993 and 1996. She taught German Law at the University of Liverpool from 1993 to 1995. She is currently working as a research assistant for a German law journal while completing her LLM thesis on gay marriage in English and German Law.

ANDREW SHARPE teaches law at Macquarie University, Sydney, Australia. He has published articles on the subject of transsexuality and the law.

STEPHEN WHITTLE is a senior lecturer in law at Manchester Metropolitan University. He is co-author of *Transvestism, Transsexualism and the Law* (Beaumont Trust, 1996), editor of *The Margins of the City: Gay*

Men's Urban Lives (Arena, 1994), and is currently editing *Reclaiming Gender: Trans-theory for a New Millennium* (forthcoming, Cassell). He is also Vice-President of Press for Change, the UK's campaign and lobby group for transgender civil rights.

PETRA WILSON is a lecturer at Nottingham University specializing in medicine and the law. She is currently working with the European Commission on matters relating to health in the European Union.

Introduction

Leslie J. Moran, Daniel Monk and Sarah Beresford

Legal Queeries brings together for the first time a diverse collection of legal scholars whose work explores the richness and complexity of the interface between perversity and legal regulation.

The essays in *Legal Queeries* are all connected by the theme of the 'outsider'. First, all are concerned with the challenge of the representation of lesbians, gay men and transgender persons as 'outsiders' within legal cultures. Second, the theme of 'outsiders' is represented in the range of essays that explore the experience of lesbians, gay men and transgender persons in other legal cultures. This comparative theme opens the Anglo-American tradition of much lesbian, gay and transgender scholarship to new perspectives and new horizons, draws attention to the idiosyncrasies of legal cultures, the capacity for difference within closely connected legal cultures and the potential for similarity across widely differing legal cultures. Third, the essays utilize and exploit the position of 'outsider' in order to explore law as a site of cultural production of legal subjects and legal objects. In this way they refuse the law/politics and law/culture distinctions that impoverish our understanding of law as an important social practice. *Legal Queeries* sets out to explore the law as a practice that is deeply embedded in culture. These essays explore the impact of wider culture upon legal rules and decisions and also look at the way law is an important site of cultural production within society. Finally, the theme of 'outsider' is also reflected in the fact that the collection goes beyond the confines of a tradition that focuses upon the decriminalization reform agenda. This collection explores the rich diversity of issues that must be considered if the law is to be taken seriously as a social practice through which the lives of lesbians, gay men and transgender persons are to be represented in society. It also departs from the traditional reformist agenda in its willingness to address matters that continue to be taboo, such as transgender issues and childhood sexuality, and problematizes progressive calls for increased engagement with law.

The opening chapter, by Leslie Moran, engages with law in a way quite distinct from the other contributions, in that it does not focus on official legal texts. At the same time, however, it exemplifies what a *legal queery* actually is and consequently demonstrates the types of original insights into law that can be achieved by such an approach. The chapter takes as its starting point 'Oscar Wilde': a name imbued with an array of cultural understandings, and misunderstandings, of law and homosexuality. Moran demonstrates how the facts and fictions, both historical and literary, surrounding Oscar Wilde's trials translate into a common 'general knowledge' of the law and in particular the legitimacy of the law's criminalization of genital relations between men. Exploring this 'knowledge' serves to identify how the experience of law as culture, both 'high' and 'low', informs and invests the formal and institutional practices of law. Of particular significance are the stories of law revealed through the study of the texts that have purported to record the story of 'Oscar Wilde'. These stories of law, which focus on the offence and act of gross indecency, the criminalization of homosexuality as an identity, and a story of law/desire/death, all have a powerful resonance with both current theoretical debates and individual and community experiences. In this way the stories, though not unproblematic in certain respects, are important in that they provide a cultural memory and, significantly, a counter memory of law to the official representation of law as impartial rule and reason. The chapter provides an important queer contribution to the increasing body of work concerned with law and literature and cultural studies and significantly widens the horizons and possibilities of legal historianship.

Andrew Sharpe and Stephen Whittle both address legal issues concerning transgendered persons. This represents a shift in focus from an engagement with an outsider of the past to explore sexual narratives and identities very much of the present, and the object recently of much judicial attention, but which are nevertheless frequently located outside of queer legal studies. While both their chapters make use of judicial decisions, they depart from traditional legal scholarship by entering the very text of law to reveal its often confused conceptualizations and understandings of transgendered people. In focusing on transgendered homosexuals and transgendered parents, respectively, they also depart from much existing work in this area, which has concentrated almost solely on the issue of legal recognition of the change of gender status. In this way both chapters challenge the boundaries of the law by interrogating both the text and practice of law from the perspective of the experiences of transgendered people's lives.

Sharpe explores, through a close analysis of recent Australian case law, how legal discourse denies the possibility of homosexuality in the construction of the transsexual as a legal object; a narrative which is far from rare amongst transgendered people. In doing so, Sharpe demonstrates how law is able to reach this conclusion through complex, and often contradictory, uses of the knowledges of cultural, medical and 'psy' discourses. Through an exploration of the complex constructions in legal reasoning of sexual desires and sexual identities, he demonstrates how the law in its attempt to preserve heterosexual hegemony actually reproduces and intensifies sexual ambiguities and consequently represents a queer site for the disruption and radical rearticulation of sexualities in general. This analysis is particularly significant in that it problematizes the 'progressive' and 'assimilationist' reform agenda, not by overlooking the potential gains but by highlighting the exclusionary effect on 'unthinkable' (trans)sexualities. In this way the contribution represents a timely, and highly sophisticated, reindorsement of a radical politics which demands the destabilizing of the hetero/homo sexual divide.

Whittle also explores an 'unthinkable' legal subject, that of the transsexual person as a parent, but he adopts a human rights approach, in contrast to Sharpe's post-structural analysis. Moving beyond the issue of the legal recogntion of transsexuals' change of gender status, Whittle questions, and indeed presents a powerful critique of, the requirement in many jurisdictions that transsexuals be sterile before being recognized in law in their new gender status. This is a requirement that is considered by many medical-legal 'experts' to be unproblematic, yet Whittle demonstrates how as an issue of reproduction rights it is intimately connected to eugenics discourses, popularly perceived as historically dormant, to the extent that the trans person is constructed as lacking an essentialist aspect of human-ness. In probing the statutes and judicial opinions in this area, Whittle highlights, like Sharpe, a prevailing ambiguity in the law's conceptualization of (trans)sexuality. It also reveals the contradictory stances governing notions of family rights and in this way makes an important contribution to current attempts to understand the 'moral panics' which dominate discussions of children alongside issues of sexuality. While Whittle utilizes the language of human rights, his approach is distinctive and more critical in that, informed by the experiences of the transgender community, it simultaneously demands a radical rethinking of the uses, and abuses, of gender and sex within legal praxis.

Sarah Beresford explores the production of lesbian identity in the law in the context of disputes that relate to the family. The lesbian mother, as a 'problematic' legal subject, has similarities with the transgendered parent, in that they both provide an opportunity to scrutinize the legal construction of legitimate and responsible parenthood. This is currently extremely pertinent because of the increasingly high profile given to 'parenting rights' in lesbian and gay campaigns, but it also has a wider significance as cultural understandings of responsible parenthood represent a contested site underlying numerous public policy debates. Beresford takes the issue of lesbian mothers beyond the claim for a right to parenthood, or custody and her detailed analysis of case law and the realities of law in practice serves to reveal a divergence, or 'gap', between the constructions, expressions and representations of women's self-identity and those that are imposed upon them by law. Beresford demonstrates how attempts to self-define are undermined and resisted and she argues that lesbian mothers are forced to inhabit a 'legal body' over which they have little control. Exploring deep into the text of law in this way is significant in that it reveals the complexities women encounter in engaging with the law in their struggle to have their lives represented within the law.

Ambivalence about engaging with law is a central theme of Judith Rauhofer's examination of the debates surrounding the possibility of a registered partnership law in Germany. The starting point for her analysis is the constitutional protection found in the German law of marriage as a (heterosexual) institution; a history and practice that demonstrates how the institution of marriage has a distinct political significance within a different cultural setting. As demands for a Bill of Rights increase in the UK, this discussion of German law, with its constitutional rights and court, provides an important reminder of how rights can serve to exclude as well as protect gays and lesbians. Cultural contrast is also evident from Rauhofer's discussion of the 'gay marriage' debates and in particular the distinct nature of the political struggles and strategies within the gay and lesbian movement(s) in Germany. Rauhofer's analysis of proposals that seek to transfer the privileges associated with the recognition of cross-sex marriage to same-sex marriage is informed by lesbian critiques of the institution of marriage. It goes beyond the assimilation versus transgression debate and instead, from a feminist perspective, raises significant concerns about the underlying structural inequalities within society which crucially challenge the notion that legal recognition of gay and lesbian partnerships is a politically 'neutral' and unproblematic demand for equality.

It is noticeable that for many people, and in a number of jurisdictions, gay and lesbian 'partnership', whether recognized by law or not, is perceived as being more acceptable and legitimate than gay, lesbian or transgender parenthood. At the heart of this antipathy towards communication, in its broadest sense, between children and queer adults are social constructions of childhood and homosexuality and, in particular, complex cultural concerns and fears of child sexuality. This is the starting point for Craig Lind's analysis of childhood and sexuality. Using work that has explored the history of sexuality and the history of the idea of childhood as innocence, Lind explores the constitution of child sexuality in the law. He demonstrates how ideas of child sexuality in the law are used, not so much to define and regulate the child, but to define and regulate adult sexuality. Consequently the child as a legal subject reflects cultural aspirations and fears regarding adult sexuality, which in part explains the 'impossibility', in law, of child queer sexualities and why the legal regulation of childhood sexuality promotes heterosexuality with such passion. Lind's analysis is particularly useful in that it reveals the strategic uses of essentialist and social constructionist understandings of sexuality, challenges the notion that childhood innocence protects children and consequently calls for a radical reassessment of legal policy.

Continuing with the theme of childhood, in the next chapter Daniel Monk focuses on the regulation of child sexuality in the specific location of school sex education. Monk seeks to readdress the law of sex education. In the recent past, analysis of this domain of law has been dominated by the decision of the British Parliament to prohibit the promotion of homosexuality in Section 28 of the Local Government Act 1988. Monk draws attention to the way this explicit and repressive method of regulation has been superseded by the use of a range of complex and subtle positive exercises of power. This approach consequently demonstrates how enhanced parental influence, the use of health professionals and curriculum categorization serve to both marginalize and to reinforce negative images of homosexuality within schools and to foreclose the possibility of radical sex education. In assessing the consequences of the new methods of control for future strategies of resistance Monk calls for the development of alternatives to strategic essentialism, despite the pragmatic advantages implicit within that approach, and argues that sex education be understood not simply as a location for the transmission of information about sexual activity but as a significant site for the production of knowledge about sexuality.

The next chapter, by Petra Wilson, also focuses on the operation of law in a particular location, but from a rather different perspective. Wilson examines the provision of legal services to those who are HIV-positive and places her analysis within the context of broader studies of access to law and unmet legal need. Issues concerning HIV/AIDS are often excluded from queer legal and political studies despite the enormous impact that HIV/AIDS continues to have on sexual politics. Those who are HIV-positive are in certain ways excluded from the mainstream gay and lesbian community and, as this study demonstrates, often have limited access to law, which consequently reinforces their status as 'outsiders'. Wilson focuses upon the early stages of the establishment of an HIV advice organization and examines the extent to which service providers are key actors in the first transformative stage of dispute resolution. She has utilized empirical work in order to explore the institutional problems of providing these services to 'outsiders'. In exploring some of the difficulties experienced by the people who use legal services, she, controversially, suggests that some of these difficulties are generated by the politics and practice of self-help organizations themselves.

The following three chapters explore experiences in legal systems and jurisdictions outside England and North America. These jurisdictions are often overlooked, but the comparative perspectives that they offer not only serve to broaden our understandings of law but, significantly, also enrich our appreciation of domestic legal cultures.

Martin Moerings examines the recent changes in criminal and civil law in the Netherlands that seek to render discrimination based upon a person's sexual orientation illegal. These new laws reaffirm the place of the Netherlands at the forefront of law reform and in a unique situation in Europe. Moerings undertakes a critical analysis of those developments, considers the value of anti-discrimination strategies for a lesbian gay and transgender law reform agenda and places the developments within the context of Dutch society. Significantly he identifies a disparity between the well intentioned laws and the actual practical usage made of them and he suggests that political compromise in their enactment is one of the causes of this discrepancy. At a moment when law reform is high on the agenda of gay and lesbian movements in many jurisdictions, this analysis provides a timely reminder of the limits of law in tackling social discrimination.

In contrast to the Netherlands, a country with a history of progressive law, in South Africa gay and lesbian sexualities have moved from being outlawed to being constitutionally protected within a very short space of time. Ronald Louw considers the formative role of law in gay and lesbian politics and identity within the context of political change in South Africa. He focuses specifically on the inclusion of sexual orientation as a ground of non-discrimination in the country's first democratic constitution and how gays and lesbians, who have been discriminated against, have been brought within the ambit of constitutional protection. The circumstances giving rise to the inclusion are outlined and placed within the broader context of the political struggle for liberation from apartheid. Louw traces the consequent formation in South Africa of the National Coalition for Gay and Lesbian Equality and discusses the particular challenges that the National Coalition faces in giving content to the constitutional protection. He also considers the issues involved in organizing within the African gay and lesbian community and particularly the argument that homosexuality is un-African. While not ignoring the various tensions involved in engaging with law, Louw is optimistic and argues that law has played a liberatory and formative role in sexual politics in South Africa since 1994.

Brian Dempsey's point of departure is as an outsider not only by virtue of sexuality but, being Scottish, by virtue of nationhood and national identity. Just as the existence of Scots law is often ignored by those trained in the English legal system, the Scottish fight for law reform is often overlooked or misrepresented by English activists and writers. Dempsey seeks to redress this position and reviews the unique experience of Scottish lesbian and gay law reform work. He traces the history of Scottish law reform initiatives and considers the work currently being carried out by groups and individuals. In looking towards the future, he discusses the possibilities offered by any constitutional changes with regard to the incorporation of A Claim of Rights for sexual minorities in a future devolved Scottish Parliament and raises the prospect of Scottish law leading the way towards openness and visibility within the United Kingdom.

From Scotland we move to New Zealand and from the overtly political to a psychoanalytic engagement with law. Elena Loizidou takes as her starting point the New Zealand film *Heavenly Creatures*, which recounts the 'true' story of a friendship between two girls and their murder of one of their mothers – a story of intimacy, criminal law and, finally, enforced separation. Loizidou uses this tale to read how the criminal justice system arrives at its decisions and locates her analysis within an emerging intertextual legal studies movement. Central to this approach is a belief that opening up the textuality of criminal law to its surroundings enables us to see that criminal law is not only not an autonomous text but also that the criminal law's denial of interdependence actually leads to various miscarriages of justice. Loizidou expands on this approach by using the cinematic text to demonstrate the processes that criminal law uses to define the bodies that come to it. Particularly illuminating is the way in which Loizidou draws on psychoanalytic and post-structural queer theorists to reveal the law's limits and exclusionary effects.

Queer theory is scrutinized again in the final chapter by Larry Cata Backer. In a bold and intricate essay, Backer challenges what he describes as a messianic temptation of revolutionary transformation within strains of queer theory. At the heart of his analysis is his belief that any theory of perfectionism ultimately carries with it a foundation for subordination. In connection with queer theory, his concern is with what he identifies as a revolutionspeak that mimics the dominating force it wishes to replace with something else. He argues that this is demonstrated through an essentializing of the dominant discourse of heterosexualism. In place of this, Backer offers a dynamic and anti-utopian theory of subversive calumny: a critical realism for modern times imbued with a capacity for irony and indeterminacy, in which modulation and revaluation replace the myth of revolution and cultural repose.

The essays in this collection vividly demonstrate the multifarious nature of law and its relationship with lesbians and gays and transgendered people. The law's ability to provoke both outrage and celebration across a wide range of jurisdictions testifies to its continual significance not only as a source of discrimination as well as protection, but also as a compelling site of cultural production. That it is, rightly or wrongly, imbued with a form of power can too easily result in experiences of law, both individual and collective, being characterized in a unitary way. The essays in this collection together present a timely and in-depth analysis of the complex nature of law. In this way *Legal Queeries* gives law reform a new form. It refuses to confine law reform activism to the democratic institutions or the streets. It takes reform activism into new places. Being a critical exploration of the minutiae of law and legal regulation as cultural production, this collection takes law reform activism into the very text of the law itself.

1

'Oscar Wilde': Law, Memory and the Proper Name

Leslie J. Moran

> I need say very little about the trials themselves; they are so well known as to be matters of general knowledge. (Plowman J in Warwick, 1967)

Mr Justice Plowman in this quotation refers to three criminal trials involving Oscar Wilde. The first was a criminal action initiated by Wilde against the Marquess of Queensbury for criminal libel. The second and third trials were criminal actions brought by the State against Wilde for the offence of gross indecency with other men. Mr Justice Plowman's observation draws our attention to the cultural significance of these trials. As 'general knowledge', these events have a very particular place within English culture and perhaps more generally, in Western Anglophone cultures. They are not known merely by a particular section of people within a community but are a common 'knowledge', widely disseminated and deeply embedded in a culture. More specifically it is a 'common knowledge' of the law, in particular law that criminalizes genital relations between men. It is on this particular 'general knowledge' that I want to focus.

As a study of the generation of a 'general knowledge' law, this chapter falls outside the traditional parameters of legal studies, which analyse codes of written law, interpret and critique the decisions of superior judges or investigate the routines of those officials who generate the day-to-day operation of the formal sources of law. My concern here is with a study of law as it is produced, disseminated and experienced within the wider culture (Chase, 1986; Redhead, 1995). My focus is on ideas of law produced and disseminated by literary criticism, autobiography and biography, political writing, the popular press and mainstream cinema. An examination of law in these texts is significant in various ways. First, it takes account of the fact that our experiences of the formal and institutional practices of law are produced outside those practices, through the diverse realms of 'high' and 'low' (popular) culture. Second, it seeks to generate information that will enable the exploration of the way in which that experience of law informs and invests the formal and institutional practices of law.

My concern is with the production and dissemination of a 'general knowledge' that speaks of the legitimacy of the law and the virtue of the law's condemnation of genital encounters between men. My analysis is also concerned with the way this 'general knowledge' has been implicated in the emergence of a critique of the criminalization of these relations in demands for reform. The first section of this chapter will consider the way in which the name 'Oscar Wilde' has come to stand as a symbol of law. The analysis will then look at some of the stories of law that have been told by way of the name 'Oscar Wilde'. I will then consider how these stories not only give form to our understanding of the interface between genital relations between men and law but generate a multiplicity of understandings and at the same time inscribe limits to our understandings. Finally, I will draw some conclusions about the interface between the name 'Oscar Wilde' and law.

The name of law: 'Oscar Wilde'

> ... the little things of life are symbols. We receive our bitter lessons most easily through them. [The] seemingly casual choice of a name [is] and will remain, symbolic. (Wilde, 1979, p. 183)

In this extract from *De Profundis* we find Wilde reflecting upon the significance of a name. At various points in that text we find Wilde documenting interaction between his name and the legal process of criminalization. Perhaps the most extreme form is illustrated by Wilde in the following extract:

> I myself, at that time had no name at all. In the great prison where I was then incarcerated I was merely the figure and letter of the

> little cell in a long gallery, one of a thousand lifeless numbers, as of a thousand lifeless lives. (*ibid.*, p. 182)

In his observation that he 'had no name at all', Wilde describes the way in which the criminal process erased his proper name. At the same time he notes that the legal process was a process that renamed him. His new name, C.3.3., is of particular significance. He is renamed as the letter and figure of his cell. His name has become the sign of his crime and punishment.[1] His name is the name of law.

In this extract Wilde describes the renaming process of law as a process of formal substitution. Wilde also draws attention to another process of renaming connected to law, the re-signification of his previous name, 'Oscar Wilde'. Wilde provides an example in the following extract:

> I have come, not from obscurity into the momentary notoriety of crime, but from a sort of eternity of fame to a sort of eternity of infamy. (*ibid.*, p. 199)

Having noted that the process of law might transform him from a position of obscurity to that of notoriety, Wilde puts the process of re-signification into the context of his own particular circumstances. 'Oscar Wilde' is a name that signifies fame by the process of criminalization. Here Wilde points to the terms of the re-signification of his name. For example, he commented that his name had come to stand for 'the weight of a terrible, a revolting tragedy, a terrible, a revolting scandal' (*ibid.*, p. 188). Another instance of this is demonstrated in his reaction to Lord Alfred Douglas's desire to dedicate a book of poetry to him. Wilde demanded that Douglas be stopped. To use the name 'Oscar Wilde', Wilde observed, would have been to give the book 'a wrong atmosphere' (*ibid.*). Such was the intensity of this re-signification that he was drawn to the conclusion that 'just as *my* name, once so musical in the mouth of Fame, will have to be abandoned by me' (*ibid.*, p. 238).

Subsequent to Wilde's death, many have noted the continuation of this reduction of 'Oscar Wilde', now by way of his writings and the story of his life, to the criminal trials. For example, writing in 1912, Ransome described this phenomenon in his observation that commentators on Wilde's writings saw 'a law court in "A House of Pomegranates", and heard the clink of handcuffs in the flowing music of "Intentions"' (Ransome, 1912, pp. 9–10). Pearson, writing in the 1940s, noted the continuation of this tendency in the context of biographical works on

Wilde. In the Prologue to his own biography of Wilde, Pearson described his project in the following terms:

> It is my desire to re-create [Wilde] first and foremost as a genial wit and humorist, because in my view the essential Wilde was expressed in spontaneous laughter, not in the pose of a martyr. I shall not dismiss the trial and its aftermath as matters of no importance, but the final phase must not be allowed to over-shadow the rest: it lasted for five years in a life of forty-six years: that is, one fifth of his manhood. (Pearson, 1946, pp. 2–3)

In contrast to the tendency in general writings about Wilde to reduce Wilde's writings and life to nothing more than a sign of the law, there is also another genre of writing about Wilde that formally focuses upon Wilde's dealings with the law. These texts have their origins in the legal process of the trials themselves and in the contemporary popular press accounts of the trials (Cohen, 1993). In addition, there is a distinct oeuvre of Wildean scholarship that focuses upon the three criminal trials and their aftermath. It is a tradition of Wildean scholarship that has been almost as durable as more general writings about Wilde's life and work. The text which is taken as the first[2] of this genre of Wildean scholarship, *The Trial of Oscar Wilde from the Shorthand Reports*, was one of the first books to be published on Wilde after his death in 1900. It was edited by Charles Grolleau and privately printed for Charles Carrington in Paris in 1906 (Grolleau, 1906). The second instance of this Wildean oeuvre is *Oscar Wilde: Three Times Tried*, published in London in 1911–12 (Millard, 1912). Montgomery Hyde's *The trials of Oscar Wilde* was first published in 1948 and subsequently reprinted in 1962 and 1973. In 1960 the story of Oscar Wilde was translated into the medium of film. While the first film to deal with this subject, *Oscar Wilde* (Ratoff, 1960), might appear to be a more general film portrait of Wilde, it follows the established practice of devoting much of the story to Wilde's encounters with the law; 37 of the 88 pages of the script are devoted to the trials. A second film, *The trials of Oscar Wilde* (Hughes, 1960), released five days later, followed the tradition of telling the story of Wilde as his encounters with the law.

The tendency to reduce the life and work of Oscar Wilde to the operation and effects of the criminal law, outlined above, draws attention to the way in which the name 'Oscar Wilde' has been generated and disseminated as a symbol of law as it impacts on genital relations between men. In this re-signification 'Oscar Wilde' has taken on a certain autonomy. While it would be wrong to conclude that this process is exclusive to the legal process, it is important to recognize that the legal process has been implicated in a significant way in the transformation of the proper name of 'Oscar Wilde'. In its repetition in law rather than being a proper noun it has become a common noun of the law. In its iteration the singularity of Oscar Wilde is erased even as it designates him (Derrida, 1989, p. 49).

The encounter with the legal process provided Wilde with a painful experience of the way that his proper name took on a life of its own. Thereby 'Oscar Wilde' has become a means for the production and dissemination of a knowledge not only of Wilde's particular encounters and their consequences but, as Mr Justice Plowman suggests, a more general knowledge of the nature and consequences of genital relations between men. As Wilde reminds us, the name 'Oscar Wilde' is a symbol by which we receive our bitter lessons (Wilde, 1979, p. 183). It is to those lessons that I now want to turn.

Telling tales of the law

In this section I want to describe some of the more common narratives of law that have been told by way of 'Oscar Wilde'. The first looks at 'Oscar Wilde' as a story about the enactment of a specific offence: gross indecency. The second looks at the use of 'Oscar Wilde' to tell a story of the criminalization of homosexuality. The third examines the use of 'Oscar Wilde' to tell a story of law, desire and death.

Gross indecency

> a victim of the Labouchère amendment (Warner, 1983, p. 79)

This quotation tells 'Oscar Wilde' as a story of a specific offence covered by 'the Labouchère amendment' formally known in law as the offence of gross indecency. Here the law of 'Oscar Wilde' is told as one particular charge found in the criminal proceedings brought against Wilde. Of central importance to this story of law is the fact that gross indecency was a relatively new offence at the time of Wilde's trial. It was created by section 11 of the Criminal Law Amendment Act 1885 which declared that:

> It is an offence for a man to commit an act of gross indecency with another man, whether in public or private, or to be a party to the commission by a man of an act of gross indecency, with another man, or to procure the commission by a man of an act of gross indecency with another man.[3]

The section was added to the draft bill at the suggestion of an MP, Henry Labouchère, and has come to be known as the Labouchère amendment (Smith, 1976; Weeks, 1981). When reduced to 'the Labouchère amendment', 'Oscar Wilde' is a story of law as a new or significant (Pearson, 1946, p. 301)[4] departure of law's expansion. Nunokawa provides a recent example of this in the following extract from his book on Wilde:

> while the law had been severe on the subject of 'buggery', it had been silent about various other kinds of homosexual practice ... 'acts of gross indecency' ... made all sexual activity between men illegal. (Nunokawa, 1995, p. 62)

For Nunokawa gross indecency expands the criminalization of 'homosexual practice'. This expansion has been explained in various ways: as a response to a new danger (Walkowitz, 1992) or a new persecution. Here the law is a new force or violence which is to be understood in terms of escalating repression and oppression focusing upon certain (newly) forbidden acts.

Homosexuality

> Wilde's trial for homosexuality (Young, 1995, p. 24)

This quotation draws attention to a second narrative. Here 'Oscar Wilde' is not so much the criminalizaton of particular acts, gross indecency, but a story of a forbidden identity, homosexuality, and its criminalization. In this scheme of things Wilde is prosecuted for 'specific crimes of homosexuality' (Nunokawa, 1995, p. 63) and is ultimately '[c]onvicted of homosexuality' (*ibid.*, p. 91). A variation on this theme is illustrated by Grey. In commenting on the writing of Hyde, Grey notes:

> in the opinion of the historian and politician H. Montgomery Hyde, [the criminal trials of Oscar Wilde] represented the 'high'

> water mark of popular prejudice against homosexuality . . . (Grey, 1992, p. 17)

Cohen has examined (and reproduced) this narrative as an analysis of popular press reports contemporary with the trials. Drawing attention to the way in which Wilde's body was made into a 'hieroglyph of the "crime"' (Cohen, 1993, p. 207), he then proceeds to tell a story of how that body came to signify homosexuality. Others have developed the theme of law as a trial of homosexuality in different ways. More recently, Sinfield's work suggests that as a trial of homosexuality the trial focused upon the gender of male homosexuality. Here the trial of homosexuality becomes a trial of competing masculinities with particular reference to the re-signification of effeminacy to signify same-sex desire (Sinfield, 1994).

Desire/death

> primeval, predatory and doomed . . . judicial murder of Wilde (Young, 1995, pp. 24, 266)[5]

These two quotations capture key aspects of the third narrative. It is a story closely connected to the law/homosexuality story set out above. I have separated it from that story in order to focus upon its particular themes. The first quotation from Young draws attention to the way in which this story tells the law/homosexuality relation by reference to homosexuality as a particular pathology with specific traits. Young's second quotation gives a particular meaning to the (inevitable) endpoint of this pathology: death. In their combination law and homosexuality express a particular relation of desire and death.

Through the emphasis of the pathological, the trials are represented in terms of just deserts; the realization of a catastrophic drive to self-destruction (Knox, 1994); a major story of the dire fate which awaits those who respond to homosexual desires (Lumsden, 1989, p. 249); a 'revolting and repellent tragedy'(Wilde, 1979, p. 173). A more recent (cynical) reading of this theme is to be found in the trials as a story of the 'myth of "gay doom"'(Duberman, 1995, p. 11).

The law/death relation might be told by way of biographical detail that stresses the proximity of Wilde's release from prison in 1897 and his death in 1900 (Knox, 1994) or by way of metaphor. Nunokawa provides an extended example in the opening chapter to his book on Wilde which is titled 'Death by shame'. Here the judge in the gross indecency trials, Mr Justice Wills, is described as 'a one man terror' and his comments to the prisoners 'were like the bullets of a firing squad' (Nunokawa 1995, p. 16). The transport used to convey Wilde from the police cells to Reading Goal is a 'hearse like conveyance' (*ibid.*, p. 17). Finally, the image of death is used to describe the sentence imposed upon Wilde:

> I have seen many awful happenings at the Old Bailey, but to me no death sentence has ever seemed so terrible as the one which Mr. Justice Wills delivered when his duty called upon him to destroy and take from the world the man who had given it so much. (unattributed quotation in Nunokawa, 1995, p. 16)

The relation of law and desire might be told in various ways. First, it might be told as a story of a struggle of law against desire (homosexuality), where death marks the defeat of homosexuality and the law's righteous victory. Here law is presented as an external force: a form of necessary repression. In other instances, rather than law being external to desire, the relation between law, desire and death is told as a story of an intimate connection. Sir Travers Humphreys in his 'Foreword' to Hyde's book of the trials provides one example: 'Oscar Wilde's talents raised him almost to the level of a genius; his mode of life dragged him down to the depths of a pathological case' (Humphreys, 1973, p. 14). As pathology, law/death is a natural part of the logic of desire. The law of desire is a force within that is constitutive of homosexual desire: 'a lethal fate, a drive toward death' (Nunokawa, 1995, p. 109; see also Dollimore, 1995).

There are many instances of this particular narrative of law/desire/death. Wilde himself tells such a story of the connection between the law and desire in *De Profundis*. In describing actions that led to the criminal libel proceedings, the first trial, Wilde explains that Lord Alfred Douglas was 'entranced at the idea of my sending lawyers' letters to your father, as well as yourself' (Wilde, 1979, p. 226). He explores the nature of this attraction to law further in the following:

> Of course once I had put into motion the forces of Society, Society turned on me and said, 'Have you been living all this time in defiance of my laws, and do you now appeal to those laws for protection? You shall have those laws exercised in full. You shall

abide by what you have appealed to.' The result is I am in gaol. (*ibid.*, p. 220)

Desire is presented here, in the first instance, as being against the law and in defiance of the law. Wilde's subsequent call upon the law brings into being the full force of the law of this desire. Yet that call to the law which is opposed to his desire appears to be inevitable, as signified by Lord Alfred's enchantment and the 'of course' of Wilde's observation. A trace of this relation is to be found more recently in Nunokawa's suggestion that in pursuing the law which condemned his practices, Wilde confused his desires with doom (Nunokawa, 1995, p. 110).

A final variation on the relation between law/desire/death shifts the meaning of death. Rather than the physical ending of a life, this death is a civil death, social exclusion which takes the form of the imposition of a silence. Ransome, having noted the way Wilde's detractors deployed the narrative of pathology in their comments that the finding of guilt at the Old Bailey was inevitable because that is where the artistic life leads a man (Ransome, 1912, pp. 18–19), comments that this inevitable death might take various forms: the physical death of the subject or a civil death of the subject, where the subject is removed from society (imprisoned) and/or erased by the destruction of his texts by fire.

We are reminded of this civil death in many ways: the censorship of reports of the criminal trials (Warwick, 1967, 515 G; Hyde, 1973, p. 20),[6] and in references to Oscar Wilde as 'the unmentionable' (see Hallidie Smith quoted in Grey, 1992, p. 45; Holland, 1954).

Making our experience of law

While these stories have been set out as distinct and separate, they join in the name of 'Oscar Wilde'. Through these narratives the status quo of the law is celebrated and the legitimacy of the law is generated and explained. However, it would be premature to limit our understanding of the significance of these stories in this way. Much of the material that has produced and disseminated these stories of the trials is to be found in texts by those sympathetic to Wilde. Many of these texts might be said to be critical of the law, either directly or indirectly, either in the specific context of Wilde or more generally in the context of the criminalization of genital relations between men. This draws attention to the way these stories have a certain ambiguity; they may explain the legitimacy of the law and at the same time be put to use to challenge that legitimacy.

Evidence of this ambivalence and its effects can be found in the day-to-day deployment of these narratives. On the one hand there is ample evidence that the stories of 'Oscar Wilde' generated fear. Oscar Wilde's downfall has been described as an 'evil stench' (Grey, 1992, p. 16) that tainted the atmosphere in which English homosexual men lived. Denton Welch noted in his journals that he was 'frightened of the prison reek all about it. I had only just heard the gruesome Wilde story, and was filled by its disgusting quality' (Welch, 1984, p. 251). Grey, a key campaigner for the reform of the law, points to the durability of these effects. Wilde, he notes, 'would occupy a prison cell for the next two years and an infamous place in social history for half a century' (Grey, 1992, p. 17).

At the same time, as Oscar Wilde himself noted, there was the potential for the same events to generate different reactions. For example, in *De Profundis* Wilde tells us that prison life, 'with its endless privations and restrictions, makes one rebellious' (Wilde, 1979, p. 203). Cohen provides a more recent expression of the violence of the contradiction: 'the anonymous ignominity in which Wilde passed the years preceding his death is still, almost a century later, both indescribably moving and indescribably painful' (Cohen, 1993, p. 210).

Another aspect of the potential for unruly and unexpected effects was described during the course of debates to extend the offence of gross indecency to women in 1921. In the House of Lords Lord Desart explained that the Oscar Wilde trials 'attracted very great public attention' and were followed by 'a perfect outburst of that offence all over the country'. 'Oscar Wilde' not only told of the criminalization of homosexual activity, but also represented its possibility, its forms and its pleasures. The trials also had another effect: they contributed to the creation amongst homosexual males of a sense of identity, and to the foundation of the early homosexual rights movement (Warner, 1983, p. 82). So the same narrative might be a story by which an experience of fear and loathing might be generated and also a story that might produce an experience of defiance and provide a source of strength and determination (Duberman, 1995, p. 9). Of particular interest here is the proximity of fear and righteous anger, of passivity and activity.

These experiences are particularly important in another way. They problematize the very idea of a 'general knowledge' of the trials. While a 'general knowledge' might refer to the production and dissemination of a particular set of stories, these do not necessarily produce a uniform 'knowledge'. The same knowledge might narrate the legitimacy of the law and at the same time tell a story of the persecution through the law and the prejudice of law. They suggest that a 'general knowledge' ought to be understood as a multiplicity of experiences, of multiple knowledges of the trials. However, following Foucault, it is important to recognize that not all of these different readings have the same status; some are disqualified (Foucault, 1980, p. 83). These disqualified knowledges are at the margins of 'general knowledge'. At the same time the fact that these marginal, disqualified, knowledges resort to the same stories which make up 'general knowledge' problematizes Foucault's spatial metaphor of centre/margin; they are both centre and margin.

Knowledge and limit

There is also a need for caution in another way. While these narratives may have been central to the generation of a rich and complex set of cultural understandings and cultural practices, both dominant and marginal, they produce very specific understandings which are problematic in various ways in both contexts. Both as dominant and marginal/disqualified knowledges, they produce knowledge by the imposition of problematic limits upon understanding.

Examples can be drawn from various contexts. While the narrative of gross indecency tells a story of the novelty of criminalization, it is far from clear that the introduction of the Labouchere amendment in general or its application in the instance of Wilde's trials was a new departure or an escalation of law's concern with male-to-male genital relations. To suggest that this amendment criminalized acts in private which had not previously been criminal is incorrect. The act of buggery and lesser offences of male-to-male genital contact had always been criminal in both public and private (Bartlett, 1997).

Aspects of the trial of homosexuality story are also problematic. While in some respects Wilde's marriage and children make his story typical of a late nineteenth-century homosexual, other homosexual characters in the trial portray a different Victorian lived experience of homosexuality (Bartlett, 1988). Likewise, to reduce all experiences of conviction to the civil death experience of Wilde, erases the lives of those who enjoyed longer and less troubled post-conviction lives. To reduce all same-sex genital practice to Wilde's particular practices and experience is an impoverishment of our knowledge of Victorian sexuality and its interface with the law.

The story of law, desire and death is problematic in other ways. For example, while the morbidity of Wilde's musing in *De Profundis* might be taken to be evidence of this narrative, that text also contains much more that disrupts that narrative. Though Wilde's state of despair owes much to the criminal trials, other legal proceedings, such as the bankruptcy and proceedings relating to his children, also had a demoralizing effect upon him (Wilde, 1979, p. 193).

Wilde also noted that factors remote from his sexuality had a significant impact upon his particular experience of criminal justice. In particular he noted the importance of class as a factor that made his experience of the law exceptional (*ibid.*). The death of his mother while he was in prison, and his continuing relations with Lord Alfred Douglas (*ibid.*) were other contributing factors that made his experience of the law distinctive.

Other problems arise in telling the story of law as the imposition of a silence. First, if this silence is taken to be an absolute prohibition on speech, this clearly misunderstands the nature of that silence and misses completely the productivity of silence. For example, while the journalists reporting the trials of Wilde were faced with the challenge of writing about matters that were not to be spoken of, journalistic practice circumvented the representational limits imposed by this injunction to silence by translating the legal utterance into printable terms (Cohen, 1993, p. 144). Journalists deployed a compensatory set of signifying practices to invoke the unprintable signifier. On other occasions Cohen notes that the unrepresentable was signified by a blank or a hyphen in the text (*ibid.*, pp. 145, 147). Here censorship is not so much a total silence as a requirement to represent the unrepresentable by a specific code and a determination to speak the unspeakable (Moran, 1996, Chapter 3). The very familiarity of the story of 'Oscar Wilde' draws attention to the fact that censorship has always been unsuccessful and that the trials have been an important vehicle through which sexuality might be put into discourse *ad nauseam* (Foucault, 1978; Hunter *et al.*, 1993).

An examination of the limits of the narratives that have been told by way of this name draws attention to the fact that this preservation is not to be reduced to that which conserves or maintains. This reference to 'Oscar Wilde' as a story about law is not to be understood as a reference to practices dedicated to the conservation or the recuperation of the 'truth' of the relationship that Oscar Wilde had with the law, be it the three criminal proceedings (one for criminal libel and two for gross indecency) or the bankruptcy proceedings or custody dispute. 'Oscar Wilde' preserves a place which is the very possibility of generating and disseminating stories about law and genital relations between men.

Conclusions: law, (counter) memory and the proper name

In general this essay seeks to begin an evaluation of the ways 'Oscar Wilde' as a name of law, still organizes our own engagements with the law/homosexuality relation (Cohen, 1993, p. 211). The production and dissemination of 'Oscar Wilde' as a symbol of law, is neither the totality of that symbol nor the totality of our understanding of the interface between genital relations between men and the (criminal) law. At the same time it is important to recognize that 'Oscar Wilde' has been and continues to be an important symbol across which struggles to (re)present the relationship between law and sexual difference and different sexualities has occurred (Fajer, 1992, p. 520). 'Oscar Wilde' has assured the preservation of particular narratives about law and genital relations between men.

Far from being stories that are only told outside the formal and institutional context of law, the stories of law outlined above also come to be told within the boundaries of legal practice. In particular they are to be found in the context of legal scholarship (Law, 1988; Fajer, 1992; Goldstein, 1993). As a study of law produced 'high' and 'low' culture this chapter seeks to promote a better understanding of the production of law in its formal and institutional practices.

The study of law as it is represented outside the formal and institutional contexts of law is important in another way. It provides evidence of the nature of law that is repressed within the 'official' representations of law; it provides a counter memory of law. The narratives outlined in this chapter describe law not as rule and reason but as violence and terror, and criminalization as a form of persecution. Rather than law's impartiality we have law's partiality: where law is a vehicle for right-wing 'queer baiting' (Lumsden, 1989, p. 247). Via 'Oscar Wilde' we can plot law as a practice and an experience of abuse and corruption. Here law is not so much right reason but a practice of official secrets and 'high' political intrigue (Hyde, 1970, p. 146; Lumsden, 1989, p. 243). Here legal order is not so much an order built on consensus but one built on sacrifice (Lumsden, 1989, p. 244), where Oscar Wilde occupies the role of the 'most celebrated victim' (Duberman, 1995, p. 11).

The significance of 'Oscar Wilde' does not reside in its capacity to resurrect a situation or a feeling that actually existed, but in its capacity to act as a constitutive act of the mind bound to its own present and oriented towards the future of its own elaboration. The past intervenes only as a purely formal element (De Man, 1983, pp. 92–3). This 'Oscar Wilde' is a practice of cultural memory and counter memory of law, where memory is the name of what is no longer only a mental 'capacity' oriented towards one of the three modes of the present, the past present, which could be disassociated from the present and the future present. As a practice of cultural memory and counter memory of law, 'Oscar Wilde' has enabled us to project ourselves towards the future, and to constitute the presence of the present (Derrida, 1989, p. 57).

Notes

1. Having described his nomination as 'no name at all', on occasion he resorted to that name (Hart Davis, 1979, pp. 280–1 and 297). A more recent re-signification of 'C.3.3.' is to be found in the play of that name (Badinter, 1995).
2. Mason's bibliography of Wilde refers to two other publications dedicated to the trials (Mason, 1914). The first is an anonymous pamphlet published in April 1895: *Just Out. Complete. The Life of Oscar Wilde as Prosecutor and Prisoner* (Anon., 1895). The second, by I. Playfair, is titled *Gentle Criticisms on British Justice* (Playfair, 1895). It is made up of ten chapters as follows: I Introduction; II General conduct of the Authorities; III Some light on the origin of the recent case of Regina v Wilde; IV A little light on Some Sources of the evidence re Regina v Wilde; V Motives of the Prosecution, or a little light on a very Dark Place; VI Methods of the Prosecution; VII The Letter – Counsels arguments; VIII The Judges summing up; IX The latter continued – Reasonable arguments; X Lord Alfred Douglas's Poems (Mason, 1914, p. 579).
3. This remains an offence and is now to be found in s.13 Sexual Offences Act 1956.
4. Though it is important to note that Pearson makes this point to counteract suggestions that the Labouchere amendment was introduced to reduce the Act to absurdity (Pearson, 1946, p. 301).
5. Young also points out that this is not the only representation of the homosexual available at the time. He describes the other as, 'the mystical/radical vision of the New Man or New Woman, the evolutionary teacher, the androgyn, the modern

shaman' (Young, 1995, pp. 34–5). However, it is important to note that this other figure of homosexuality has no overt relation to law.

6. Hyde's reference for this is Session papers, cxxi, 531–2.

References

Anon. (1895) *Just Out. Complete. The Life of Oscar Wilde as Prosecutor and Prisoner.* Published for the proprietors at 43 Stanhope Street, Clare Market, London.

Badinter, R. (1995) *C.3.3.: précédé de Oscar Wilde ou l'injustice.* Paris: Actes Sud.

Bartlett, N. (1988) *Who Was That Man? A Present for Mr Oscar Wilde.* London: Serpent's Tail.

Bartlett, P. (1997) 'Sodomites and the pillory', *Social and Legal Studies*, **6**(4).

Chase, A. (1986) 'Towards a legal theory of popular culture', *Wisconsin Law Review*, 527–57.

Cohen, E. (1993) *Talk on the Wilde Side: Towards a Genealogy of a Discourse on Male Sexualities.* London: Routledge.

De Man, P. (1983) *Blindness and Insight: Essays in the Rhetoric of Contemporary Criticism*, 2nd rev. edn. Minneapolis: University of Minnesota Press.

Derrida, J. (1989) *Memories for Paul De Man.* Rev. edn. New York: Columbia University Press.

Dollimore, J. (1995) 'Sex and death', *Textual Practice* **9**(1), pp. 27–53.

Duberman, M. B. (1995) 'Gay, straight and in between', in J. Nunokawa, *Oscar Wilde.* New York: Chelsea House Publishers.

Fajer, M. A. (1992) 'Can two real men eat quiche together? Storytelling, gender-role stereotypes, and legal protection for lesbians and gay men', *University of Miami Law Review*, **46**, pp. 511–651.

Foucault, M. (1978) *The History of Sexuality*, Vol. 1. London: Penguin.

Foucault, M. (1980) *Power/Knowledge: Selected Interviews and Other Writings 1972–1977*, ed. Colin Gordon. Brighton: Harvester Press.

Goldstein, A. B. (1993) 'Reasoning about homosexuality', *Virginia Law Review*, **79**(7), 1781–1805.

Grey, A. (1992) *Quest for Justice.* London: Sinclair-Stevenson.

Grolleau, C. G. (1906) *The Trial of Oscar Wilde from the Shorthand Reports.* Paris: privately printed.

Hart-Davis, R. (1979) *Selected Letters of Oscar Wilde.* Oxford: Oxford University Press.

Holland, V. (1954) *Son of Oscar Wilde.* London: Rupert Hart-Davis.

Hughes, K. (1960) *The Trials of Oscar Wilde.* London: Warwick.

Humphreys, T. (1973) 'Foreword', in H. M. Hyde, *The Trials of Oscar Wilde.* London: Dover.

Hunter, I. *et al.* (1993) *On Pornography.* London: Macmillan.

Hyde, H. M. (1948) *The Trials of Oscar Wilde.* London: William Hodge.

Hyde, H. M. (1962) *Famous Trials 7: Oscar Wilde.* London: Penguin Books.

Hyde, H. M. (1970) *The Other Love. An Historical and Contemporary Survey of Homosexuality in Britain.* London: Heineman.

Hyde, H. M. (1973) *The Trials of Oscar Wilde.* London: Dover.

Knox, M. (1994) *Oscar Wilde: A Long and Lovely Suicide.* New Haven: Yale University Press.

Law, S. A. (1988) 'Homosexuality and the social meaning of gender', *Wisconsin Law Review*, pp. 187–237.
Lumsden, A. (1989) 'Westminster barbarism', in S. Shephard and M. Wallis (eds), *Coming on Strong: Gay Politics and Culture*. London: Unwin Hyman.
Mason, S. (1914) *Bibliography of Oscar Wilde*. London: Werner Laurie.
Millard, S. (1912) *Oscar Wilde: Three Times Tried*. London: Ferrestone Press.
Moran, L. J. (1996) *The Homosexual(ity) of Law*. London: Routledge.
Nunokawa, J. (1995) *Oscar Wilde*. New York: Chelsea House.
Pearson, H. (1946) *The Life of Oscar Wilde*. London: Methuen.
Playfair, I., otherwise Wilson, J. H. (1895) *Gentle Criticisms on British Justice*. Newcastle-upon-Tyne.
Ransome, A. (1912) *Oscar Wilde A Critical Study*. London: Methuen.
Ratoff, L. (1960) *Oscar Wilde*. London: Rank.
Redhead, S. (1995) *Unpopular Culture: The Birth of Law and Popular Culture*. Manchester: Manchester University Press.
Sinfield, A. (1994) *The Wilde Century: Effeminacy, Oscar Wilde and the Queer Moment*. London: Cassell.
Smith, F. B. (1976) 'Labouchère's amendment to the Criminal Law Amendment Bill', *Historical Studies*, 17 (6/7), 165–75.
Walkowitz, J. R. (1992) *City of Dreadful Delight: Narratives of Sexual Danger in Late-Victorian London*. London: Virago Press.
Warner, M. (1983) 'Parliament and the law', in B. Galloway (ed.), *Prejudice and Pride: Discrimination against Gay People in Modern Britain*. London: Routledge & Kegan Paul.
Warwick (1967) *Warwick v. Eisenger* [1967] 1 Chancery Division (Law Reports) 508.
Weeks, J. (1981) *Sex, Politics, Society*. London: Longmans.
Welch, D. (1984) *The Journals of Denton Welch*, ed. M. De la Noy. London: Allison and Busby.
Wilde, O. (1979) *De Profundis*, in *Selected Letters of Oscar Wilde*, ed. R. Davis, Oxford: London.
Young, I. (1995) *The Stonewall Experiment*. Cassell: London.

2

Institutionalizing Heterosexuality: The Legal Exclusion of 'Impossible' (Trans)sexualities

Andrew N. Sharpe

> [T]hough homosexualities of all kinds in this present climate are being erased, reduced, and (then) reconstituted as sites of radical homophobic fantasy, it is important to retrace the different routes by which the unthinkability of homosexuality is being constituted time and again. (Butler, 1991, p. 20)

This chapter attempts to trace one, relatively recent, route through which the unthinkability of homosexuality has been constituted in law. It explores the relationship in law between heterosexuality, homosexuality and transsexuality.[1] Using Australian criminal law and social security law cases dealing with male-to-female transsexual persons, the chapter focuses upon how the shifting medico-legal uses of homosexuality and transsexuality operate to produce an ideal of heterosexuality within that jurisdiction. It explores the way this heterosexuality then comes to set parameters within which the transsexual subject is given a presence in the law and whereby that person might make legal claims. The chapter will highlight how legal attempts to preserve heterosexual hegemony in the face of the sex claims of transsexual litigants have, paradoxically, led to the denaturalization of both sex and heterosexuality. Far from resolving the 'ambiguity' which the transsexual is considered to pose, legal reasoning will be shown to reproduce and intensify that 'ambiguity' and to have created a legal space for the disruption and radical rearticulation of (trans)sexualities.[2] In this respect the chapter aims to take law reform activism into the very text of law where legal discourse is implicated in the production and non-production (Butler, 1993, p. 8) of identity categories. Conversely, the traditional gay reform agenda, with its 'progressive' and 'assimilationist' tendencies, is viewed as problematic. Indeed, it is precisely this sort of approach that has led to the legal exclusion of 'impossible' transsexual homosexuality in the discursive production of the male-to-female transsexual as female.

However, while homosexuality is excluded in transsexual legal subject formation, the category of heterosexuality is reversed, inverted, literally turned inside out by legal reasoning. It will emerge that in the context of transsexuality, heterosexuality escapes its mooring to biological sex and is reinvented through, and rendered intelligible by, recourse to psychological sex. At this new psychological site law continues to insist upon a mutually exclusive relation of sex identity and sexual desire (Butler, 1993). In other words, while medico-legal discourse has reformulated the categories of sex, gender and heterosexuality, their interrelationship remains unaffected. Unsurprisingly, legal discourse does not permit a parallel reconceptualization of homosexuality. It is through a differential deployment of biology and psychology across the hetero/homo divide that a homosexual/transsexual dichotomy is constituted in medico-legal discourse. In this way a tension is produced between transsexuals and lesbians and gays around the possibility of the transsexual homosexual. On the one hand, transsexuals are encouraged to define themselves in opposition to homosexuality, while on the other, the image of the transsexual homosexual threatens to destabilize the 'coherent' identities formulated by the traditional gay law reform agenda. Thus, within this legal framework transsexual homosexuals come to represent a threat not only to heterosexual hegemony but also to homosexual and transsexual 'coherence'.

For those of us who would like to bring the hetero/homo sexual division to the point of collapse, it may be that progress in this direction can best be achieved by working on the insides of our inherited sexual vocabularies and turning them inside out to the point of exhaustion as a prerequisite to their transformation (Fuss, 1991, p. 7). This chapter will highlight how this queer process is already underway in the context of transsexual case law. Legal reasoning, through seeking to maintain heterosexual hegemony in the face of the transsexual litigant, has produced unintended consequences which offer opportunities for resistance (Stychin, 1995, p. 140). The multiplication of such opportunities might best be achieved through the acceleration and proliferation of these emerging forms of legal reasoning.

The Australian cases to be considered are of particular interest because they serve to illustrate the problematic nature of the traditional law reform agenda. In departing from the landmark English decision in *Corbett* v. *Corbett* ([1970] 2 WLR 1306), the Australian courts, as the cases referred to here indicate, have rejected the notion that 'sex is determined at birth' in favour of a story of 'psychological and anatomical harmony' whereby transsexual persons who have undergone sex reassignment surgery have been granted legal recognition. However, it is important to resist the temptation to simply characterize this Australian trend as 'progressive', to be contrasted with a 'repressive' English scenario (Foucault, 1981), for legal recognition of transsexual sex claims has proved possible only through the simultaneous production of a constitutive and abjected transsexual 'outside' – a domain of 'unintelligible' bodies, 'impossible' (trans)sexualities and 'incoherent' (trans)gender practices. It is important to consider these exclusionary effects for, as Butler points out:

> it is not enough to claim that human subjects are constructed, for the construction of the human is a differential operation that produces the more and the less 'human', the inhuman, the humanly unthinkable. (Butler, 1993, p. 8)

While the various components of a legally produced transsexual 'outside' interconnect and overlap, this chapter will focus primarily upon the ways in which sexual 'otherness' is reproduced through legal discourse. Before proceeding to analyse the case law in this area, it is instructive to consider how transsexuality is conceptualized in medical discourse as medical 'knowledge', as this has proved particularly significant in informing legal debate.

(Trans)sexuality: the medical gaze

While the phenomenon of 'transsexualism' has perhaps a long and complex genealogy, the term itself dates to 1950s America where it emerged as a definitional precursor to the medical colonization of the phenomenon (King, 1993). Since that time, medical epistemology has produced two broad narratives for conceiving of transsexualism which have, in different ways, served to constitute and maintain a homosexual/transsexual dichotomy that has proved central to understanding (trans)sexuality and to reproducing heterosexual hegemony. The first medical narrative to emerge was the 'discovery story of transsexuality' (Benjamin, 1953; Stoller, 1968) while the second, and since the early 1970s increasingly dominant, narrative is generally referred to as 'gender dysphoria syndrome' (Fisk, 1973; Laub and Gandy, 1973).

According to the discovery story, the 'true' transsexual is to be distinguished from the 'pseudotranssexual' for the purpose of surgical intervention. In particular, this approach scripts homosexuality as a sign of pseudotranssexuality in a candidate for sex reassignment surgery (Stoller, 1968). However, the medical deployment of homosexuality in this context proves curious, as it is asserted in two different and contradictory senses. On the one hand homosexuality is utilized to cast doubt upon the male-to-female candidate's heterosexual desire for men, while on the other it is used to invalidate the sex claims of those male-to-female candidates whose sexual desires are directed towards women. The medical deployment of homosexuality in the former sense appears to have been activated by (trans)sexual practice rather than desire. In other words, a male-to-female candidate's sexual desire for men is consistent with heterosexuality, whereas pre-operative sexual practice with men tends to be read as evidence of homosexuality, thereby rendering inauthentic claims of heterosexual desire. It was precisely this type of analysis that led in the *Corbett* decision (*ibid.*, at 1310) to April Ashley being diagnosed as a 'constitutional homosexual' prior to reassignment surgery.

In the present era medical discourse on sex reassignment has been dominated by the 'gender dysphoria' paradigm, which deploys homosexuality only to cast doubt upon desire for opposite (biological) sex sexual relations. According to this narrative, inquiry into the nature of a male-to-female candidate's sexual desire for men becomes of less concern. Rather, an attempt is made to ascertain the sex in which it is best for a person to live and is therefore capable of considering 'effeminate homosexuals' and 'atypical transvestites' to be suitable for sex reassignment surgery (Koranyi, 1980, p. 156). However, as in the discovery story of transsexuality, a homosexual/transsexual dichotomy remains central to contemporary medical understandings of (trans)sexuality. Thus while the basis for 'appropriate' heterosexual desire is relocated from biology to psychology, 'inappropriate' homosexual desire continues to be grounded in, and governed by, biological sex.

Accordingly, within this borderline (trans)sexual category heterosexuality is considered to be the desire for same (biological) sex sexual relations. Here the male is considered to be the appropriate sexual object choice for a male-to-female candidate, as she regards herself as female (Benjamin, 1966; Walinder *et al.*, 1978; Bolin, 1988, p. 55). Indeed, the absence of sexual relations with a male is for a male-to-female candidate viewed by some as an adverse sign (Koranyi, 1980, p. 31). Curiously however, desire for opposite (biological) sex sexual relations is negated through displacing psychology and reinscribing biology as the mooring for sexuality. Thus a 'lesbian' sexual object choice is considered to contraindicate surgery. Compared to the 'heterosexual', the lesbian, and indeed the bisexual, male-to-female candidate is considered a poor risk for surgery in the sense of satisfaction with surgical outcome (Bolin, 1988, p. 63). Moreover, the male-to-female candidate who considers herself to be lesbian is most likely to be considered a transvestite or a heterosexual with impotence problems (Koranyi, 1980, p. 89). While medical discourse conceives of (trans)sexuality as being grounded in psychological sex, suggestions of homosexuality (in the psychological sense) serve to place psychological sex in issue. In these circumstances psychological sex claims are interpreted as inauthentic and recourse is made to biology to establish the 'truth' of sexuality. In other words, (trans)sexuality is always read, and can only be read, as heterosexual. Homosexuality and transsexuality are simply not commensurate.

In a sense the psychoanalytic theory of 'sexual inversion' (Freud, 1975), as applied historically to homosexuals, is re-enacted in the transsexual context. However, the figure of the transsexual homosexual serves, much like the macho gay and lesbian femme, to expose the inability of inversion theory to account for or contain the fluidity of gendered and sexual subjectivities, and represents a refusal to have non-heterosexual desire reinscribed as heterosexual. In this regard, medico-legal strategies of containment and erasure of homosexuality generate their own unmangeability, for the heterosexual matrix proves to be an imaginary logic (Butler, 1993).

Indeed, Bolin in her study of male-to-female transsexuals found only one of her population of seventeen to be exclusively heterosexual, with six identifying as exclusively lesbian (Bolin, 1988, p. 63). Similarly, Lewins in his study of male-to-female transsexuals found less than half of his sample to be heterosexual, with 31 per cent clearly identifing as lesbian (Lewins, 1995, p. 95). While these findings might be viewed as casting doubt upon the 'truth' of transsexuality in individual cases, they might more persuasively be used to challenge the coupling of transsexuality and heterosexuality as 'truth'. In the meantime, transsexuals identifying as lesbian, gay, bisexual or queer and seeking reassignment surgery and legal recognition must continue to pass as heterosexual before a medical gaze.

While medical discourse and practice significantly inform legal discourse on (trans)sexuality, legal discourse is nevertheless an important site in its own right for the constitution, consolidation and regulation of sexuality, and in particular the hetero/homo dichotomy (Stychin, 1995, p. 7). It will become apparent that sexuality in law is tied to the legal determination of sex, a determination that proves to be influenced by capacity and desire for heterosexual intercourse, and by the further considerations of the subject matter of litigation and the law/fact distinction. It is to these influencing factors that my attention now turns.

Heterosexual intercourse: the capacity and the desire

Prior to 1988 no Australian court had occasion to determine the 'legal sex' of transsexual persons. In that year, in the case of *R* v. *Harris and McGuiness* (17 NSWLR 158; [1989] 35 A Crim R 146) the New South Wales Court of Criminal Appeal was required to consider whether a male-to-female transsexual was a male person within the meaning of (the now repealed) section 81A of the Crimes Act 1900 (NSW). At trial Lee Harris (a post-operative male-to-female transsexual) and Phillis McGuiness (a pre-operative male-to-female transsexual who proposed to undergo surgery) (*ibid.*, at 173) had been convicted of procuring 'another' male person to commit an act of indecency contrary to the legislation. A majority of the appeal court held that a male-to-female transsexual who has undergone 'full' sex reassignment to align her genital features with her psychological sex is to be regarded as a female for the purposes of the criminal law. Here 'legal sex' is reworked so that present 'psychological and anatomical harmony' supplant chromosomal, gonadal and genital congruence at birth as governing criteria. Accordingly, Lee Harris fell outside the ambit of the legislation, while the conviction of Phillis McGuiness was upheld.

The nature and significance of surgical intervention as a precondition for legal recognition needs to be emphasized. In the first place, surgery emerges in medical practice as a prize (King, 1993, p. 85) conferred upon those who have successfully accomplished pre-surgical medical rites of passage, thereby satisfying medical experts that they will blend into society post-surgery. In this respect, legal recognition serves to endorse and retrospectively legitimate a medical model with inbuilt notions of gender and sexuality (*ibid.*, p. 185). In the context of sexuality, law presupposes that medicine has already established the heterosexuality (in the psychological sense) of the post-operative transsexual who stands before the court and asks for legal recognition of her sex claims.

However, heterosexual desire by itself has proved insufficient for legal recognition. Rather, it is surgical intervention in its own right, rather than anything it presupposes, which has proved crucial. Moreover, the type of surgical intervention that law requires is specific in nature. The legal recognition conveyed upon Lee Harris proved dependent not merely on genital surgery but upon 'full' sex reassignment involving the construction of a vagina. While Matthews J pointed out that Lee Harris had been deprived of 'the capacity to procreate or to have normal heterosexual intercourse in her original sex' (*ibid.*, at 194), and while the prospect of having a sexually/procreatively functional male classified as female concerned the court, these forms of irrevocable loss do not ground the decision. Rather, it is the capacity for heterosexual intercourse that 'full' sex reassignment provides that proves crucial.

While Matthews J refused to treat as significant the 'temporary' inability of Lee Harris to have sexual intercourse as a female, caused by a closing-up of her surgically constructed vagina (*ibid.*, at 194), it would seem that a permanent inability to do so would fall short of 'full' sex reassignment. It should be borne in mind that the type of operation for male-to-female transsexuals is not a uniform procedure and may be little more than full castration (*ibid.*, at 168). It would seem that male-to-female transsexuals undergoing this latter type of procedure would fall outside the scope of the decision, as it would fail to produce a capacity for heterosexual intercourse as a female. In short, the capacity for heterosexual intercourse comes to set the parameters within which the transsexual subject is given a presence within the law. Further, because law views sex reassignment surgery as authenticating the psychological sex claims, and therefore the sexual desires, of transsexual persons, the sex claims and sexual desires of pre-surgical subjects are immediately problematized.

Thus legal recognition of transsexual sex claims has proved conditional upon the establishment of both heterosexual desire (presumed to be established within the medical arena) and heterosexual capacity (demonstrated by specific surgical procedures). Accordingly, the possibility of transsexual homosexualities is negated. This is achieved through invoking a homosexual/transsexual dichotomy whereby a mutually exclusive relation of sex identity and sexual desire is insisted upon (Butler, 1993). From this perspective 'homosexuality' serves to cast doubt on the psychological sex claims of the transsexual and therefore upon homosexuality itself. In other words, law, like medicine, interprets the male-to-female transsexual's sexual desire for women to be evidence that her psychological sex is really male and her sexual desires therefore really heterosexual (in the biological sense). The invocation of this homosexual/transsexual dichotomy finds legal expression in the judgment of Matthews J: 'Transsexuality is quite different from homosexuality which relates to sexual preference rather than gender identity' (*ibid.*, at 173).

While this may seem axiomatic upon first reading, the view that homosexuality has nothing to do with gender identity actually serves to foreclose the possibility of transsexual homosexualities. Further, the legal exclusion of these 'impossible' homosexualities illustrates how strained legal reasoning has become in this area. That is to say, how is it possible for a male-to-female transsexual to be viewed as heterosexual if sexual preference has nothing to do with sex identity? Legal logic is seen to break down here under the strain of maintaining the hegemony of an increasingly malleable heterosexuality. In short, the medico-legal insistence upon the 'truth' of (trans)sexuality as unproblematically heterosexual generates its own unmanageability (Butler, 1993).

In the wake of *Harris* other decisions have emerged endorsing the story of 'psychological and anatomical harmony' as the legal test for sex. Thus in *Secretary, Department of Social Security* v. *HH* ([1991] 13 AAR 314) the Administrative Appeals Tribunal upheld a decision of the Social Security Appeals Tribunal that a male-to-female post-operative transsexual was a woman and was therefore entitled to an age pension at 60 rather than 65.

As in *Harris*, the decision serves to circumscribe (trans)sexuality through the insistence upon a homosexual/transsexual dichotomy. Thus O'Connor J and Muller assert that transsexuals desire surgical assistance, something which they both view as an affirmation of psychological sex (*ibid.*, at 321), 'in order that they may enter into heterosexual relationships' and that 'homosexuals are satisfied with their anatomical sex and are only attracted to people of the same (by which they mean biological) sex' (*ibid.*, at 317). Here transsexual homosexualities are scripted as being 'impossible' because they entail both anatomical dissatisfaction and sexual desire for persons of the opposite biological sex. In view of the claim that transsexuals undergo surgery 'in order that they may enter into heterosexual relationships' and the further claim that 'homosexuals are satisfied with their anatomical sex', the male-to-female transsexual who considers herself to be lesbian emerges in legal discourse as neither transsexual nor homosexual, but rather as male and heterosexual. In short, lesbian desire serves to render psychological sex claims inauthentic.

However, the decision in *HH* proves dependent upon more than a clear delineation of 'appropriate' sexuality. Thus O'Connor J and Muller express the view that anatomy must be the overriding factor in sex determination if 'overwhelmingly contrary to the assumed sex role' (*ibid.*, at 320). This contention that the female sex role can only be properly fulfiled with the 'right' anatomical parts, specifically a vagina, assumes that the role requires penetrative sex. This view of the female sex role finds further expression in the assertion that after reassignment surgery the male-to-female transsexual is 'functionally'(*ibid.*, at 320) a member of her 'new' sex. As in *Harris*, it is the capacity for heterosexual intercourse that proves decisive in the determination of 'legal sex', even though this would seem to be somewhat superfluous in the context of entitlement to an old age pension.

More recently, in *Secretary, Department of Social Security* v. *SRA* ([1992] 28 ALD 361) the Administrative Appeals Tribunal upheld a decision of the Social Security Appeals Tribunal that a pre-operative male-to-female transsexual was a woman and was therefore entitled to a wife's pension. In rejecting the distinction drawn in its own previous decision in *HH* between post- and pre-operative transsexuals, the tribunal took the view that biological considerations could be overridden when presented with 'psychological, social and cultural harmony' (*ibid.*, at 367). Here in determining 'legal sex' the court dispensed with anatomical considerations and by implication the capacity for heterosexual intercourse. The tribunal's willingness to divorce sex, and therefore sexuality, from genital insignia is a significant legal step. It is the closest the law has yet come to locating sexuality in the subjective feelings and personal experiences of individuals.

Any cause for celebration, however, was to be short-lived, as the Federal Court of Australia held on appeal that SRA was not a woman as a matter of law. The argument that 'legal sex' could be determined by reference to psychological, social and cultural factors alone was firmly and unanimously rejected (*ibid.*, at 471). As in *Harris*, the Federal Court would not countenance a mixing of genres (Derrida, 1980) in the sense of upsetting the couplings of man/penis and woman/vagina. The court went on to approve of the *Harris* decision, making it clear that a person who was both anatomically and psychologically female, and therefore harmonious, would be covered by the social security provisions (*ibid.*, at 496).

However, while 'legal sex' has been subject to reformulation and while that reformulation has been paralleled by a relocation of heterosexuality from its anchorage in biology to a new psychological site, the new understandings of sex and sexuality thereby produced prove quite unstable in legal discourse.

Womanhood and the subject-matter of litigation

While recognizing Lee Harris as a woman as a matter of law, the court in *Harris* was careful to confine the scope of its decision to the criminal law (*ibid.*, at 189). In particular, the court drew a clear distinction between the criminal law and the issue of marriage:

> No question is raised in these appeals as to the sex of marriage partners. Marriage involves special considerations and it is obvious that the determination of these appeals will have no direct application to the law of marriage. (*ibid.*, at 189)

This concern over marriage was echoed by the Federal Court in *SRA* even as that court stressed the need for legal consistency (*ibid.*, at 495). The insulation of the institution of marriage from these decisions is particularly curious when one considers that the story of 'psychological and anatomical harmony', upon which the court relied, was borrowed from United States decisions in which the sole issue was marriage.[3] Further, it is especially ironic that a test for 'legal sex' which has been predicated upon the capacity for heterosexual intercourse should be dispensed with in the context of marriage, an area where that capacity would seem to have, at least in legal discourse, particular relevance.

Implicit within this potential for differential treatment of transsexual sex claims across subject matters, is the notion that the 'legal sex' of transsexual persons is capable of variation. The possibility for variation in determinations of 'legal sex' reveals the contingency of both sex and heterosexuality serving to 'denaturalize' both categories. This is particularly ironic in the context of marriage, where the rationale for differential treatment appears to lie in the attempt to retain the idea of the naturalness of heterosexuality (Sharpe, 1997a). It would seem that at the very moment Lee Harris is recognized in law as a 'coherent' heterosexual female subject, that 'coherence' disintegrates. The legal reasoning in *Harris* appears to envisage a situation where the same transsexual person might be viewed as a heterosexual female (in the psychological sense) for one legal purpose and a homosexual male (in the biological sense) for another. This possibility implicates law in a sublimely queer legal moment as the spaces of both 'inside' and 'outside' come to be inhabitated by the transsexual.

Further, it would appear that the possibility for differential treatment of transsexual sex claims across subject matters is not confined to the issue of marriage. Thus in *HH*, while HH was recognized to be female for the purposes of an old age pension, Brennan in a separate judgment stated that she would have found HH to be a male person for the purposes of the Social Security Act generally despite sex reassignment surgery (*ibid.*, at 325). Drawing upon Ormrod's analysis in the English decision of *Corbett* (at 1324), she took the view that while biological sex was 'irrelevant' in the context of an old age pension it was 'relevant' to, and perhaps an 'essential determinant' of, other relationships covered by the legislation (*ibid.*, at 325). Thus the potential for schizophrenic legal determinations of sex and sexuality, across subject matters, which is apparent in *Harris* becomes possible in Brennan's judgment within the context of a single subject matter.[4]

Legal woman versus factual woman

The lead case of *Harris*, however, proves to be an unreliable barometer, even in the context of criminal law, in assessing the likelihood of legal recognition of the sex claims of transsexual persons. While the majority[5] in *Harris* accepted the determination of 'legal sex' to be a question of law, doubt has been cast upon the correctness of that view (Sharpe, 1994). In *R* v. *Cogley* (41 A Crim R 198), a case involving an appeal against conviction for assault with intent to commit rape upon a post-operative male-to-female transsexual on the grounds that the victim was not a woman, the Victorian Court of Criminal Appeal, while upholding the conviction upon other grounds, unanimously held that the determination of the complainant's 'legal sex' was 'a question of fact to be determined by the jury' (*ibid.*, at 198).[6]

Here, then, competing judicial understandings of the law/fact distinction threaten to further queer sex, and therefore sexuality. That is to say, if the reasoning of the appeal court in *Cogley* is adopted, then the 'legal sex' of transsexual persons may prove variable, as juries can be expected to differ as to findings of fact. Thus a jury given a direction on the basis of *Harris* might conclude that genital features and psychological sex have not been brought into conformity. Indeed, Carruthers J, dissenting in *Harris*, expressed doubt as to whether conformity of this type could ever be achieved (*ibid.*, at 163).

The uncertainty regarding whether 'legal sex' is to be determined by reference to law or fact was compounded further by the Federal Court in *SRA*. In considering whether a male-to-female transsexual person was a 'woman', a 'female' or a member of the 'opposite sex' was one of law or fact, the Federal Court, following *Harris*, took the view that it was a question of law alone (*ibid.*, at 480). However, in response to counsel for the respondent's argument that the words 'woman', 'female' and the phrase 'opposite sex' are ordinary English words, not technical terms, and their meaning therefore a question of fact, Justice Lockhart expressed the view that:

> the crucial question for present purposes is . . . whether or not the evidence before the court *reasonably admits of different conclusions* as to whether certain facts or circumstances fall within the ordinary meaning of the relevant word or phrase. That is a question of law. If different conclusions are reasonably possible, it

> is necessary to decide which is the correct conclusion and that is a question of fact. (*ibid*., at 480, my italics)

The Federal Court took the view that on the facts of the case only one conclusion was reasonably open, namely that a pre-operative male-to-female transsexual was not a 'woman' for the purposes of the Social Security Act 1947 (Cth) and therefore no question of fact arose for decision. The court went on to hold that the ordinary meaning of the words 'woman' and 'female' include a post-operative male-to-female transsexual who is both psychologically and anatomically female. Yet the claim that different conclusions are precluded in respect of both pre- and post-operative transsexuals is hardly persuasive in view of Carruthers' dissenting judgment in *Harris* and the Victorian Court of Criminal Appeal's view in *Cogley* that:

> it can [not] be asserted that the arbitary selection of satisfaction as to the existence of two factual requirements, viz., 'core identity' and 'sexual re-assignment surgery' thereupon necessarily determines as a matter of law the sex of a transsexual. (*ibid*., at 204)

The legal reasoning of the Federal Court in *SRA* around the law/fact distinction opens up possibilities for resistance, subversion and the proliferation of queer legal arguments designed to free sexuality from the constraints of biological and anatomical destiny. In a sense the court invites the assertion of alternative factual conclusions regarding the 'legal sex', and therefore the sexuality, of transsexual persons. This is an invitation that ought to prove irresistible to queer legal activists and theorists alike.

Conclusion

It should be clear by now that law as a locus of struggle over sexuality can be dynamic, unstable and unpredictable. In the context of transsexuality the attempt by the Australian judiciary to reproduce heterosexual hegemony has led to a queering of the notions of both sex and sexuality. That is to say, these notions have been reinvented, inverted, turned inside out by forms of legal reasoning which insist on the 'normality' of heterosexuality and the 'abnormality' of homosexuality. Butler has asked:

> [if] sexuality is to be disclosed, what will be taken as the true

> determinant of its meaning: the phantasy structure, the act, the orifice, the gender, the anatomy? (1991, p. 17)

In the present context the 'true' determinant of the meaning of sexuality in law proves to be not one thing, but rather all the things Butler identifies and more. It is phantasy structure (psychological sex), act/orifice (the capacity for heterosexual intercourse), gender (pre-surgical medical rites of passage) and anatomy (sex reassignment surgery). However, determinants of the meaning of (trans)sexuality also include considerations of subject matter and the law/fact distinction. While the Australian judiciary have sought to maintain the hetero/homo sexual division and while that division persists, the forms of legal reasoning adopted nevertheless contain the possibility for its subversion. If the criteria for establishing sexual subjectivity continue to proliferate, then distinguishing the content of homosexuality from that of heterosexuality, and therefore any meaningful difference(s) between them, may become increasingly difficult.

In any event, irrespective of the implications transsexual case law has for the hetero/homo sexual division, one of its effects is to offer the possibility for a radical rearticulation of (trans)sexuality (Butler, 1993). The legal recognition of transsexual sex claims has involved the loosening of 'legal sex' from a specific temporal moment – birth – and from a strict grounding in biological determinism. The emergence of psychology as an integral component in 'legal sex' determinations has created a legal space for the constitution and consolidation of sex and sexuality around the subjective feelings and experiences of individuals. Legal argument along these lines would seek to overcome legal insistence on the necessity of anatomical and sexual specificity as prerequisites for legal recognition of sex identity. It is encouraging that such an approach, at least in the anatomical context, has received some legal endorsement in the form of the Administrative Appeals Tribunal decision in *SRA*.

However, even here a cautionary note is warranted, for legal recognition of SRA as female proved contingent upon her acceptance of a medico-legal 'wrong body' story and the adoption of an apologetic stance towards her own 'wrong body' (Sharpe, 1997a). Accordingly, the discursive production of SRA as female serves to clarify the 'unknowability' of the pre-surgical body even as it enables SRA to assume a presence within the law. In the last analysis the tribunal decision provides a perfect illustration of the inadequacy of a traditional law reform agenda premised upon 'progress' and highlights the need for an analysis which recognizes law as an important site of cultural production. While the traditional law reform agenda looks to potential gains, it is equally important, if not more so, to consider the potential exclusionary costs of engaging law.

Notes

1. In medical and legal discourses transsexuals are generally considered to be those persons who possess a chromosomal, gonadal and genital structure that is congruent at birth, consider themselves to be men or women despite official designation to the contrary and who have either undergone reassignment surgery or have manifested a desire for such surgery.
2. Brackets are used to draw attention to the sexualities of transsexual persons in addition to the phenomenon of transsexuality more generally.
3. *Re Anonymous* 293 NYS 2d 834 [1968]; *MT* v. *JT* 355 A 2d 204 [1976].
4. It should be pointed out that some Australian jurisdictions have enacted legislation which, subject to certain conditions, conveys full legal recognition upon post-operative transsexuals. However, such legislation has failed to overcome the schizophrenia and equivocality of legal reasoning. Indeed those tendencies have in some respects become more pronounced (see Sharpe, 1997b).
5. Carruthers J dissenting (*ibid.*, at 171) viewed the determination of 'legal sex' as involving a question of fact rather than law.
6. The question whether the determination of 'legal sex' is a question of law or fact is an important one. If a question of fact, the possibility of setting a precedent whereby transsexual sex claims are recognized is precluded.

References

Benjamin, H. (1953) 'Transvestism and transsexualism', *International Journal of Sexology*, 7(1), 12–14.

Benjamin, H. (1966) *The Transsexual Phenomenon*. New York: Julian Press.

Bolin, A. (1988) *In Search of Eve: Transsexual Rites of Passage*. Massachusetts: Bergin & Garvey.

Butler, J. (1991) 'Imitation and gender insubordination', in D. Fuss (ed.), *Inside/Out: Lesbian Theories, Gay Theories*. London: Routledge.

Butler, J. (1993) *Bodies That Matter: On the Discursive Limits of 'Sex'*. New York: Routledge.

Derrida, J. (1980) 'La loi du genre/the law of genre', trans. Avital Ronell, *Glyph*, 7, p. 176 (French), p. 202 (English).

Fisk, N. (1973) 'Gender dysphoria syndrome. (The how, what and why of a disease)', in D. R. Laub and P. Gandy, *Proceedings of the Second Interdisciplinary Symposium on Gender Dysphoria Syndrome*. Stanford: University Medical Center.

Foucault, M. (1981) *The History of Sexuality: An Introduction*, Vol. 1. London: Penguin.

Freud, S. (1975) *Three Essays on Sexuality*, trans. James Strachey. New York: Basic Books. (First published 1905.)

Fuss, D. (1991) 'Inside/out', in D. Fuss (ed.), *Inside/Out: Lesbian and Gay Theories*. London: Routledge.

King, D. (1993) *The Transvestite and the Transsexual*. Avebury.

Koranyi, E. K. (1980) *Transsexuality in the Male: The Spectrum of Gender Dysphoria*. Springfield, IL: Charles C Thomas Publishers.

Laub, D. R. and Gandy, P. (1973) *Proceedings of the Second Interdisciplinary Symposium on Gender Dysphoria Syndrome*. Stanford: University Medical Center.

Lewins, F. (1995) *Transsexualism in Society: A Sociology of Male-to-Female Transsexuals*. London: Macmillan.

Sharpe, A. N. (1994) 'The precarious position of the transsexual rape victim', *Current Issues in Criminal Justice*, **6**(2), 303–7.

Sharpe, A. N. (1997a) 'Anglo-Australian judicial approaches to transsexuality: discontinuities, continuities and the wider issues at stake', *Social and Legal Studies*, **6**, 51–78.

Sharpe, A. N. (1997b) 'The transsexual and marriage: law's contradictory desires', *Australasian Gay and Lesbian Law Journal*, **7**, 1–14.

Stoller, R. J. (1968) *Sex and Gender*. New York: Science House.

Stychin, C. F. (1995) *Law's Desire: Sexuality and the Limits of Justice*. London: Routledge.

Walinder, J., Lundstrom, B. and Thuwe, I. (1978) 'Prognostic factors in the assessment of male transsexuals for sex reassignment', *British Journal of Psychiatry*, **132**, 16–20.

3

Gemeinschaftsfremden[1] – or How to Be Shafted by Your Friends: Sterilization Requirements and Legal Status Recognition for the Transsexual

Stephen Whittle

This chapter explores the problem of 'demanded sterilization' that arises when seeking to legislate for transsexual 'rights' in the light of the recent movements within the transgender[2] community towards self-definition, both legally and medically. By concentrating on the matter of reproduction rights, it highlights how eugenics discourses, which are thought to be historically dormant, still govern the policy processes which take place within the contradictory stances that govern notions of family rights. It illustrates the hegemonic processes of government that continue to set the boundaries within which normalization and absorption into society are allowed for 'outsiders'. To the extent that the 'trans' person is to be given limited acceptance, those limits exclude what is constructed as their potential invasion of the bodily integrity of others, in this case, children. It has not proved easy for non-trans people to acknowledge both the imperative existence of trans-people and their claim to the law's protection, but it has proved even harder for them to accept fully the consequences of the 'discourse interruptus' that the community is offering in their new theorizing of sex and gender roles, because of that theory's mandatory removal of gender and sex from legal praxis. This persevering failure to comprehend the reconstructive nature of such a stance has instead meant that the 'gender neutral' or 'gender crossing' sites of trans-bodies are still seen as lacking some essential aspect of human-ness.

Resisting the issue

The 1990s have seen increasing calls from transsexual people, throughout the world, for legal recognition of their gender status in their new role. A question that has arisen is whether the transsexual person who is seeking legal recognition, for example, birth certificate amendment, should be certified as being permanently sterile at the time of recognition. The legislation from several jurisdictions including Germany, Sweden, Holland and some North American states requires this to be certified as a matter of course before a legal change of 'sex' or 'gender' will be allowed. For example, the German legislation (TSG) requires that the transsexual person be 'continuously non-reproductive' (TSG (1980) Second Section 8.1 (iii)).

In the UK a similar provision was included in the initial draft of an unsuccessful private Members' Bill, presented by Alex Carlisle MP in February 1996. But it was removed after prompting by the transsexual members of the cross-party Parliamentary Forum. They argued that, in reality, most transsexual people will be medically sterile as a result of their treatment and surgical reassignment, so to talk of a sterile post-operative transsexual person is a tautology. However, on a very rudimentary level, they also asked 'who else *has* to be sterilized before they are allowed to take up their full legal rights and responsibilities?'

At the 1993 XXIII Colloquy on European Law, 'Transsexualism, Medicine and The Law', Professor Michael Wills of the University of Berne, a rapporteur (expert witness) took the view that 'sterility [of the transsexual person] must be absolutely certain and permanent' (Council of Europe, 1993, p. 88) before a full recognition of gender change is afforded in law. However he did not explain his reasoning; it is presented as a common-sense assumption and it is shared by many of the medical practitioners who provide gender reassignment treatment. At the 1993 Colloquy no fewer than four rapporteurs mentioned the sterility requirement without 'batting an eye' (Wills, Hage, Delvaux, Doek in Council of Europe, 1993).

This assumption of sterility before legal recognition begs certain questions. It seems an almost obsessional demand, since in almost all cases it is a *de facto* consequence of the treatment and surgery undertaken.

There are, however, some transsexual people who for health reasons cannot take the high hormone levels normally prescribed, nor can they necessarily undergo extensive surgery. Should they then, by virtue of being unable to be rendered permanently sterile, be denied recognition? Furthermore, should female-to-male transsexuals be forced into undergoing a hysterectomy, a major surgical procedure that involves some high level of risk, for no therapeutic reason other than to qualify for a legal 'sex change'?

There are, also, those people who identify as transsexual but who do not wish to undergo the surgical procedures involved in gender reassignment. The development of the 1990s term 'transgendered'[3] in the trans-communities specifically caters for the inclusion of these people in the political processes concerned with access to health care, anti-discrimination and anti-hate crime policies and practices.

The legislative requirements for sterility and specific surgical procedures clearly illustrate the medico-legal discourse of the transsexual body, which highlights the ways in which particular bodies are constructed and controlled by the state. Further, they throw light on the particular eugenics and mental hygiene discourses that still surround deviant bodies.

The eugenics movement, which built on Galton's principle of enhancing a biological group on the basis of alleged hereditary merit,[4] was heavily grounded in Social Darwinism and was a powerful force well into the twentieth century. It is today all too often seen as a thing of the past which resulted in either a series of monumental policy mistakes, as in the United States Supreme Court decision in *Buck* v. *Bell* (274 US 200, 1927) in which it was held that 'three generations of imbeciles are enough', or the Nazi sterilization and killing programmes of the 1930s and 1940s. Yet while the eugenics movement[5] may have apparently disappeared, its principles live on. Smith (1994) argues that eugenics continue to influence attitudes and behaviour towards people who are perceived to be non-productive or defective. Worldwide, court decisions concerning the non-consensual sterilization of the intellectually disabled indicate that the 'basic right to reproduce' becomes largely irrelevant when considering the best interests of such women (Little, 1992). Such best interests are defined and delineated by 'qualified experts' who are, of course, medical experts.

Medical experts, both scientists and physicians, in fact have had a long and dishonourable history in the field of eugenics, creating a common discourse on degeneracy and the role of both hereditary and environmental factors in the production of 'deficiency' (Smith, 1993; Garton, 1994, p. 181). As Rafter (1992) explains, no longer did science (eugenics) go through a claims making process, which was then endorsed, thereby creating a response, but rather the claims are made, the response follows and this provides the endorsement.

Throughout the Western world and up until the 1960s, the sexuality of people of racial and social difference was regulated in order to control their reproduction (Kempton and Kahn, 1991). The 'deficient' body became the origin of deviance and the site of control. As Rafter states, the early eugenics campaigns: 'constituted a very early attempt to criminalize not an action, but the body itself' (Rafter, 1992, p. 17). In this way the body itself is the social problem and the solution to social problems is to prevent their (re)production by ensuring that the body can no longer reproduce. The relationship between the state, science and the individual was irrevocably changed through early eugenics. This paradigm shift may have been questioned, in terms of practice, but it has by no means dissipated as we approach the next century.[6]

Indeed the theoretical discourses of the 'hereditarily deficient' are still extremely powerful. Whether looking at the family planning threads within the 1994 Cairo World Conference on Population and Development or at the social theories of Charles Murray (1990), they bear reminders of some of the theoretical underpinning devised and promoted by eugenics movements throughout history.[7] Negative eugenics (which are being discussed here as opposed to positive eugenics) are fundamentally concerned with the prevention of reproduction to deplete certain societal groups. In turn, this was adapted by the mental hygiene movement into a movement concerned with controlling who could become a parent and the ways in which parenting was to be practised.

Transsexual concerns

Transsexual people may appear to have more to worry about than their right to reproduce. A significant number of jurisdictions now provide various judicial or legislative solutions for transsexual people (Whittle, 1995). Yet as problem areas are gradually surmounted, the agenda is being widened, by members of the community, to include other issues that are seen as fundamental human rights.

Furthermore, the community has itself undergone great changes in the last six years (Whittle, 1996a), and many of these changes of self-identification, alongside new reproductive technologies, have led to the possibility of procreation no longer being excluded from the post-transition transsexual person. Transsexual parenthood, albeit not genetic, is certainly on the agenda, as witnessed by the case of *X., Y. and Z.* v. *The United Kingdom* (App. 21830/93, 1995) before the European Court of Human Rights.

These issues cannot be viewed in isolation; the 'common sense' discourses that surround the drafting of any legislation relating to transsexual people can be seen to be informed by eugenic principles. Such principles are concerned with the idea that some people are less worthy people than others, and because they are lesser people (and by that I mean 'less human') they have less of a right to reproduce, to become a parent, and to practise parenting.

Lesser people – the transgendered movement

Transsexualism is currently being redefined to come under an umbrella term transgenderism, a larger group which is no longer medically defined (Whittle, 1996b), and hence body form is less prescriptive and more flexible, so enabling the physiology for procreation to be retained. There are a variety of reasons, relevant to this discussion, that contribute to this redefinition. First, the strong transsexual activist movement in the United States has had to come to terms with the fact that as medical costs spiral, and Medicaid and other insurance schemes will not finance gender reassignment surgical procedures, there are an increasing number of self-identified transsexual people who are living their lives as members of their opposite natal sex designated grouping without taking up surgical sex reassignment procedures. Similarly within the United Kingdom local Health Authorities are increasingly refusing to fund gender reassignment treatment, arguing that it is a treatment similar to cosmetic vanity surgery (Press for Change, 1995, p. 5). Because transsexual people are viewed as 'less worthy', it becomes easy for refusal to become institutionalized. Transsexual people are increasingly having to resort to privately funded, expensive, treatment; to 'sex work' to fund reassignment; or to cope with the alternative – living in role without surgical reassignment. Thus the trans-community has had to redefine its own definitions of what it means to be a transsexual person, from the 1980s view that it was someone who sought reassignment surgery, to a 1990s self-identification category based on mental rather than body morphology.

Second, despite legal recognition in the United States, to date, no court has found Title VII of the 1965 Civil Rights Act applicable to discrimination cases brought by transsexual people. From the first reported case of *Voyles* v. *R. K. Davies Medical* (403 F. Supp. 456 N. D. Cal, 1975), in which an employer was granted permission to dismiss a transsexual woman who requested that she be called by her new name, to the decision in *Kirkpatrick* v. *Seligman & Latz Inc.* (M. D. FL 1979, 636 F. 2d 1047), in which a beauty salon employee was dismissed, the courts have: 'gone out of their way to find that existing federal non-discrimination laws do not apply to transgendered individuals' (ICTLEP, 1993, p. A6-2). The courts have repeatedly held that the word 'sex' in Title VII is to be given its plain meaning and is not to encompass transsexual people, the major thrust of the legislation being to provide equal opportunities for women. Protection under state employment practices acts and non-discrimination laws has also proved elusive, as in the case of *Sommers* v. *Iowa Civil Rights Commission* (337 N. W. 2d 470, 1983). Similarly, laws protecting disabilities in particular have proved of little help (*Jane Doe* v. *Boeing Co.*, 823 P. 2d 1159 Wn. Ct. App., 1992).[8] Thus status recognition has proved grossly inadequate, and transsexual people have realized that the law provided by others fails to comprehend their issues of import.

Third, a growing theoretical (and personal/emotional) movement argues that gender is merely socialized performativity. As an imaginary concept, it is used to oppress rather than being a means of self-expression (Bornstein, 1994). Therefore transsexual people have become involved in calls for empowerment to decide and formulate their own gendered position. Gender expression becomes an entirely arbitrary identifier, personal and belonging to the self. As in other anti-discrimination movements, arbitrary identifiers should not be used to exclude people from the basic forms of social interactivity such as getting and keeping a job, bringing up children or registering relationships. Therefore the body has to be extracted from gender praxis.

The removal of the body from status means that judgments based upon status, but imposed upon the body, become problematic. Negative eugenics practice is based substantially within jurisdictions over the body. If the normative organizations, status and identity fail the jurisdictional site, then the structural value of the 'hereditarily deficient' theses is faulted. Mainstream academic theories of deviance such as the Durkheimian tradition or labelling and Foucauldian or feminist theories of deviance, locate identity as a formulation of later life, of cause and effect rather than of ancestry and birth. It may be the case that transgender theorists may deny gender as cause and effect (Whittle, 1996a), but neither do they see it in terms of biological process. The new formulations are attempting to move beyond either definitional point, and to go into Bornstein's (1994) third space in which 'our own patchwork individual identities have come together to form a brilliant complex mosaic of theater for our day' (Bornstein, 1994, p. 165). Consequently the new transgendered community when faced with bodily control, whether medical, legal or social, fights back, refusing to accept values which devalue the individual body.

Parenthood: a natural state of affairs?

Generally the law might now be said to prevent interference in the right of the individual to become a parent; from the decision in *Roe* v. *Wade* (410 US 113–152, 1973), where the US Supreme Court held that a woman's reproductive rights were protected under the privacy clause of the Constitution, to Article 12 of the European Convention on Human Rights, which protects the right to family life.

However, we must not make the assumption that everybody has the right to become a parent – the right to found a family is principally 'a negative right – a right to be free of state interference' (Feldman, 1993, p. 906). Yet this freedom from state interference is not available to all and, in the United Kingdom as elsewhere, judicial paternalism plays a significant role in authorizing the sterilization of women who would be unable to adequately care for any resultant children.[9]

Mother or father?

The notion of what is meant by parentage itself, until very recently, has not been in question, with legal systems generally regarding it as a factual progenitory relationship (unless resulting from statutory adoption).

However, in England, The Children Act 1989 by emphasizing parental responsibility, as opposed to parental rights, has gone some way to conceding and granting that there is a concept of social parenthood that may be worthy of recognition.

Furthermore, recent advances in reproductive technology have led to a questioning of what exactly is meant by the terms 'mother' and 'father' (McKnorrie, 1994). Again, in English law, The Human Fertilization and Embryology Act 1990 has removed the genetic imperatives that used to signify parentage and there is no longer any requirement for a legally recognized father to be the person who performed the fecundatory role in the conception of a child, nor does a mother have to have any genetic or birth relationship with a child. However, public and private presumptions still prevail in that a father is required to be a man, and a mother a woman. There are problems with this view, and in law the question of what is a man or a woman still requires a tremendous amount of clarification, particularly with regard to transsexual people as can be seen in the case of *X., Y. and Z.* v. *The United Kingdom*.

Man or woman?

The judgment of Ormrod LJ, in the now infamous case of *Corbett* v. *Corbett* ([1970] 2 All ER 33) which removed the right to marry from heterosexual transsexual people, gave the courts an opportunity to define what is meant by 'man' and 'woman'. *Corbett* concerned the marriage of April Ashley, a male-to-female transsexual. On the breakdown of the marriage her husband petitioned for nullity on the ground that the respondent remained a male and hence the marriage was void. Ormrod LJ decided the sexual status of April Ashley by devising a three-point test based upon the chromosomal, gonadal and genital features at the time of birth. These were established as being 'male' at the time of Ashley's birth. However, rather than deciding whether she was then a man, Ormrod LJ held:

> Since marriage is essentially a relationship between man and woman, the validity of the marriage in this case depends, in my judgement, on whether the respondent is or is not a woman. I think with respect this is a more precise way of formulating the question than that adopted in para. 2 of the petition, in which it is alleged that the respondent is male. (*Corbett* at 48)

One of the problems with any analysis of Ormrod LJ's judgment is that he constantly mixed the notions of 'male and female' with those of 'man and woman'. For example, he states in conclusion to this question: 'the respondent is not a woman for the purposes of marriage but is a biological male and has been so since birth' (*Corbett* at 49). He did not attempt to categorize Ashley as a man, but argued that marriage is a relationship based on sex rather than gender, and consequently needed to consider her to be a 'man'. Almost certainly Ormrod LJ was faced with a dilemma that arose from his being unable to define the person in front of him as a man, yet he felt unable, in law and because of the test he had devised, to call her a woman.

Thus, irrespective of any reconstructive surgery, the transsexual woman is not a woman and has at all times been a biological male. The decision in *Corbett*, despite not being considered by the higher courts, has been highly influential, not just in family law cases, and the United Kingdom government has supported this definition of sex in all of the 'transsexual' cases going to the European Courts.

The neither man nor woman in law

The definitional problems associated with the dichotomous view of gender, and in particular the right to reproduce, are not confined just to the United Kingdom. To illustrate the issues, I will look at two particular instances: a state that requires sterility in its legislative provision for transsexual people, and one that does not.

The German legislation requests that the transsexual person has

> undergone an operation to alter their other sexual marks, so that a visible closeness to the appearance of the other sex has been achieved. (TSG (1980) Second Section, SS 8. 1(iv))

but it does not specify that the operation be penectomy and vaginoplasty, or hysterectomy and phalloplasty. Nevertheless, in the case of *OLG Zweibruken* (7.5.1993, OLGZ 1993), concerning a transsexual man who had undergone a bilateral masectomy, the courts asked to ascertain what the law required for a 'clear approximation' to the opposite sex, decided in favour of the transsexual man (Council of Europe, 1995, p. 89). Interestingly, one of the courts' reasons was that occlusion of the vagina was unnecessary, as hormone therapy would diminish the size of the vagina, thereby precluding sexual activity as a woman. This makes several false assumptions, first that the vagina diminishes in size, second that women always have vaginal intercourse, and third that transsexual men are never gay (see Sharpe in this collection). The decision and commentary on it by Wills (Council of Europe, 1993) are indicative of the lack of understanding of transsexualism, its features and the effects of reassignment treatment, and they highlight the continuing problems of ignorance in this area.

An earlier German case concerned a transsexual man who had undergone a bilateral mastectomy but was unable to continue hormone therapy and unwilling to undergo any further surgery. The legislation requires that the transsexual person be completely non-reproductive. In this case the courts granted a name change, but would not allow the change of sex designation because regular menstruation showed that the applicant was still fertile. In obiter, the court held that a reversible interruption of the fallopian tubes might be sufficient, because a transsexual man would be very unlikely to seek such a reversal (OLG Hamm, 15.2.1983, OLGZ 1983). However, Wills argues that this does not preclude the possibility of in-vitro fertilization, and that such practice ought not to prevail (Council of Europe, 1993, p. 88).

It may stretch the imagination to think of a man giving birth, or a woman impregnating and fathering a child, yet where does the law define that a mother must be a person of xx chromosomes with a womb and vagina and a father a person of xy chromosomes with testes and a penis? For that matter, where does it define a man as having xy chromosomes, and a woman xx chromosomes? It is in Ormrod LJ's decidedly problematic decision in *Corbett* that we see these criteria being upheld.

The requirement that the transsexual person should not be able to reproduce through the biological mechanisms concordant with their natal sex designation is not the only issue. What if future surgical techniques enable a transsexual woman to carry a child – should this be restricted?

In contrast, it is possible in various states in the United States and Canada to obtain legal recognition of a new gender status without having to undergo sterilization. In British Columbia an unmarried transsexual may apply to the Director of Vital Statistics to 'change the sex designation on the registration of birth of such a person in such a manner that the sex designation is consistent with the intended results of the transsexual surgery' (*Revised Statutes British Columbia*, 1974 Section 21a(1)) and there is no specific requirement of sterility. However, the problems that have arisen under German law have also arisen under Canadian law. In two Canadian cases, *C(L) v. C(C)* (Ont. C. J. Lexis 1518, 1992) and *B. v. A.* (29 RFL (3d) 258, 1990) transsexual men were held not to be spouses/ husbands for the purposes of marriage and family law, albeit they were so held for other purposes. If the only surgery they had undergone was a bilateral mastectomy and a hysterectomy they could become men but not husbands. The courts, both in Ontario, followed the doctrine in *Corbett*. If not a man for the purposes of marriage, are they a man for the purposes of fatherhood? They certainly would not be men if they retained their reproductive facilities.

The International Bill of Gender Rights

The International Bill of Gender Rights (IBGR) is one way in which the transgender community promotes the issues relating to the community's legal and social status. The most recent version (adopted in Houston, Texas, USA, 17 June 1995) is a theoretical proposal that formulates basic human rights from a transgender perspective. These rights are not seen as special rights, but rather as universal statements of human rights and consequently the customary labels – gay, lesbian, bisexual, transgendered, transsexual, transvestite, bi-gendered, crossdresser – are deemed unnecessary. The tenth right states:

> individuals shall not be denied the right to conceive, bear or adopt children, nor to nurture and have custody of children, nor to exercise parental capacity with respect to children, natural or adopted, on the basis of their own, their partner's, or their children's chromosomal sex, genitalia, assigned birth sex, initial gender role, or by virtue of a self-defined gender identity or the expression thereof. (ICTLEP, 1995)

Thus it states that the right to be a parent should not be dictated by gender identity, and that living in an oppositional gender role should not prevent, in law, the procreation, conception or bearing of children. This means that an individual who lives as and is legally recognized as a male, but who for some reason has not taken enough hormones, nor undergone enough surgery to render it otherwise, could bear a child.

Research has shown that the children of transsexual parents are just as likely to grow up well adjusted (and as heterosexual) as any other child (Green, 1978). However, it becomes illogical to discuss the 'best interests' of the child, if the child can never be born. Just as in eugenics, if the claim is made that transsexual people are not suitable for parenthood, then they are refused access to parenthood, and this supports the claim because there is no evidence to the contrary. The English case of *Re D (a minor) (wardship: sterilisation)* ([1976] 1 All ER 326) held, on interpretation, that any sterilization performed in the absence of consent and for non-therapeutic reasons involves a deprivation of the right to reproduce (Lee and Morgan, 1989, p. 136). The International Bill of Gender Rights argues for a recognition of that basic human right in the 'revolutionary' framework of a unified humanity. Lee and Morgan feel that the argument that liberties are dependant upon usages that others consider reasonable or valuable is a dangerous one, and they cite Bernard Williams:[10] 'there is no slippery slope more perilous than that extended by a concept which is falsely supposed not to be slippery' (Lee and Morgan, 1989, p. 152 n. 25). Assuming that the surgically reassigned transsexual person has voluntarily given up a right to reproduce begs the question whether there is little, if any scope, for the giving or refusal of consent. The individual is faced with the lesser of two evils, a choice of choosing to live as a whole person or to reproduce and give life to another person at the cost of one's self. There is no real choice if we do not provide in law (or medicine) either a space in which the legal status change sometimes afforded to the gender reassigned does not require procedures demanding sterility or, alternatively, a universal framework in which sex or gender is no longer a delineator in law. The International Bill of Gender Rights promotes a vision of the world in which child-bearing and child-rearing are by and about the development of people rather than by and about the development of men and women. This vision is symbolic of the reconstructive project of the new trans community; going beyond the deconstructive enterprise of postmodernity.

Science and society are changing too rapidly to know what will lie in the future, but it is not so long in the past that negative eugenics, the forced sterilization of unfit, asocial groups of people was accepted medical practice in some countries. Undoubtedly the discourses that led to the 'hygienic' practices of the past are still just bubbling under the surface. The transsexual/transgendered person could be regarded as the ultimate non-being, neither man nor woman, a-gendered and hence asocial, therefore a danger to all our futures. Yet, just like the rest of us, throughout history they have been carrying their genes alongside ours.

> The only way to oppose eugenics is to ensure that human rights come first. The idea of scientifically manufacturing a set of people exclusively composed of individuals with certain characteristics must be outlawed because it runs counter to the dignity of human beings, who are unique, free and responsible for their actions. . . . In the words of the American novelist Paul Auster 'Each man is the entire world, bearing within his genes a memory of all mankind.' (Elnadi, 1994, p. 5)

Notes

1. *Gemeinschaftsfremden* is the title of the 1943 Nazi draft law on the 'handling of social aliens', which provided the framework for the compulsory castration of homosexual men in Nazi concentration camps.
2. The term 'transgender' is inclusive, and includes a wide range of people including transsexual people who seek gender reassignment, both surgically and legally.
3. For an explanation of the term 'transgendered' see Whittle, 1996a.
4. Francis Galton coined the word 'eugenics' in his 1883 book *Inquiries into Human Faculty and Its Development*, reprinted in 1973 by AMS Press, New York.
5. The eugenics movement might be best defined as a Euro-centric collection of campaigning groups, individual physicians and policy-makers, who throughout the late nineteenth century and twentieth century held that racial miscegenation and 'poor breeding' were the causes of poverty, mental health problems, people with learning difficulties, and other sorts of 'social disease'. In the later twentieth century, many aspects of their theories, although seen to be racist or bigoted at an intellectual level, have entered the social discourses surrounding parenting rights.
6. The controversies surrounding theoretical eugenics are still very much with us, as could be seen with the publication of the book *The Bell Curve* (Hernstein and Murray, 1994), the withdrawal from publication of Edinburgh University's Christopher Brand's book (Ofori, 1996), and the criticisms of the Pioneer Fund funding of American and European Academics (ABC News, 1994; *Irish Times*, 1994).
7. In 1995 China's new law promoting the sterilization of people suffering from genetic disorders (Agence France Press, 1995) was justified as being, 'aimed at improving China's population both in quantity and quality' (Maier, 1995).
8. For example, the 1995 Disability Discrimination Act includes in its definition of disability 'mental impairment' if the illness is a clinically well-recognized illness. As gender dysphoria, which is seen as a pre-essential to receiving treatment for transsexualism, is included in the Diagnostic Statistical Manual IV (1994) of the American Psychiatric Association, transsexuals could argue that it is a disability under the Act as long as it has had a substantial and long-term adverse effect on their abilities to carry out normal day-to-day activities, and therefore they should

be afforded the protection given under the Act in the areas of employment and the provision of goods and services.

9. For an example see *Re: F (mental patient: sterilisation)* 1990 2 AC 1.
10. In B. Williams, 'Which slopes are slippery?', in M. Lockwood, (ed.), *Moral Dilemmas in Modern Medicine* (London: Oxford University Press, 1985).

References

ABC News (1994) 'Bell Curve and the Eugenics Foundation', Tonight Program, 22 November.

Agence France Press (1 June 1995) 'Chinese minister defends new eugenics law'.

Bornstein, K. (1994) *Gender Outlaw: On Men, Women and the Rest of US*. New York: Routledge.

Council of Europe (1993) *Proceeding of the XXIII Colloquy on European Law: Transsexualism, Medicine and Law*. Strasbourg: Council of Europe.

Elnadi, A. B. Noelle Lenoir (1994) *Unesco Courier*, Iss 0304–3118, pp. 5–9.

Feldman, D. (1993) *Civil Liberties and Human Rights in England and Wales*. Oxford: Oxford University Press.

Garton, S. (1994) 'Sound minds and healthy bodies: re-considering eugenics in Australia 1914–1940', *Australian Historical Studies*, **26**(103), 163–81.

Green, R. (1978) 'Sexual identity of 37 children raised by homosexual or transsexual parents', *American Journal of Psychiatry*, **135**(6), 692–7.

Hernstein, R. J. and Murray, C. (1994) *The Bell Curve: Intelligence and Class Structure in American Life*. London: Free Press.

ICTLEP (1993) *Proceedings from the Second Conference on Transgender Law and Employment Policy*. Houston: ICTLEP.

ICTLEP (1995) *International Bill of Gender Rights*. Houston: ICTLEP.

Irish Times (1994) 'Of race and right', *Irish Times Education and Living*, 6 December 1994.

Kempton, W. and Kahn, E. (1991) 'Sexuality and people with intellectual disabilities: a historical perspective', *Sexuality and Disability: Special Issue: Sexuality and Developmental Disability*, **9**(2), 93–111.

Lee, R. and Morgan, D. (1989) *Birthrights, Law and Ethics at the Beginning of Life*. London: Routledge.

Little, H. (1992) 'Non-consensual sterilisation of the intellectually disabled in the Australian context: potential for human rights abuse and the need for reform', *Australian Year Book of International Law*, pp. 203–26.

McKnorrie, K. (1994) 'Reproductive technology, transsexualism and homosexuality: new problems for international private law', *International and Comparative Law Quarterly*, **43**, 757–75.

Maier, S. (1995) 'Preventative eugenics', *World Press Review*, **26**.

Murray, C. (1990) *The Emerging British Underclass*. London: The IEA Health and Welfare Unit.

Ofori, T. (1996) 'Where only the gowns are black', *Guardian Education*, 7 May 1996.

Press for Change (1995) *Newsletter No.4*. London: Press for Change.

Rafter, N. (1992) 'Claims-making and socio-cultural context in the first U.S. eugenics campaign', *Social Problems*, **39**(1), 17–34.

Smith, D. J. (1993) 'Institutionalization, involuntary sterilization, and mental retardation: profiles from the history of the practice', *Mental-Retardation*, **31**(4), 208–14.

Smith, D. J. (1994) 'Reflections on mental retardation and eugenics, old and new: Mensa and the Human Genome Project', *Mental-Retardation*, **32**(3), 234–8.

Whittle, S. (1995) *Transvestism, Transsexualism and the Law*. Belper: The Gender Trust.

Whittle, S. (1996a) 'Gender fucking or fucking gender', in R. Elkins and D. King (eds), *Blending Genders: Social Aspects of Cross Dressing and Sex Changing*. London: Routledge.

Whittle, S. (1996b) *The Trans-Cyberian Mail Way* (unpublished).

4

The Lesbian Mother: Questions of Gender and Sexual Identity

Sarah Beresford

This chapter is concerned with lesbian identities in law and the lesbian mother in particular.[1] My analysis examines the 'gaps' between constructions, expressions and representations of a mother's self-identity and those that are imposed upon her by law. These matters will be considered by way of a series of legal judgments concerned with parental responsibility for the child of the family and the child's residence.[2] These cases suggest that the law's concept of lesbian identity cannot be easily reconciled with the diversity of women's experiences and sexual identities. Lesbian mothers are forced to inhabit a 'legal body' not of their own making and construction. In this context I understand the 'legal body' as a cultural and legal construct. It is composed of numerous aspects of identity, for example gender, nationality and ethnicity, which together combine to (re)produce an overall sense of self. This 'body' can be viewed as an outward expression of identity – an expression of a particular way of being 'one's self'. This body can also be viewed as an inner source of self-identity. Within the context of these issues, the term 'body' is capable of being interpreted as generating and containing a multiplicity of meanings. In this particular context, my use of 'legal body' refers to the individual person as she appears to the court and to law – a person who is 'fully constituted' to bring matters of legal dispute before the authority of the court and the legal process. In other words, a person who is capable of enjoying legal rights, or is subject to legal duties.

Through an analysis of the 'gaps' between how an individual perceives and constructs herself, and how that individual is constructed and then represented in law, I will draw attention to the continuing difficulty that women, as legal subjects, have in authenticating their identity and exercising control over it. In particular I will consider the ways in which law impoverishes our understanding of identity by way of an extremely limited range of imposed alternatives. I will illustrate the many ways in which self-identity is excluded from law, by law, and by the imposition of an identity different to that constructed by the subject herself, and the extent to which a subject's attempts to 'self-define' her identity are undermined and resisted by law seeking to impose its own constructions.

Female identity as 'property': the principle of marital unity

A preliminary matter that needs to be addressed in this context is the relation between the identity of the subject in law and the 'control' and 'ownership' of that identity. This is of particular concern for women, as the law has traditionally treated the woman as the property of the man. The clearest example of this is to be found in the principle of 'marital unity':

> the husband and wife are one person in law: that is, the very being or legal existence of the woman is suspended during the marriage, or at least is incorporated and consolidated into that of her husband: under whose wing, protection, and cover, she performs everything. (Blackstone, 1769, pp. 441–2)

While 'marital unity' addresses the ownership and control of woman's identity in the context of marriage, the principle of 'ownership' and 'control' that is described here is not limited to the woman as wife, but it also applied to woman as daughter and woman as mother. In the context of marriage, having no independent legal existence produced various effects. It meant it was legally impossible for a husband to commit rape against his wife (Hale, 1678, p. 629). Being 'one person' in law, marital rape was taken to be an act of rape by the husband upon himself – a legal impossiblility.[3] Further, if a wife was sexually assaulted or raped by a man other than her husband, only the husband had legal redress in the form of tortious action for interference with property rights. Sexual violence was treated as a *property* crime.

As property, a woman's gender and sexuality might be not so much matters that she herself determined and controlled, but matters subject to the control of men, sanctioned and enforced in law by men. She had little or no effective control, possession or ownership of her sexual and gender identity. Historically, the 'legal body' of a woman was considered as 'property'. All of these examples draw attention to the legal tradition which denied women the possibility of an autonomous self presence in the law and formally subjected them to the control of men. As I will illustrate in this chapter, women still experience considerable difficulties in their attempts to control the way they are represented in the law.

Invisible identities?

Lesbian identities and experiences,[4] have a long cultural history, although much of that history remains undocumented, concealed or invisible (Faderman, 1985; Donoghue, 1993). In a legal context, those identities and experiences can be said to have a relatively short history, having been rendered invisible by, and displaced from, legal culture (Robson, 1992). However, there are signs that lesbian identity is gradually becoming more visible both on a wider scale and more particularly within legal culture. This appears to reflect a social and legal reappraisal of lesbian identity. For example, the media appear to have had (and are still having), a field day with lesbians generally, promoted largely by the emergence of 'lesbian chic' or the 'lipstick' lesbian (Cindy Crawford and k.d. lang on the front cover of *Vanity Fair* appears to be the most famous example). On the other hand, there is still evidence that this shift is relatively limited. One example where the limit of changes is to be found is in the context of lesbian motherhood.

Constructing the body of the lesbian mother

Recent press coverage given to lesbian mothers has provided the following headlines:

> Should Lesbians Have Children? (*Daily Express*, 22 June 1994),
> Court Says That Lesbian Can Be 'Father' (*Daily Mail*, 30 June 1994)
> Gay Culture Will Never Beat Nature (*Daily Mail*, 23 January 1995)

These newspaper headlines illustrate the continuation of negative social constructions of lesbian mothers, which is generated by attaching a particular significance to her sexuality. This is in sharp contrast to 'traditional motherhood' where (heterosexual) women are perceived as non-sexual beings.

When it falls to law to determine and assess 'parental suitability' or the child's residence, those mothers who express a sexuality other than heterosexuality, again find that their sexuality assumes an importance not deemed relevant to heterosexual mothers. It is to these matters that I now want to turn.

The case I want to consider is *Re C* (1994). This decision was the first to grant a lesbian couple joint parental responsibility for a 22-month-old boy. Despite this, *Re C* did not find its way into the law reports (the hearing was held 'in camera', and only a short statement was authorized by the judge). As such, its status as a precedent is problematic, further adding to the invisibility of lesbian motherhood to academics and practitioners alike. However, the media provides some insight into some of the problems that arise in the context of establishing lesbian motherhood in law.

While the actual decision was welcomed by many, there were some who were not quite so enthusiastic. Harry Greenway, a Conservative MP, commented 'It's very unfair on the child. He should have a father as well as a mother. There should be an appeal without delay' (*Daily Mirror*, 30 June 1994). The late Sir Nicholas Fairbairn, former Conservative Solicitor General for Scotland, observed 'It's ridiculous. We don't put children in the hands of the insane. Why should we put them in the hands of the perverted? Surely the child should have a normal upbringing not an abnormal one' (*Daily Express*, 30 June 1994). These statements about the case are of interest in various ways. They set up the distinction between lesbian and heterosexual by resort to a series of polar opposites: the perverted and the normal, 'gay' versus 'straight', 'good' versus 'bad'. The establishment of 'gay' as a polar opposite of 'heterosexual' is particularly important in the context of the term 'lesbian mother'. In this context 'lesbian mother' is an oxymoron. For the lesbian to be a 'mother', she has to 'mimic' the construction of 'woman' as heterosexual. As 'motherhood' is understood in terms of heterocentric normativity, the sexuality of motherhood is rendered invisible. Lesbian mothers upset the relation between sexuality and gender, rendering motherhood sexualized and thereby problematic.

More generally within the context of that amorphous body called 'Family Law', the heterosexualist imperative in law reiterates and imposes 'norms' that make up the idea of 'parent'. Generally speaking, in all jurisdictions, it will be the mother who is more likely to have custody of the children, and therefore it is the lesbian mother who is placed under greatest scrutiny. As Edwards notes, 'Lesbianism has been considered as axiomatically antipathetical to the interests of the child and incongruous with the construction of motherhood' (Edwards, 1996, p. 69). What appears to be a common thread throughout residence and responsibility cases, is the almost exclusive reliance on the heterocentric imperative. Accordingly, families are (in a legal sense) essentially heterosexual, and a woman's sexual identity is heterosexual. This, as O'Donovan points out, is because of the perceived 'dissonance' between 'mother' and all that the word implies, and 'lesbian' which carries a different set of resonances. It is for this reason that a lesbian mother's application for residence in respect of a child is difficult for family law judges to come to terms with.

> Faced with this problem of dissonance, courts resort to the external environment and general social attitudes. ... So although the mother may be seen by the court as better qualified for child care than the father by reason of past experience or a 'natural bond', her femininity, which is affirmed by such a perception, is opened to question by sexual preferences. (O'Donovan, 1993, p. 84)

As a mother, a woman is further constructed according to the distinction 'married' or 'unmarried', which in turn are made to signify respectively 'good mother' or 'bad mother'. Here we have categories of mother which are defined not in terms of the relationship between the child and the mother, but by reference to the marital status of the mother, a role that has traditionally been subordinated to that of 'husband/father'. Because many lesbian mothers are legally unmarried,[5] or are in the process of divorce, they are placed into the category of a 'bad' mother due to the law's construction of unmarried mothers as 'bad', and married mothers as 'good' (see Wallbank, 1997). As such, a lesbian's sexual identity threatens to disrupt the heterocentric logic of identity.

At the same time, the more a lesbian conforms to the pre-existing legal attributes conventionally associated with the construction of 'woman', the more likely she is to be successful in any residence case. The pressure to conform can take several guises. For example, prior to the case reaching the court room, the woman's solicitor may advise her to wear a skirt, or to apply make-up. If the case ends up in court, the identity of the particular woman is further constructed and restrained by enquiries into the mother's lifestyle, with invasive questioning regarding lifestyle and shows of physical affection in front of the child(ren), and concern about the 'minutiae of who was in which bedroom, whether or not the women slept in the same bed' (Crane, 1982, p. 103). Questions such as 'Will you have sex in front of the children?' or 'Do you make a noise when you have sex?' (*Guardian*, 5 December 1990) are not uncommon.

The 'catch-22' situation for the lesbian mother is that for as long as she 'refuses' to adopt the hetero-identity the law has constructed for her, she faces an uphill battle in trying to convince the court that she is a 'suitable' parent. Her lesbian sexuality becomes 'relevant' though if she were a heterosexual mother sexuality would have no such similar 'relevance'. If she adopts the hetero-identity constructed for her, she does appear to stand a greater chance of success, but at the cost of denying her self-identified sexual identity.

In this context, the 'appearance' of the lesbian is all-important to legal culture. Law appears more concerned with the so-called 'butch' lesbian, than it is with the so-called 'feminine' lesbian (Creed, 1995). The latter presents a 'lesser' threat to the dominant male ideology than the former. This is due to a greater 'sameness' – the 'feminine lesbian' body physically presents herself as visibly little different from her heterosexual counterpart. The 'butch' lesbian body presents herself with a greater degree of difference. However, although physical sameness is one factor, more important, perhaps, is 'lifestyle', which is understood by reference to a public/private distinction found within legal discourse.

The public/private distinction is also a distinction between good and bad. In the reported case of *B* v. *B* (1991) the judge drew the distinction between 'lesbians who were private persons who did not believe in advertising their lesbianism . . . and militant lesbians who tried to convert others to their way of life'. Here the private lesbian was praised (the good lesbian), while the militant (public) lesbian was regarded with suspicion (the bad lesbian). In contrast to the lesbian, the existence of heterosexual orientation presents no such dichotomy. A distinction between 'private' heterosexuals and 'public/militant' heterosexuals makes no sense. By way of these distinctions the lesbian identity is constituted as both other to heterosexuality and other to itself. Both work to render lesbian identities largely invisible. In turn that which is visible is forced to 'conform' to the 'accepted' expectations of female gender identity expression: the 'feminine' female. The expression of sexual identity has to 'conform' with the expression of gender identity. In other words, legal culture expects and requires conformity to its own constructs of sexual and gender identity. Where an individual's expression of sexual identity does not conform, that sexual identity is perceived by legal culture as 'deviant'. The constructed legal body is the only body that legal culture is able to recognize and respond to – given the prejudicial criteria for visibility. 'Lesbian bodies' are constructed as 'outsiders'.

We can make a link with this and the previous point about appearances. There, the 'feminine' was 'good, invisible and private' as opposed to the 'butch' which was 'bad, militant and public'. The former appears to be more 'accepted' than the latter. However, the problem is slightly more subtle than this. As Creed notes, 'to function properly as ideological litmus paper, the lesbian body must be instantly recognisable' (1995, p. 23). As such, appearance is never always irrelevant. Where the lesbian body is other, exposure is always already a possibility. In this context, 'control' over identity lies with the law, not the individual.

The decision in *Re C* appears to be at odds with previous cases where lesbianism was considered legally relevant to questions relating to a child's residence, or parental responsibility. An interesting feature of *Re C* is the lack of consideration given to sexual orientation. In this context, the lack of consideration given to sexual orientation is similar in nature to applications by heterosexual women. In fact, it was not considered at all. But we can also say of this decision that although sexual identity might have been considered relevant, it was not considered problematic. The press release at the time gave the impression that the mother's sexual identity was not considered problematic because no legal representation was made regarding this issue. (The Official Solicitor who represented the child's interests was in favour of the application.) In one respect, it can be argued that this case is a step forward, for sexual identity was not considered legally problematic. However, the outcome of this case does not mean that the obsession, in legal culture, with non-heterosexual identity has magically disappeared. The absence of discourse on the relevance of lesbianism to parenting in this case can be seen as a positive omission, but there remains that which was *not* stated. The case did not expressly state that sexual orientation is irrelevant and unproblematic to parenting. Thus it is (unfortunately) still open for future cases to consider a lesbian identity as a legally relevant consideration, illustrating the law's determination to continue constructing identity and imposing that construction upon its subjects.

This particular point is one that should, in the first instance, be analysed in terms of equality. In terms of assessing parental suitability, sexual orientation is at present only considered relevant where that sexual orientation is not heterosexual. In this context, it is possible to view this case from another angle. If we assume that the court is preoccupied with lesbianism, then why not emphasize this in order to illustrate to the court the advantages for a child of being brought up in a lesbian household? In other words, this approach would acknowledge the court's *de facto* interest in the mother's lesbianism, and would use this to emphasize the positive aspects of lesbian parenting as opposed to heterosexual parenting. While this idea holds some attraction, I remain unconvinced that emphasizing lesbian identity to the court would necessarily produce 'better results'. A significant majority of such custody cases revolve around a dispute between a lesbian mother and her estranged male heterosexual partner. A potentially significant danger here is that lesbian sexuality would be placed in a competitive arena with heterosexuality. Such a context would necessitate portraying lesbian sexuality as 'better' than heterosexuality – a sexual identity 'competition'. This, in my opinion, would be an unnecessary focus. What is important is not necessarily what sexual identity is 'better' than another, but the quality of parenting.

At this juncture, a distinction needs to be made between 'sex' and 'gender'. Obviously the terms 'sex' and 'gender' will have different meanings for different people, but there does appear to be a relatively common understanding that there is a division in the distinction between sex and gender. It is a widely held view that the terms 'sex' and 'gender' do not have the same meaning. And what purpose does making this distinction have? The distinction appears to serve the argument that whatever fixed characteristics sex (as a biological phenomenon)[6] may, or may not, have, as a cultural construct gender can take as many different forms as there are possible variations in cultural ways of life. Thus, gender is neither the causal result of sex nor as seemingly fixed as sex. If we accept the argument that sex denotes physical characteristics, hormones, chromosomes and so forth, then gender still remains something else other than sex. Gender is usually said to be expressed by those personality traits and behaviour patterns associated with the cultural constructs of 'masculinity' and 'femininity'. Therefore, a biological sexed 'man' can be 'effeminate', and a biologically sexed 'woman' can be identified as 'masculine'.

Furthermore, even if the sexes appear to be unproblematically binary (which cannot be assumed),[7] there is no reason to assume that gender must necessarily be unproblematically binary. The presumption of a binary gender system implicitly retains the ideological belief in gender 'mimicking' or being defined by sex. When the constructed status of gender is theorized and *lived*, as being totally independent of sex, gender is again recognized as a free-floating artifice (see the articles by Sharpe and Whittle in this collection). The paucity and narrowness of the 'binary' approach to sex and gender leave us little room for manoeuvre outside of the predetermined compound. If we wish to explore the extent to which the individual can have genuine self-determination with respect to sexuality and gender, thinking in terms of universal, narrow, binary opposites does not allow for much diversity, and again leads to essentialism.

From a position outside the heterosexual norm, the lesbian lives a paradox. While the lesbian sense of self may be more of a 'product' of the lesbian herself than the sense of self of her heterosexual counterpart, the more she identifies with a lesbian body, the greater the gap will be between her self-defined identity and the identity which law constructs for her. Furthermore, the less likely she is to receive formal recognition of that lesbian body and the greater the regulation and control. Viewed in this way, 'control' and 'ownership' of the sexual body and the expression of identity are separated from self-determination and autonomy. The law's concern here is not so much 'truth' as one truth, one legal body, one legal identity, which exludes other senses of self.

Some conclusions

While it can be argued that greater visibility for lesbians and lesbian motherhood is a 'good thing',[8] greater visibility does not necessarily mean greater subjective control over identity. While the boundaries of lesbian identities may have widened or moved (which remains to be seen), this has not necessarily been the result of a re-evaluation of the strategies employed in constructing those identities, and this may partly explain why the 'new' lesbian identity is largely as stereotypically limited as the legal construct of 'wife', or 'mother', 'husband', 'father' and so forth.

The idea that sexuality or sexual identity is a social construct is nothing new, but as with any construct, what must be remembered is that the construct cannot exist independently as a 'thing in itself'. Without its constructors, it has no 'independent' existence (Caplan, 1987; Frosh, 1994). Without law as the constructor, the boundaries of identity cease to have importance or relevance.

If law is to continue to exercise control over the formation and expression of identity, it must enforce and preserve the exclusive parameters of identity. The gaps separating imposed identity and self-defined identity, essential to the maintenance of its own control, must be maintained and enforced by a process of exclusion, definition and ownership.

'Lesbian identity' in motherhood presents an interesting legal construction because it crosses the boundaries of legal identity. In terms of 'control' or 'ownership' of identity, the experience of the lesbian mother can uncover the law's pervasiveness in not just the construction of identity, but also the control over the expression of identity. The lesbian mother may have control over her appearance, and she may have the appearance of control, but she faces a severe uphill struggle to gain legal representation and recognition of her lesbian body unless she complies with a predetermined construction of identity.

Notes

1. The term 'lesbian mother' obviously has essentialist connotations, and while I am reluctant to place reliance on essentialism, this chapter concentrates upon the *law's* essentialist constructions of identity. Indeed, this point illustrates the limitations placed upon us by language; there must surely be a suitable alternative terminology available that encompasses the extremely wide-ranging and diverse group of women whose sexuality and sexual existence, not being heterosexual, is questioned and controlled by legal culture.
2. Since the introduction of the Children Act 1989, the terms 'custody' and 'access' have been replaced by 'residence' and 'contact' respectively.
3. The erasure of women's identity within the context of 'the marital rape exemption' only came to a formal end in the case of *R* v. *R* [1991] 3 Weekly Law Reports 767.

4. I use this phrase to include the widest possible variety of female same-sex relationships.
5. In legal terms, the lesbian mother cannot adhere to the prescribed formal rules for the legal recognition of her partnership (if she has one). And while two 'parents' are generally considered to be 'better' than one, this refers only to a man and a woman. Consequently, it is not only in connection with the formal rules that the lesbian partnership is not recognized.
6. Butler has argued that 'Sex is an ideal construct which is forcibly materialised through time. It is not a simple fact or static condition of a body, but a process whereby regulatory norms materialise "sex" and achieve this materialisation through forcible reiteration of those norms' (Butler, 1993, p. 1).
7. See for example the *Independent*, 9 October 1994, which highlights the growing number of individuals who wish to create and become part of the third gender – neither male nor female.
8. By a 'good thing', I mean that lesbians are at least becoming part of the discourse, having been previously ignored in comparison to, for example, gay men.

References

Blackstone, W. (1769) *Commentaries on the Laws of England Volume 1*, reprinted 1979. London: University of Chicago Press.

Butler, J. (1993) *Bodies That Matter: On the Discursive Limits of 'Sex'*. London: Routledge.

Caplan, P. (1987) *The Cultural Construction of Sexuality*. London: Routledge.

Crane, P. (1982) *Gays and The Law*. London: Pluto Press.

Creed, B. (1995) 'Lesbian bodies', in *Sexy Bodies – The Strange Carnalities of Feminism*. London: Routledge.

Donoghue, E. (1993) *Passions Between Women. British Lesbian Culture 1668–1801*. London: Scarlet Press.

Edwards, S. M. (1996) *Sex and Gender in the Legal Process*. London: Blackstone Press.

Faderman, L. (1985) *Surpassing the Love of Men: Romantic Friendships and Love Between Women from the Renaissance to the Present*. London: Women's Press.

Frosh, S. (1994) *Sexual Difference, Masculinity and Psychoanalysis*. London: Routledge.

Hale, M. (1678) *Pleas of the Crown, A Methodical Summary of the Principle Matters Relating to the Subject*, 1982 reprint. London: Professional Books.

O'Donovan, K. (1993) *Family Law Matters*. London: Pluto Press.

Robson, R. (1992) *Lesbian (Out)Law*. Ithaca, NY: Firebrand.

Wallbank, J. (1997) *Reconstructing Mothers and Fathers in Contemporary Debates on Child Support and the Lone Parent Family*, PhD dissertation, University of Lancaster, Lancaster.

5

The Possibility of a Registered Partnership under German Law

Judith Rauhofer

Over the past few years, some European countries have introduced so-called 'registered partnerships' that enable gay and lesbian couples to obtain some form of legal recognition and protection for their relationships.[1] The lesbian and gay movements that fought for these laws have seen this as an instrument for achieving the broader acceptance of their relationships and for obtaining the rights and privileges granted to (heterosexual) married couples. In Germany, because of the political climate and the different organization of the gay and lesbian movement, the question of 'gay marriage' has not been on the agenda. Only since the early 1990s have discussions taken place about introducing such an institution under German law. This chapter focuses on 'gay marriage' debates in Germany and explores the constitutional problems facing law reform in this context. It pursues this objective by way of lesbian and gay critiques of these proposals that seek to transfer the privileges associated with the recognition of heterosexual marriage to same-sex marriage.

The protection of 'marriage'[2] in the German Grundgesetz (GG)[3]

According to Article 6 I GG 'marriage and family shall enjoy the special protection of the State'. The 'fathers of the Constitution' thereby created an area of legal protection for a certain form of relationship between two people. Looking at the concept of 'marriage' as it is protected in Article 6 GG, three questions are evident. First, how was 'marriage' defined? Second, what effects does the special protection of 'marriage' have for those who take advantage of it? And last, how does this affect other forms of relationships, especially same-sex relationships?

Definition of 'marriage' according to the Constitutional Court

The Federal Constitutional Court Stated in 1959 that 'marriage as the object of state protection is as a rule the lifelong association of one man and one woman in a relationship' (BVerfGE 20, 59, 66).[4] This means that even though it is not defined in the Constitution itself, the partners of a marriage have to be of a different sex. This is generally acknowledged as an indispensable pre-condition. This can be verified by looking at the history of Article 6 1 GG (BVerfGE 6, 55). In the original proposal for a new German Constitution after the Second World War, the wording of Article 119 1, 11 of the Weimar Constitution was used as the basis for the new definition. It stated that 'marriage as the legal form of an on-going relationship between man and woman ... enjoy(s) the special protection of the Constitution'. The General Editorial Committee for the Creation of a New Constitution, however, clearly aimed for a shorter version of the clause. It reasoned that 'no special reference to the legal form of an on-going relationship between man and woman is needed if marriage itself is to be protected by the State' (Report of the Parliamentary debates: PR-Drucks. No. 370, 13.12.48).

In the final version of Article 6 1 GG 'marriage' was therefore understood as the term for a heterosexual relationship and any further definition with regard to the sex of the partners was deemed to be an unnecessary tautology. This attitude was the basis for any future interpretation of the law and, by definition, excluded same-sex couples from a range of rights and privileges.

However, having regard to the changes occurring in society, the continued validity of this definition can be questioned. In contrast to the time of the adoption of the German Constitution, 1949, marriage today has ceased to be the standard form of relationship in Germany. According to the latest estimate based on an official micro-census, the number of cohabiting couples has more than tripled in the past decade (from 516,000 in 1982 to 1,582,000 in 1993) while only 50.2 per cent of men and 46.8 per cent of women remain married. In addition, the stated purpose for the protection of marriage, the conception of and caring for children, is no longer limited to married couples. Approximately a quarter of all cohabiting couples have children. Cohabitation and single-parent families are equally acknowledged by large parts of society. The number of marriages is decreasing while the number of divorces is rising steadily. Under these circumstances one has to look at the validity of the concept that is protected by Article 6 1 GG and whether it is possible to adapt the interpretation of 'marriage' to the changed situation in society.

'Marriage' as a guaranteed institution

In doing this one must first look at the function of Article 6 1 GG as a basic human right.[5] Like many human rights Article 6 1 GG was originally conceived of as an individual's defence against state interference. It achieves this to the extent that it guarantees the freedom of two people to enter into a relationship without the state being able to prevent them from doing so or to regulate the details of this relationship in an oppressive manner. Apart from that, however, Article 6 1 GG has another recognized function within the frame of the Constitution (Friauf, 1986). It is recognized as a human right which guarantees a legal institution. In the commonly adopted terminology of Schmitt, certain core values of society can be protected as 'institutional guarantees' (Schmitt, 1973). Their interpretation, then, is not at the disposition of the legislation or the courts.[6] Guaranteed institutions are known to have a conserving content:

> Admittedly, the legislation is not deprived of every possibility to change the social and legal shape which marriage and family as an institution have achieved but the essential core of these institutions must remain intact. (Pieroth and Schlink, 1986)

The Constitutional Court has stated that any legislation which contributes to the state's regulation of 'marriage' must observe the structural principles that determine the institution of 'marriage' and that these regulations must comply with Article 6 1 GG (BVerfGE 36 146, 162).

Examples that determine the inaccessible core of the institution 'marriage' include monogamy, consent at the beginning of the marriage and the principle of lifelong commitment (BVerfGE 341, 58, 59, 53, 224, 245). Although the prevailing opinion always was that the different sex of the partners is also one of these core prerequisites, until lately, this had never been mentioned by the Constitutional Court (Friauf, 1986). In

1978 the Constitutional Court even applied this formula to a relationship between a man and a male-to-female transsexual. Contrary to English law it allowed a marriage between the two, arguing that their relationship was a heterosexual one as:

> according to scientific knowledge the male transsexual does not want to have a homosexual relationship but is looking for an association with a heterosexual partner and is able, after a successful genital changing operation, to have normal intercourse with a male partner. (BVerfGE 49, 286, 300)

Some have argued that this decision has redefined the concept of 'marriage' because it allows the union of an originally biological male with another male. However, it is important to realize that the heterosexual nature of 'marriage' remains untouched in this decision and is even used as a justification. The court sought to include male-to-female transsexuals by allowing them to legally redefine their sex and thereby to fit into the concept of heterosexuality. This becomes clearer in a comparison between this decision and the position in the United Kingdom. In the case of *Corbett* v. *Corbett*[7] no such redefinition was permitted and accordingly the right of a male-to-female transsexual to marry a man was denied. Ormrod J, just as his German colleagues, justified this with the heterosexual nature of marriage. This is to show that it is not 'marriage' that is on the line here, but heterosexuality itself.

If the concept of 'marriage' as an institution guarantees the unalterableness of its basic features and thus prevents the legislation and the courts from applying it to any other form of relationship, for example gay and lesbian partnerships, the question arises: why does this happen and what effects does it have for those who take advantage of it and for those who are barred from doing so?

Reasons for protection

Various reasons are given for the special protection and promotion of marriage. Traditional values, religion, morality and control of procreation are usually named by the more conservative groups. Liberal theory on the other hand emphasizes the economic implications and a person's right to privacy, that is their right to marry the person of their choice.[8]

In radical feminist theory the concepts of 'marriage' and 'heterosexuality' have been closely connected. It has been argued that in capitalist and patriarchal society heterosexuality must be the social norm, the common consensus that is not questioned or reflected upon, that is not even perceived as a concept, but as something 'natural', something that came before all society. According to Honore, homosexuality is seen as a threat to marriage because 'acceptance of homosexuality would mean that men would no longer support women in marriage' (Honore, 1976, p. 104). Collier (1995) rightly argues that this argument is based on the assumption that men in general support women economically and that implicitly the differentiation of male/female activities along the male breadwinner/female child-bearer dualism is accepted and the legal denial of legitimacy is justified because homosexual men are less likely to marry and support wives. For Collier this explanation fails to account for the social nature of law and masculinity, which he sees as the core problem of the issue. Collier himself, however, is too focused on the role of the man and the construction of (heterosexual) masculinity in society, and he does not complete his analysis through paying more attention to the role and the social construction of 'femininity' in law. The concept of 'marriage' is not only connected to the concept of 'man' but also the concept of woman, which has been created to justify oppression instead of acknowledging that it is the invention of the concept of 'woman' that creates oppression. Monique Wittig, a leading French feminist theorist, argues that this thought, based on the primacy of difference, is the thought of domination. Here the gender/sex order and the division of labour within it is represented as a natural order (Wittig, 1992, pp. 4–5). But it is also more than that. As Wittig states, 'The refusal to become (or to remain) heterosexual always meant to refuse to become a man or a woman, consciously or not' (Wittig, 1992, p. 13). It also relates to sexuality. Wittig calls the social consciousness that creates and maintains the 'norm' of heterosexuality the 'straight mind':

> the straight mind develops a totalizing interpretation of history, social reality, culture, language, and all the subjective phenomena at the same time. I can only underline the oppressive character that the straight mind is clothed in its tendency to immediately universalise its production of concepts into general laws which claim to hold true for all societies, all epochs, all individuals. (*ibid.*, p. 27)

Marriage as well as heterosexuality are part of the power structure in society. The industrial State depends on the gender-specific division of labour, where women do their part without pay. A social order based upon capitalism strives to concentrate wealth and the means of production in the hands of only a few people, mostly excluding women. Last but not least, the concept of marriage has a distracting function for those men who do not directly benefit from capitalist society, in that they still have a form of power over another human being that they do not have in any other area of life. Homosexuality here works to confirm the concept of heterosexuality by distracting the heterosexual person from the fact that they, too, are relatively powerless in a capitalist and patriarchal society (Wittig, 1992, pp. 28–9).

Marriage as the manifestation of heterosexuality and the basis for the nuclear family is therefore an important institution upholding the present economic political and social systems. The concept of 'gay' or 'lesbian' defies the belief which is central to heterosexualism, that is that man and woman are two halves that make a whole and need to complement each other to function. To question that belief or to draw attention to any other possible way of living is to question, even threaten, the social consensus of what is 'normal'. Therefore, by existing, lesbians and gay men are a threat to this system in that they represent a deviation.

Gay and lesbian politics that focus on merely sharing rights and privileges that come out of the heterocentric system deny themselves the opportunity to make a difference and are still confined to heterocentric thinking based on the nuclear family. The main task, therefore, is to differentiate between those rights and privileges that are in themselves heterosexist and therefore not worth fighting for and those that are applicable to everybody regardless of their marital status.

Current positions in the lesbian and gay movement: new developments in the 1990s

In the 1990s the position of the lesbian and gay movement in Germany regarding 'gay marriage' has been bitterly contested. There is a definitive split between the gay and lesbian positions, at least as far as the political parts of the movement are concerned. Gay men's organizations seem to be much more in favour of codified regulation that enables same-sex relationships to enter at least a so-called registered 'partnership' that would entitle them to some of the privileges of heterosexual marriage. There are also distinct differences between the various gay men's groups. Some of them will at least acknowledge that the claim for extending the rights of unmarried people should at least in theory take priority over claims for a 'gay marriage'.

In a protocol of a seminar that was held by the Bundesverband Homosexualität (BVH – Federal Association Homosexuality), a more progressive gay men's organization, and the Lesbenring[9] (LR – Lesbian Association), a nationwide lesbian organization, it was stated that what started as a 'politics for the unmarried' has changed to a 'lifestyle politics' that seeks the inclusion of the rights of everybody, whether they wanted to marry or not, regardless of whether they were gay/lesbian or straight:

> What matters here is neither the introduction of marriage for gay men and lesbians nor equality between married and unmarried couples; our ideas go far beyond that. We want the equality of all life styles. (Behrmann and Trampenau, 1991)

In 1991, the LR started a discussion about their catalogue of demands, including the question of whether they should add the claim for 'gay marriage'. At the General Meeting in June 1991 they decided to carry out a survey among their members. During this time the question was fiercely debated in their monthly newsletter. For example, in a letter in August 1991, a woman who advocated 'gay marriage' argued that the possibility of marriage was a right, not an obligation, and that people were still free to stay unmarried. She reasoned that opening the institution of marriage to gay and lesbian couples would eventually dissolve its nature of 'compulsory heterosexuality' and therefore benefit all gay men and lesbians (*Lesbenring-Info*, July 1991). The possibility of such marriages, she argued, would end the silence and the taboo that has been built around homosexuality and would lead to approval and acceptance within society. Calls for the abolition of marriage as a legal institution, she concluded, are unrealistic and she advocated reform from within.

Others argued that assimilation and adaptation to heterosexual values would necessarily lead to a loss of lesbian culture and thought. In addition, one would then discriminate against those who did not intend to marry in any case and would thereby split the lesbian movement into 'good and bad daughters of the patriarchal'. They argued that 'gay marriage' should not be on the agenda when all the marriage privileges have been abolished (*Lesbenring-Info*, July 1991). In October 1991 the results of the survey were published. They showed that 93 women had voted against putting 'gay marriage' on the agenda of the LR, 49 had voted in favour and 10 had abstained. The LR therefore did not see the need to change their policy.

In 1992 one of the most prominent founding members of the LR, the only out MP in the German parliament, Jutta Oesterle Schwerin, published an article in which she demanded the abolition of Article 6 1 GG from the Constitution. This happened in conjunction with the first meeting of the 'Committee for a new Constitution', which had become necessary after German reunification.

At the same time, lesbian and gay couples started a new initiative to force the Constitutional Court to decide on the constitutionality of 'gay marriage'.[10] They went to the registry offices to give notice that they intended to marry and upon refusal took legal action against the respective States. It was clear that under the current interpretation of the law the courts would not be able to uphold their complaints, but they had to exhaust all legal remedies before they could call on the Constitutional Court. When these initiatives reached the Constitutional Court in October 1993, that Court decided that the applicants were not able to marry under German law because marriage 'implied' that the partners were of a different sex. Any other regulation would violate Article 6 1 GG. The Court also ruled that the various discriminations that lesbians and gay men encountered could violate other Articles under the Constitution: Article 2 1 (General Freedom of One's Actions) and Article 3 1 GG (Equality before the Law). However, the Court was unable to decide on these matters because they had not been the object of the complaint and an *obiter dictum* would not have constituted a valid precedent (BVerfG Streit 94, 176). The future will have to show if these instructions will be taken up by the legislation and if it will cause them to reflect on the privileges as a whole or not. In the meantime discussion about 'gay marriage' was taken up in other contexts.

Legislative initiatives to promote a 'registered partnership'

In 1990, the Green Party drafted 'A Bill regarding the rights of gay men', which among other things (such as the age of consent) dealt with the possibility of 'gay marriage'. Unfortunately they did not have the chance to introduce it into the Federal Parliament because they were not re-elected in the General Elections in December 1990. This was followed, in 1991, by a second initiative presented by the Schwulenverband Deutschland (SVD – German Association of Gay Men). This Bill related to 'Marriage for people of the Same Sex' and a second draft added 'registered partnership'.

More recently the BVH produced 'A Bill on a Registered Partnership'. They proposed conditions under which a same-sex relationship could be legally recognized with certain rights resulting therefrom. The registration procedure was loosely based on the procedure that had been introduced by the Danish and Dutch governments, that is a formal registration where both partners had to declare their consent in the presence of a notary. The Bill included a proposed change to the Code of Criminal Procedure, and granted a residence permit to partners of German nationals. Furthermore it proposed changes to the Civil Code regarding the law of succession (by granting to the surviving partner a statutory right to a share in the late partner's estate) and family law (by establishing an obligation to help each other financially in times of need but no obligation to pay maintenance). Even though the draft leaves a lot to be desired under close revision, it is the one that focuses most on the rights of the partners as individuals. It is therefore clearly meant as a body of regulations for a transition period, a point stressed in the introduction to the draft:

> The question whether the institution of civil marriage should be opened for lesbians and gay men has been widely discussed in the media recently. The BVH rejects this aggravated and one-sided position as politically unsuccessful. It cannot be the foremost and only priority to transfer the only form of relationship that has been legally sanctioned and is therefore socially acknowledged to lesbians and gay men and thereby purely extending the group of people who are privileged when it comes to the legal provisions that safeguard their relationships without creating new legal rules for the living together of people as such.

In 1994 the Green Party introduced a Bill that aimed to change article 1353 of the Civil Code that rules civil marriage so that the institution would be open to gay and lesbian partners. The accompanying reasoning lists many of the discriminations gay men and lesbians encounter every day and demands complete equality between heterosexual and same-sex relationships. In doing this, however, the Bill embraces the concept of marriage, not unconditionally, but to a wide extent. In a way it expresses an opinion that was predominant in the early stages of the discussion, that is that lesbians and gay men 'should be allowed to do every silly thing that heterosexuals can do as well'. Apart from the fact that, under the current conservative government, there is no realistic chance of this Bill ever being enacted by Parliament, it betrays the lesbian and gay community in that it does not reflect any of the discussions that have taken place over the past few years. It is in my opinion a strategic move that was aimed clearly at provoking more conservative Members of Parliament in order to promote a discussion. But it is doubtful whether it could achieve much more.

The latest approach to introduce a new legal institution of 'registered partnership' has come from the Lower Saxony State government. In June 1995 they drafted a bill that would create such an institution under German civil law. The government is planning to convince the Upper House of Parliament (Bundesrat) to use its rights to introduce bills in the parliament to introduce this draft.

The Bill deals with the proceedings of registering a same-sex partnership, the prerequisites and the ways to end it. The only effects it states so far are a form of equal treatment of these partnerships in matrimonial property law. It includes an obligation to pay maintenance in case of a break-up under certain conditions and enables the partners to legally act for one another during the partnership.

In general, it includes nearly all the provisions that have been questioned by feminists in the past twenty years concerning an individual's property and their partner's access to that. Every other area of law where lesbians and gay men are discriminated against have been left aside so far, stating that they will be decided in a later bill. A schedule lists other legal areas where the government wants to achieve changes. That list includes claims of putting 'registered partnerships, on an equal footing with married couples in civil service payment regulations, health insurance, pensions, criminal procedure, residence permits, naturalization and capital transfer tax. This list seems solely to enumerate all the legal areas where married couples enjoy special privileges. The one exception was income tax law, where it was decided not to adopt it for the partnership, not because it was unfair but because the Constitutional Court had ruled it out for unmarried couples because it was based on the concept of 'marriage' as it is protected in Article 6 1 GG.

At this point it is difficult to offer the draft Bill wholehearted support because it does not reflect upon or question the privileges of matrimony and their effects on unmarried people who remain single or who chose a different style of relationship. Instead it seeks to guarantee that gay and lesbian couples have full access to them as far as the Constitution will allow this at this point.

While the gay movement, especially the BVH and the gay sector of the Green Party, is campaigning on behalf of the Lower Saxony Bill, the lesbian movement has still not voted in favour of any of these proposals. There has been little discussion of the issue at the annual 'Lesbian Spring Meetings'[11] in Hamburg (1995) and Munich (1996), which is an indication that the matter is not a priority for most politically active lesbians in Germany. The question was also discussed in a workshop held at the 1996 Feminist Lawyers Conference in Cologne. While the opinions there seemed to move towards a more open approach to the matter, the final plenary session passed a resolution that held that the claims for so-called 'gay marriage' or 'registered same-sex partnership' (which have predominantly been made by gay men) ought to be rejected, as they essentially contradict feminist beliefs and support unwanted structures of dependency. Reform of the law should respect individual choices of lifestyle and the form of relationships should be a matter determined by negotiation between individuals.

Following a similar line of thought, LR recently published a booklet that gives information about the possibilities of contractual agreements between the partners of a relationship to achieve a form of security within this relationship and in relation to outside authorities. These contracts 'will be entered into by mutual consent as and when they are deemed to be necessary.' They altogether reject a 'package version' of state regulation which leaves no room for deviant[12] agreements. The approach of the lesbian movement is therefore much more focused on individual self-determination, the reason for which can be found in the movement's strong roots in the feminist movement.

Concluding remarks

Compared to some European countries, the legal situation of lesbian and gay couples in Germany is much more uncertain and unprotected. The question of 'gay marriage' has not been on the agenda of the gay or the lesbian movement until quite recently. The German gay movement has been too engaged in the fight for decriminalization of male homosexuality and the effects of HIV/AIDS to pay much attention to lifestyle politics. The lesbian movement, being closely entwined with the feminist movement, is too critical of the institution of 'marriage' to actually claim it for themselves.

With other countries now providing legal safeguards for gay and lesbian partnerships, the German movement seems to feel it has in some way been left behind. Many lesbians remain critical of the idea of state regulations for their relationships, particularly when discrimination against lesbians and gay men is such an important and damaging part of our day-to-day lived experience. While a registered partnership might in the short term resolve many of these conflicts, it is my opinion that instead of jumping on the European bandwagon in this matter, we should utilize our 'being behind' to critically reflect upon our aims and objectives and to observe the changes that these laws have brought about in other countries. In Scandinavian countries there have already been complaints by the lesbian and gay movement that these changes have led to a loss of lesbian and gay culture. Even if a registered partnership made a positive change in the life of lesbian and gay couples, we must not forget that our community includes millions of people who are not prepared to make this commitment and who would be even further excluded from certain rights which should be granted to everyone.

Notes

1. For example Denmark, Sweden, the Netherlands.
2. I put marriage in quotation marks when I refer to the concept of 'marriage' as it has been defined by the Constitutional Court.
3. The 'Grundgesetz' is the German Constitution, which was enacted in 1949, that is after the Second World War. It contains basic human rights as well as rules of state organization. It is the most important body of regulations in Germany, with which all other laws have to comply. The controlling authority is the Federal Constitutional Court (Bundersverfassungsgericht).
4. A decision of the Federal Constitutional Court, Volume 10, page 59 (decision starts), see page 66.

5. Articles 1–20 GG contain a catalogue of so-called basic rights (Grundrechte) which are understood as human rights (Menschenrechte) if they apply to everyone and civil rights (Burgerrechte) if they only apply to German nationals.
6. The power of the Federal Constitutional Court to determine these core values only goes so far as its interpretation of the Constitution represents concepts as they are understood in society.
7. [1971] All England Law Reports 33.
8. While this angle doubtlessly became very important in post-war Germany after a period where numerous marriage prohibitions had been in force, it is not central to the question at hand, that is, why marriage as one of many forms of human relationships should be given preference by the state.
9. The lesbian movement in Germany was traditionally always closer to the feminist than to the gay movement. It is hard to say where the reasons for that development lie. It could partly be due to the joint campaigning, especially on behalf of abortion rights in the early 1970s. It could also be that in Germany gay men and lesbians were never 'united' by a common cause, as was the case with the 'Clause 28 campaign' in the UK. Lesbians mainly seemed to identify as women-identified-women who were conscious of their dual oppression as women and as lesbians.
10. Other developments include a 'Resolution of the European Parliament on the Equality of Gay Men and Lesbians', where member states and the Commission were asked to enact laws that abolish the discrimination against gay men and lesbians and to allow them to get married or enter a similar relationship (BT-Drucksache 12/7069).
11. The Lesbian Spring Meeting is a three-day conference that is held in a different city every year. Approximately 3500–5000 lesbian and bisexual women meet to take part in workshops, rallies and cultural events.
12. 'Deviant' here can be understood as 'individually negotiated agreements', but also as a reference to a deviant sexual lifestyle.

References

Behrmann, L. and Trampenau, L. (1991) *Mit der Doppelaxt durch den Paragraaphendschungel*. Hamburg: Fruhlingserwachen.

Collier, R. (1995) *Masculinity, Law and the Family*. London and New York: Routledge.

Eckert, B. (1983 ongoing) *Gemeinschaftskommetar zum Arbeitsfordenungsgesetz*. Neuwied: Luchterhand.

Friauf, C. (1986) 'Verfassungsgarantie und sozialer Wandel – das Beispiel von Ehe une Familie', *NJW*, 2595 [2600].

Honore, T. (1976) *Sex Law*. London: Duckworth.

Maunz, D. and Durig, M. (1958 ongoing) *Grundegesetzkommentar*. Munchen: CH Beck.

Pieroth, B. and Schlink, L. (1986) *Staatsrecht II – Grundrechte*, 2nd edn. Heidelberg: Juventa.

Schmitt, C. (1973) *Verfassungsrechtliche Aufsatze*. Berlin: Duncker and Humbolt.

Schwegmann, L. and Summer, D. (1975 ongoing) *Kommentar zum Blundesbesoidungsgesetz*. München: Rehm.

Wittig, M. (1992) *The Straight Mind and Other Essays*. New York and London: Harvester Wheatsheaf.

6

Law, Childhood Innocence and Sexuality

Craig Lind

'Sex' and 'childhood' are characteristics that seem to have an essence that cannot be dislodged. 'Sexuality' and 'innocence' in childhood, on the other hand, cannot simply be seen as biologically inevitable or immutable. Social philosophers of both the left and the right have taken this view. In this chapter I want to consider the social construction of sexuality and of childhood innocence, and go on to reflect on the role of law in supporting these constructions. I also want to consider the way in which the construction of sexuality and innocence may be less determinative than those who use law as a mechanism of control seem to accept that it should or can be.

Equality, sexuality and children

It is now common to find support for the argument that queer people, and in particular, lesbians, bisexuals and gay men, ought to enjoy a life free from discrimination based on their sexual orientation or identity. The reason often given is that sexuality is naturally predetermined: that queer people are as little able to determine or change their sexual identity as straight people are able to determine or change theirs. In these circumstances it is unjust to prejudice people on the basis of personal characteristics over which they have no control (Wintermute, 1995, esp. ch. 7). This kind of argument appears to be on the political ascendance in many (particularly Western) democracies, and has already received legislative and judicial support in some of them (Rubin, 1993, p. 270; Wintermute, 1995, p. 145). But enthusiasm for the idea that it espouses, and for the legal and social changes that it proposes, appears to be entirely lacking when the sexuality of children is in issue. Political opinion, and consequently law, retains its antipathy towards diverse sexual practices and identities when their potential manifestation in childhood is under consideration. In fact, modern Western tradition dictates that childhood should be a period when sex and sexuality are irrelevant. It is only once the innocence of childhood has passed that these matters became relevant attributes of the person (Foucault, 1976; Evans, 1993).

While this view of human sexuality in childhood is waning (especially in adolescence: Moore and Rosenthal, 1993), queer sexuality in young people remains a strictly controlled and under-researched subject (Goggin, 1993). Where the law regulates sex or sexual information made available to children, it retains an antipathetic view of queer sexuality, despite its apparent acceptance of the inevitability of queer sexuality in adulthood.

The social construction of sexuality

The most appealing explanation for this negative attitude towards the sexuality of queer children is to be found in the central weakness of the argument for queer equality outlined above, that is its bland acceptance of the immutability of human sexuality. The presumption that the sexuality of a person is inevitable and unchangeable (whether for reasons of biology or early psychological development), while ascending politically, is not universally accepted, particularly in academic circles (Scruton, 1985; Weeks, 1991; Gray, 1993; Rich, 1993; Rubin, 1993; Scott, 1993: esp. chs. 4 and 5). The attempt to exclude particularly adolescent children from minority sexualities is a clear acknowledgement of an alternative to the essentialist view of sexuality. That alternative most frequently describes sexuality as being socially constructed. A large and still growing body of literature has begun to explore the ramifications of this kind of theory (Foucault, 1976; Scruton, 1985; Weeks, 1989, 1991; Caplan, 1987; Gray, 1993; Halperin, 1993; Scott, 1993). The most prominent investigations have been historical. Theses studies suggest that whereas Western societies have in almost all periods concerned themselves with the regulation of sexual activity (Brundage, 1987) it was not until the late nineteenth century that that activity began to be perceived (and spoken of) as the hallmark of a particular kind of person. It was not until then that, as a result of the proliferation of the criminal and medical discourses on the subject, people began to be defined (and ultimately to define themselves) by reference to the sexual acts in which they preferred to engage (Foucault, 1976, pp. 43, 101; Weeks, 1989).

This argument, with its powerful use of historical evidence, presents a convincing picture of the social construction of clear categories of sexual identity. But it is less clear on the mechanisms by which individual people come to inhabit a particular category: how individual desire is 'constructed'. In some instances it sometimes appears to accept the inevitability of desire, which echoes an essentialist model.

If this were the full extent of social construction theory on sexuality, the social and legal reform arguments against prejudice remain as strong as they ever were. If the characteristics that result in people adopting a particular sexual identity are innate, and if the identity category itself is a mere creation of a particular society and not their own, it would be iniquitous to prejudice those for whom the identity is appropriate, in much the same way as it is argued to be unacceptable to prejudice people because of their race or gender.

But that is not the full extent of constructionist theory. The assault on essentialism is much more radical. In the words of Rubin:

> It is impossible to think with any clarity about the politics of race or gender as long as these are thought of as biological entities rather than as social constructs. Similarly, sexuality is impervious to political analysis as long as it is primarily conceived as a biological phenomenon or an aspect of individual psychology. Sexuality is as much a human product as diets, methods of transportation, systems of etiquette, forms of labor, types of entertainment, processes of production, and modes of oppression. (1993, p. 10)

From a different political standpoint Roger Scruton argues that 'Sexual desire is a social artefact. Like language, and like morality, it is born from the social relations between human beings, and adds to those relations a structure and firmness of its own' (1985, p. 348). These arguments suggest that while sexuality is inculcated in early psychological development (and thereby might be experienced as innate), desire itself is a social creation. What differentiates this view from its essentialist counterpart is that the process of construction, which is both historical and contemporary, is never complete. Sexuality is capable of perpetual flux; individual sexual identity is fluid across the established categories and is even capable of reforming categories by defying contemporary categorization. It is never inevitable. Rearing, biology, social circumstance, and the processes of construction themselves, are all elements contributing towards the creation of individual sexuality. This assertion does not, despite seeming to, claim all people for bisexuality. It merely believes all people to be potentially multi-sexual. They may belong to a single category of sexuality at any one time, but they may also move across categories at any time, sometimes blurring the distinction between them (as bisexuality does, and transsexuality often does) (Kinsey, 1948, p. 659; Moran, 1996, p. 86).

It is clear that this fluidity of outcome for the sexuality of people in Western jurisdictions has, by modern history and tradition, been deemed to be unacceptable. The legal regulation of their sexuality bears the hallmarks of a determination to construct a heterosexual society. Thus in various spheres, family law, military law, criminal law, law of taxation, social security law, immigration law, public housing law, employment law, to name only a few, heterosexuality is promoted and queer sexuality is discouraged. The legal regulation of childhood sexuality is no exception, and is, arguably, the sphere in which the passion for the promotion of heterosexuality is most striking.

Regulating childhood sexuality

The most obvious attempt to control childhood sexuality occurs in the criminal law. It sets out to prevent the majority of children from making decisions about their sexual experience and is particularly imposing in the case of sexual decisions to engage in male homosexual conduct, which in the United Kingdom is no longer criminal providing that both parties are over eighteen years of age, consent to the acts and perform those acts in private (sections 6 and 12 to 15, Sexual Offences Act 1956, read with section 1, Sexual Offences Act 1967, as amended by the Criminal Justice and Public Order Act 1994; following the recent vote in the House of Commons in June 1998, the age of consent for homosexual activity will soon be lowered by statute to the age of sixteen).

In the context of medical advice, on the other hand, the law enables some younger children to control their own sexual health. Since *Gillick* v.

West Norfolk and Wisbech Area Health Authority[1] 'mature' children have been able to receive medical advice concerning their sexual conduct (even when their parents would object or where it is apparent that they are committing a criminal offence by being sexually active). However, their self-control, as Monk explores in more detail in Chapter 7 in this collection, is dependent upon a doctor's assessment of their 'maturity and understanding'.

Where local authorities are involved in the care or rearing of children, their legal responsibilities relating to their sexuality are somewhat schizophrenic. If children are in their care under Parts III, IV or V of the Children Act 1989, they are required to demonstrate a remarkably understanding and tolerant attitude towards the queer sexuality of any of their charges (Department of Health, 1991: Vol. 4, paras. 7.50 and 7.53 and Vol. 3, paras. 9.50 and 9.53). In other respects, however, local authorities conduct themselves in the shadow of the notorious section 2A of the Local Government Act 1986 (inserted by Section 28 of the Local Government Act 1988). While the section has negligible legal effect, it is an important piece of symbolic legislation and its practical impact should not be underestimated (Thomas and Costigan, 1990). Its object, to prevent local authorities from promoting homosexuality or from teaching the 'acceptability of homosexuality as ... pretended family relationship[s]', undermines any desire within local government to be positive about queer sexuality.

In one respect the section may, however, have been intensely 'positive'; Section 28's attack on queer identity and the protests that resulted from it were significant factors revitalizing proactive queer politics in Britain in the mid-1980s. Moreover, together with the campaign to equalize the gay male 'age of consent', the Section 28 debate placed childhood queer identity on the political agenda.

As Monk argues in Chapter 7 in this collection, the regulation of sex education in schools is likely to limit any debate about the queer sexuality of children: it is conducted by adults; it restricts the variety of sexual information that will be made available; it is antipathetic to queer sexuality; it is designed to keep queer children securely closeted (Department for Education, 1994; Lind and Butler, 1995).

In all these instances the law tries to protect the deemed innocence of childhood by controlling access to sexual knowledge and experience. This control is particularly secure where queer sexuality is concerned.

While there is an, arguably grudging, acceptance of the growing sexuality of children in late adolescence, in that education policy provides for sex education, the courts permit independent medical advice to older children, and the criminal law permits some sexual experience, that acceptance does not extend comfortably to queer sexuality. The legal wall that attempts to protect the sexual innocence of queer children remains largely intact (Lind and Butler, 1995).

The social construction of childhood innocence

But the concept of 'innocence' as it is associated with childhood is controversial. It has, increasingly, been subjected to close psychological, sociological and historical scrutiny (Ariès, 1960; Hunt, 1970; deMause, 1974; King, 1981; Shahar, 1990; Evans, 1993; Moore and Rosenthal, 1993). As in the debate on the origins of sexuality, essentialist postures may have clouded the issue. While it may be reasonable to claim that innocence in childhood is natural (of the essence of childhood) because of the innate lack of experience of infants, and even older young people, the need to 'protect' that innocence to the limits of adulthood is not an easy deduction. Even on essentialist reasoning, this innate childhood innocence is naturally eroded by the gradual accumulation of knowledge and experience throughout childhood (and into adulthood). The desire to enclose and protect innocence from the effects of the inevitable acquisition of experience is, therefore, suspect (as being contrary to nature).

That those who would promote such an approach to childhood innocence do so unflinchingly can only be attributed to their acceptance of the proposition that our conception of innocence in childhood is no more than a construct of our society. And it is this approach which is acquiring greater currency in socio-theoretical and socio-historical thought.

According to Ariès childhood itself (not unlike sexuality) is a construct with a relatively short history (Ariès, 1960). His reading of the past suggests that children in as late a period as the late Middle Ages were still being treated as adults. They had no special protection based on their youth, nor did anyone think it odd that they should be treated in this way. Thus, the young Louis XIII was able to enjoy an active sex life even in his infancy (apparently masturbating openly and without adult opprobrium before he was a year old) (Ariès, 1960, p. 98; deMause, 1974, p. 21). Ariès maintains, then, that the total absence of a concept of innocence associated with childhood undermines the idea of childhood itself entirely.

Many have not been convinced by these views (suggesting, as they do, the invention of childhood in the early modern period) (Hunt, 1970; deMause, 1974; Shahar, 1990), but none seem to deny (and it seems hard to imagine that anyone could) that the significance of childhood is historically contingent. The consensus seems to be that while childhood has existed as a social category for much longer than Ariès was prepared to accept, the characteristics of childhood, and particularly the attribute of innocence, have been differently constituted by different societies (both historically and geographically). While childhood may have been shorter, and characterized by speedy progress towards adulthood in the Middle Ages, by the modern period childhood was lengthening, and acquiring the formal trappings of innocence. This meant that children were increasingly protected in law from their own errors of judgement caused by their youthful inexperience of life. Their liability in, for example, the criminal law and contract law started to differ from adult liability. Whereas adults could, by virtue of their life experience, take care of themselves, children were 'innocent' and needed protection. The extent to which that protection was needed, and the ages at which it was terminated, have been and continue to be in an almost perpetual state of flux, illustrating most forcefully how societies have, over time, changed their perceptions of the innocence of children. While children just a few centuries ago worked as adults did and were criminally liable as adults were (Wagg, 1988), their position now is vastly different (Thane, 1981).

Whether the legal protection afforded to childhood innocence is regarded as progressive, neutral or retrogressive over time, few doubt its increased significance into the twentieth century, and that its focus is now on the protection of children from the harm to which their inexperience may subject them. The current social aim of the constructed innocence of children, therefore, is to protect their welfare (Barton and Gillian, 1995).

For this reason current English law regulates childhood to release children from the burdens of responsibility that are associated with adulthood. But it also recognizes that the boundary between adulthood and childhood cannot be easily or simply delineated. While a formal age of majority does dictate an end to childhood, the law, in various spheres, recognizes the variability of innocence. This variability occurs both within fields of law, and between different areas of law. Thus while the criminal law absolves children under ten from liability entirely, and partially absolves children under fourteen from liability, its treatment of older children differs from adult treatment only at the sentencing stage (Smith and Hogan, 1996, p. 194). In medical law, younger children (under sixteen, this time) are given partial responsibility for decisions concerning their health, while older children have a much greater determinative capacity and so on through the different legal territories. At various points in their childhood children are accorded greater responsibility because their maturation towards adulthood is recognized at that time, and in that respect, to be complete (Thane, 1981; Freeman, 1983; Eekelaar, 1986).

But some of their incapacities are less obviously protective, and seem more concerned to prepare children for an appropriate adulthood. Compulsory education and restrictions on employment are the most obvious examples in this respect. Another is the regulation of their sexuality. In these respects the state takes it upon itself to order the acquisition of knowledge and experience so as to channel children into a particular kind of adulthood.

Childhood 'innocence', sexuality and law

The historical presumption of innocence in childhood, particularly in the Victorian era (Foucault, 1976), resulted in the assumption that children were pre-sexual, or sexually innocent. That assumption was a preoccupation both of law and of various other social discourses, and was most powerfully manifested in the silence surrounding childhood sexuality in the home (Evans, 1993) and the attempted enforcement of innocence in the public domain (see, for example, the crusades against masturbation: Weeks, 1989, p. 48). Since the zenith of the constructed innocence of children's sexuality corresponded with the period during which sexuality itself was only just beginning to emerge as stratified into polarized sexual identities, it has been suggested that there was no consideration of the potential for a distinctive childhood sexual identity (Goggin, 1993).

But sexual innocence in childhood has, in the last 30 years (and even in the Victorian era), been revealed to be more imagined than real (Foucault, 1976; Moore and Rosenthal, 1993). Empirical evidence suggests that children are reaching sexual maturity earlier than they were just decades ago, and increasing numbers of them, at ever younger ages, are engaging in sexual activity, which is both heterosexual and homosexual (Schofield, 1965; Moore and Rosenthal, 1993).

One peculiar quality of the modern renewal of 'childhood immodesty' (Ariès, 1960), however, is the persistence of the rhetoric of childhood innocence. Because sexual maturation is complex and causes confusion in adolescence, there is considerable fear that children may venture into dangerous sexual territory. For this reason, while the developing sexuality of children is increasingly recognized in social and legal policy, that sexuality remains rigorously controlled. The ability of children to confront issues of their sexuality is delayed as much as possible by delaying their acquisition of sexual knowledge as much as possible, and by a socialization aimed at creating sex-negative impressions in their minds (Moore and Rosenthal, 1993).

Any confusion regarding sexual identity is resolved by a kind of 'conscription' into the single appropriate sexuality (Goggin, 1993). Only determined 'conscientious objection' is tolerated, and then only in the very limited circumstances and subject to the very tight behavioural controls described earlier. Children who know themselves to be in any way queer, and who insist on their queer identity, may do so, but quietly and, for the most part, provided they abstain from any sexual conduct and refrain from asking for information or advice.

Cause and effect: arguing for law reform

It seems clear that the law adopts, for the most part, a radically constructionist stance towards sexuality. In promoting heterosexuality in childhood, it demonstrates its belief in the possibility of the social construction of desire, and evidences a determination to perpetuate a society inhabited by heterosexual adults.

The difficulty for queer law reformers is that this view of sexuality creates a serious obstacle to arguments for social (and hence legal) tolerance. If a tolerant society could, potentially, yield a greater number of queer individuals, political decisions to prevent that outcome become defensible (Scruton, 1985; Ireland, 1997). A majoritarian, democratic society may reasonably wish to circumscribe the knowledge and experience of its children so as to foster its favoured outcome for their sexuality (which is acknowledged to be socially constructed) in much the same way as it imposes a particular ideology of education and socio-political involvement on them as they grow up.

That the processes by which sexuality is constructed are not fully understood may not be a sufficient reason to prevent restrictive regulation. Our society may have produced diverse minority sexualities, but they remain minorities. Unrestrained sexual tolerance may produce divergent sexualities on a much larger scale. The inherent uncertainty of a move to unrestrained tolerance is, in the minds of many, enough to justify the conservative restraints on the developing sexuality of children. In this way it may be hoped that sexual minorities will remain just that.

The problem for an argument of this sort is to be found in the circumstances in which diverse sexualities emerged in their categorical form in our societies. Social historians (Foucault, 1976; Weeks, 1989) have demonstrated that queer identities emerged when formal tolerance was at its lowest ebb. This suggests that our ability to control the constructs (of sexuality, in this instance) of our society is doubtful. The consequences of regulating desire are (inevitably) unforeseen; some may be benign, but most are not. They range from injury to individual psychologies to the stratification of society on the basis of constructed categories of desire. Furthermore, that stratification itself has given rise to the aggressive (direct action) politics and social behaviour ('queer bashing') with which we are now so familiar. Moreover, in raising the profile of these strata this process has contributed to (if not caused) the (apparent) increase in the numbers of people who adopt sexually diverse identities, as well as the proliferation of categories of sexuality themselves.

The rising tide of childhood activism

If the desire of repressive legal strategies, then, is to construct the vast majority of people into heterosexuality, it appears to be failing. The ultimate effect of deliberate attempts to direct sexuality seems most often to be the reverse (or something like the reverse) of what may have been intended. Tolerance recommends itself, then, as the safest, and perversely, most conservative, alternative.

A further development in the ongoing history of sexuality also recommends legal tolerance. From its history we know that the existence of law regulating childhood sexuality is likely to contribute towards the stratification of the categories of sexuality into which *children* define themselves (or are defined). In the current era the politics of adult sexuality and the legal regulation of that sexuality must be considered in the search for factors that will influence the construction of individual sexualities in childhood.

The problem for law and policy is that, while the law on childhood sexuality restricts children from manifesting diverse sexualities in their childhood,[2] they are also more likely now than ever before to encounter positive views of those various sexualities during their childhood. Lesbian and gay pride, together with a series of high-profile political campaigns to reform legal, and even private, regulation restricting the rights of queer people, have seen to it that almost every sphere of public life – and most prominently the news and entertainment media – offers news about and models of alternative sexual expression.

The result is, and will increasingly become, that the apathy of children concerning their sexuality, straight-jacketed as it is by law, will dissipate and be replaced by a kind of activism similar to that which occupies older individuals determined to equalize the status of their sexual identity. The increasing recognition of their sexual status and of the troubles that it causes for them because of the law – ranging from bullying to the disadvantages (both physical and psychological) that they must suffer because of the enforced silence on issues of queer sexuality in school – must, in time, become the subject of political action by those who are suffering.

The gay male age of consent is already the subject of such an altered attitude (Stonewall, 1996). Subjects of controversy, like the inadequacy of the general age of consent of sixteen and the powerlessness of children to influence the extent to which they should receive sex education at school, are likely to be taken up in the same way in the near future by a more proactive youth (Diffeliciatonio and Wagner, 1994; Tatchell, 1996). Bullying and the reticence to deal comprehensively with information on sexually transmitted diseases are also likely candidates for action. Perhaps most interesting is that these proactive political steps are likely to be taken by children's groups that are not defined solely by the sexual identity of their participants. The concerns that they encompass will often be relevant to all children. In this respect the politics of childhood sexuality are potentially different from the politics of adult sexuality. Alliances may be differently struck, and mutual understanding more easily attained.

Conclusion

That children are already taking on sexual identities (learned from knowledge of adulthood much more open to them now than a century ago), and that they are becoming politically active about those identities, should serve as a warning that intolerant legal regulation is likely to have an explosive effect on the politics of childhood as well as on the number of queer children emerging from the closet in the future. If we add to this an acknowledgement that many of these children are seriously harmed (sometimes by their own suicide attempts – Rubenstein, 1993) and that the aim of the construction of innocence in childhood is to protect them from harm, then we have established a clear case for the reform of law, affecting both childhood and adulthood, which constrains diverse sexualities.

As we do not understand the way in which the social construction of sexuality works, and as attempts to stem the growth of minority sexualities have failed, persistent efforts to oppress those sexualities by legislating for their prejudice (or by not legislating for their protection from prejudice) is simply unjust. That we acknowledge the 'fact' of the social construction of sexuality does not address, and certainly cannot undermine, the equal 'fact' that the sexuality outcome for individuals is very real. In the words of Jeffrey Weeks:

> most individuals do not feel 'polymorphously perverse'. On the contrary they feel their sexual desires are fairly narrowly organised, whatever use they make of those identities in real life. Moreover, a social identity is no less real for being historically formed. Sexual identities are no longer arbitrary divisions of the field of possibilities; they are encoded in a complex web of social practices – legal, pedagogic, medical, moral, and personal. They cannot be willed away. (1991, p. 84)

The failure to protect children from the prejudice which their desire meets does not sit easily in an era in which the innocence of children is constructed as a protective device. It is clear that our legal policy on sexuality generally, and on queer sexuality in particular, needs to be reassessed.

Notes

1. (1986) AC 112. In *Gillick* a mother had tried to argue that doctors could not give contraceptive advice to her daughters under the age of 16 without her consent. The House of Lords held, by a majority, that a child of sufficient maturity could give the required consent herself.
2. While the premise of this essay has been that where children engage in (or wish to engage in) sexual activity, their desire is to involve other (similarly situated) children, the analysis it offers is no less viable in the context of children who desire sexual relations with 'adults' (even those much older than themselves). In the constructionist thinking that serves as the foundation upon which this essay is based, there is nothing inherently 'corrupting' about sexual relations between young people and older people (no matter how old or young they are). However, the real disparities of power that exist between adults and children, it is submitted, justifies a presumption that sexual relations between children and adults are imposed upon children (against their wills). Where the notion of childhood sexual innocence is still so powerful (as it is in our culture, particularly with younger children) it would be immensely damaging to children to remove that presumption. But that does not mean that the facility to overcome the presumption (by producing convincing evidence of valid consent) should never be available. This argument acknowledges – contrary to popular bigotry – that children are not necessarily (and need not necessarily be) sexually passive. But it also wishes to refrain from accepting that paedophile conduct (read to mean the abuse of power to impose sexually upon children) must be incorporated into any discussion that deals with the sexuality of children in a queer context. In the face of overwhelming evidence that paedophilia is predominantly a crime of fathers in traditional heterosexual families the homosexualization of paedophilia seems wholly unjustifiable, and seems destined to undermine any attempt to take the sexuality of children seriously so as to offer them the best protection and development that can be made available to them.

References

Abelove, H., Barale, M. A. and Halperin, D. M. (eds) (1993) *The Lesbian and Gay Studies Reader*. New York: Routledge.

Ariès, P. (1960) *Centuries of Childhood*. Harmondsworth: Penguin Books.

Barton, C. and Gillian, D. (1995) *Parenthood and the Law*. London: Butterworths.

Brundage, J. A. (1987) *Law, Sex and Christian Society in Medieval Europe*. Chicago: University of Chicago Press.

Caplan, P. (ed.) (1987) *The Cultural Construction of Sexuality*. London: Tavistock Publications.

Collier, R. (1995) *Masculinity, Law and the Family*. London: Routledge.

deMause, L. (ed.) (1974) *The History of Childhood*. London: Souvenir Press.

Department of Health (1991) *The Children Act 1989: Guidance and Regulations*, Volumes 3 and 4. London: HMSO.

Department for Education (1994) *Education Act 1993: Sex Education in Schools*, Circular 5/94.

Diffeliciatonio, T. and Wagner, J. (1994) *Over the Rainbow: Generation Q*. London: Testing the Limits Productions and Channel 4.

Eekelaar, J. (1986) 'The emergence of children's rights', *Oxford Journal of Legal Studies*, **6**, 161–82.

Evans, D. T. (1993) *Sexual Citizenship: The Material Construction of Sexuality*. London: Routledge.

Foucault, M. (1976) *The History of Sexuality: Volume 1: An Introduction*. London: Penguin Books.

Freeman, M. D. A. (1983) *The Rights and Wrongs of Children*. London: Frances Pinter.

Giddens, A. (1992) *The Transformation of Intimacy*. Cambridge: Polity Press.

Goggin, M. (1993) 'Gay and lesbian adolescence', in S. Moore and D. Rosenthal (eds), *Sexuality in Adolescence*. London: Routledge, pp. 102–23.

Gray, J. (1993) *Post-Liberalism: Studies in Political Thought*, London: Routledge.

Halperin, D. M. (1993) 'Is there a history of sexuality?', in H. Abelove, M. A. Barale and D. M. Halperin (eds), *The Lesbian and Gay Studies Reader*. New York: Routledge, pp. 416–31.

Hunt, D. (1970) *Parents and Children in History: The Psychology of Family Life in Early Modern France*. New York: Basic Books.

Ireland, P. (1997) 'The endarkenment of the mind: Roger Scruton and the power of law', *Social and Legal Studies*, **6**, 51.

King, M. (ed.) (1981) *Childhood, Welfare and Justice: A Critical Examination of Children in the Legal and Child Care Systems*. London: Batsford Academic and Institutional.

Kinsey, A. C., Pomeroy, W. B., and Martin, C. E. (1948) *Sexual Behaviour in the Human Male*. Philadelphia: W. B. Saunders Company Ltd.

Lind, C. and Butler, C. (1995) 'The legal abuse of homosexual children', *Journal of Child Law*, 7, 3–9.

Moore, S. and Rosenthal, D. (1993) *Sexuality in Adolescence*. London: Routledge.

Moran, L. (1996) *The Homosexual(ity) of Law*. London: Routledge.

Rich, A. (1993) 'Compulsory heterosexuality and lesbian existence', in H. Abelove, M. A. Barale and D. M. Halperin (eds), *The Lesbian and Gay Studies Reader*. New York: Routledge, pp. 227–54.

Rubenstein, W. B. (1993) *Lesbians, Gay Men, and the Law*. New York: The New Press.

Rubin, G. S. (1993) 'Thinking sex: notes for a radical theory of the politics of sexuality', in H. Abelove, M. A. Barale and D. M. Halperin (eds), *The Lesbian and Gay Studies Reader*. New York: Routledge, pp. 3–44.

Schofield, M. (1965) *The Sexual Behaviour of Young People*. London: Longmans.

Scott, J. W. (1993) 'The evidence of experience', in H. Abelove, M. Barale and D. M. Halperin (eds), *The Lesbian and Gay Studies Reader*. New York: Routledge, pp. 397–415.

Scruton, R. (1985) *Sexual Desire*. London: Weidenfeld and Nicolson.

Shahar, S. (1990) *Childhood in the Middle Ages*. London: Routledge.

Smith, J. and Hogan, B. (1996) *Criminal Law*. London: Butterworths.

Stonewall (1996) *Newsletter*, **4** (2), May, p. 6.

Tatchell, P. (1996) 'Is fourteen too young for sex?', *Gay Times*, June 1996, p. 36.

Thane, P. (1981) 'Childhood in history', in M. King (ed.), *Childhood, Welfare and Justice: A Critical Examination of Children in the Legal and Child Care Systems*. London: Batsford Academic and Institutional, pp. 6–25.

Thomas, P. and Costigan, R. (1990) *Promoting Homosexuality: Section 28 of the Local Government Act 1988*. Cardiff: Cardiff Law School.

Wagg, S. (1988) 'Perishing kids? The sociology of childhood', *Social Studies Review*, 3, 126.

Weeks, J. (1989) *Sex, Politics and Society*, 2nd edn. London: Longman.

Weeks, J. (1991) *Against Nature*. London: Rivers Oram Press.

Wintermute, R. (1995) *Sexual Orientation and Human Rights*. Oxford: Clarendon.

7

Beyond Section 28: Law, Governance and Sex Education

Daniel Monk

Sex education is aspirational; it represents, amongst other things, an attempt to construct a particular type of sexual citizen. Consequently the provision of sex education is inherently political and its structure and content are intimately linked to and act as an indicator of the current struggles and concerns within society about sexuality and sexual activity. Sex education is therefore not simply a location for the transmission of information about sex, but significantly represents a contested site for the production of knowledge about sex. In recent years it has been a site of highly visible struggles reflecting the wider political debates concerning education (Bash and Coulby, 1989) and 'moral panics' surrounding issues of sexuality (Durham, 1991, pp. 99–122; Meredith, 1992; p. 65; Thomson, 1993, 1994). Throughout these struggles much attention has focused on the law and this chapter attempts to demonstrate the ways in which law operates and has been used both to marginalize and to reinforce negative images of homosexuality within school sex education. It concludes with an assessment of current strategies of resistance.

For many people, including informed lesbians and gays (Powell, 1996), the infamous Section 28 of the Local Government Act 1988[1] is perceived as the main legal restriction to the inclusion of a progressive or radical approach to homosexuality within sex education; yet while it is far from unimportant, its effect on the sex education curriculum is severely restricted.[2] Significantly the focus on Section 28 has resulted in overlooking the less visible, more subtle, and in practice often more effective, ways by which sex education is controlled.

Drawing attention to these other measures requires looking beyond provisions, such as Section 28, which seek to impose a sexual norm through repressive commands and instead involves focusing on more positive exercises of power. This approach consequently examines how terms such as 'biology', 'health' and 'child sexuality' are contested and given specific meanings by competing discourses, which translate into, often conflicting, programmes of sex education. In particular, it identifies the role that law plays in bringing these programmes into reality through the utilization of a variety of techniques of government, such as the structure of the curriculum and the legitimization of the expertise and knowledge of parents, governors and health professionals in particular locations within the curriculum. (This approach utilizes a method of analysis developed by sociologists Miller and Rose (1992).)

The legal framework

English legislation concerning sex education is complex and was frequently amended throughout the 1980s and early 1990s, after highly politicized debates in which opposition to progressive sex education policies by traditionalists[3] and the tabloid media challenged pragmatic approaches to concerns about HIV/AIDS and the high rate of teenage pregnancies (Thomson, 1993, 1994). The current law is contained in the Education Act 1996[4] and the government circular *Education Act 1993: Sex Education in Schools* ('the Circular'); which in effect provide for sex education in three distinct locations.

The first is biology lessons, the content of which are prescribed by the National Curriculum for Science. This aspect of the curriculum is compulsory and centrally controlled by the Secretary of State for Education (Meredith, 1992, pp. 77–88). Its content is restricted to biological aspects of human sexual behaviour (Section 356(9)(c); Lenderyou, 1994, p. 139). 'Biological' is not defined by statute, but information about HIV/AIDS and other sexually transmitted disease is specifically excluded (Section 356(9)(a)(b)).

Second, the non-biological aspects, referred to as 'sex education' (Section 252(1)(c)), are located in the basic curriculum. This aspect of the curriculum is under the control of school governing bodies (Sections 371(3), 372(4)(a)). Governors have discretion as to the provision of sex education in primary schools (Section 371(3)) but it is compulsory in secondary schools (Section 352(1)(c));[5] nevertheless parents have an absolute right to withdraw their children from this aspect of the curriculum (Section 405). Statute requires that it includes information about 'HIV/AIDS and other sexually transmitted disease' (Section 352(3)) and is 'given in such a manner as to encourage ... pupils to have regard to moral considerations and the value of family life' (Section 403(1)). More detail as to its content is provided by the Circular which, although only guidance, has 'had a significant impact on the way in which school sex education was and continues to be perceived' (Thomson, 1994, p. 20).[6]

Third, the Circular makes a distinction between sex education within the curriculum and individual advice to pupils (Paragraph 38). While not referred to by statute, advice outside of the classroom is an important and distinct location for the provision of sex education.

In the following sections these three locations are explored in more depth and the various techniques of government at play are identified.

Science lessons and the uses of 'biology'

In 1991 Kenneth Baker, then Secretary of State for Education, under pressure from the Department of Health, amended the National Curriculum for Science to include study of the 'ways in which the human body can be affected by ... HIV/AIDS'.[7] This caused a political storm, which resulted in the removal of HIV/AIDS from the science curriculum by the Education Act 1993 (Thomson, 1994). Implicit, and at times explicit, within the objections made by traditionalists to Baker's action was the fear that teaching about HIV/AIDS would involve children being 'exposed' to homosexuality. In particular, the Department of Education pamphlet *HIV and AIDS: A Guide for the Education Service* came under much criticism for being 'amoral' and 'judgement free' and for reassuring pupils of the safeness of masturbation and for 'explicitly describing oral sex' and 'deviant sexual practices' (Hansard HL 5/3/92 cols 977–8). These debates indicate that the meaning of 'biology', in the context of sex education, is not solely a matter of scientific knowledge, but is contested and constructed in ways which enable it to perform distinct functions.

Removal of HIV/AIDS from the science curriculum ensures that the 'biological aspects' of sex education are restricted to human reproduction and exclude reference to non-reproductive sex such as masturbation and homosexuality, together with practical advice about contraception and sexually transmitted diseases. These exclusions support the traditionalists' aim that sex education be a programme of moral education. This programme upholds the belief that sexual activity is permissible only within marriage and the discursive construction of children as sexual innocents and homosexuality as unnatural, sinful and associated with physical and mental illness and social decay. Consequently within this programme practical advice to children on sexual matters and a positive approach to homosexuality are deemed highly inappropriate and potentially dangerous.

This curriculum categorization and definition of 'biology' represents a particularly effective technique for the marginalization of homosexuality within the classroom because of the privileged position that the National Curriculum occupies within the curriculum as a whole. Examinations in core subjects increasingly, through league tables, form the basis on which schools are judged and it consequently has a detrimental impact on the time and resources available to schools for subjects outside of it, such as sex education within the basic curriculum. Furthermore, because of its highly prescriptive nature, there is less opportunity for teachers to respond imaginatively with issues relating to gender and sexuality within National Curriculum subjects such as history and English. Similarly providing information about sex through the language of science in biology undermines the possibility of pupils developing an awareness of the socially constructed and contingent aspects of sexuality.

The sex education curriculum

The uses of 'parent power'

One of the major criticisms of Baker's positioning of HIV/AIDS in the National Curriculum was that it undermined parental influence over sex education. Indeed it was perceived as being in conflict with earlier provisions that had enhanced parental influence by increasing the numbers of parent governors, transferring control of sex education from Local Education Authorities (LEAs) to the governors and by requiring governors to be more accountable to parents. (These measures were introduced in 1986 and are now contained in the Education Act 1996, Sections 371, 404(1).) The subsequent restrictions to the remit of the

National Curriculum and the establishment of a parental right to withdraw a child from sex education within the basic curriculum, introduced in 1993, further increased parental influence. Consequently parent power in this area of the curriculum is real and more than political rhetoric.

Increasing parental influence has been a clearly identifiable policy throughout the education reforms in the last decade (Meredith, 1992; Harris, 1993). The significance attached to this enhanced role for parents owes much to the ideas of what is broadly characterized as the 'New Right' and in particular to the political discourse of neo-liberalism (Quicke, 1988; Bell, 1993; Barron 1996). Within this discourse, welfare intervention is perceived as having 'a morally damaging effect upon citizens, producing a "culture of dependency" based on expectations that government will do what in reality only individuals can' (Miller and Rose, 1992, p. 198). Consequently 'parent power' is upheld as a policy to simultaneously strengthen parental responsibility and to provide a check on both central and local government intervention. The neo-liberal construction of parents as active participants in their children's education, as opposed to passive recipients of services, can be seen to translate into policies that attempt to place education within a free-market economy (Bash and Coulby, 1989). Significantly, however, within this framework it is parents and not pupils who are the 'consumers'.

Inherent within this approach is the conceptualization of the parent/child relationship as private, self-regulating and operating outside of the state-regulated public sphere. This results in a public/private dichotomy which has been the object of much academic thought. Family law critiques have emphasized that the dichotomy is a social construction, 'not fixed by nature' (Freeman, 1985, p. 170), in order to explain why the privacy of the parent/child relationship is at times legitimized, for example in the context of sex education, but is at other times rejected, as is the case with compulsory education and increasingly with the physical abuse of children by parents. A further critique demonstrates that it serves to perpetuate a particular set of power relations, in particular that of men over women (O'Donovan, 1985) and, in the context of sex education, that of parents over their children.

An alternative approach suggests that the state, by utilizing independent agents that are distinct from its own institutions, does not so much relinquish power but governs through them (Foucault in Burchell, Gordon and Miller, 1991, pp. 87, 103; Dean, 1994, p. 174). Miller and Rose describe this as a technique of government that enables modern liberal states to 'reconcile the principle that the domain of the political must be restricted, with the recognition of the vital political implications of formally private activities' (1992, p. 179). Consequently parental influence is in part legitimized by being presented as depoliticizing education. This is particularly apparent in the context of sex education and especially so with regard to homosexuality, where the portrayal of parents as non-political is contrasted with the converse portrayal of progressive teachers and 'loony left' LEAs as 'corrupters of youth' and their policies as subversive political programmes for sexual indoctrination (Thomson, 1994; Sanderson, 1995; Cooper, 1994). However, it is clear that the government calculated that parental influence would have a particular impact on the content of sex education. Indeed the government initially opposed Section 28 of the Local Government Act on the basis that central government restrictions on 'immoral' sex education were unnecessary, as LEA influence had been replaced by parental control (Colvin and Hawksley, 1989, Durham, 1991, p. 113) – a strategy which clearly indicates that 'laissez faire is not so much practised as used' (Bell, 1993, p. 594).

The parental right to withdraw a child from sex education can similarly be interpreted as a means of restricting the teaching of controversial subjects such as homosexuality and not, as has been suggested, a provision enabling governors more flexibility in developing the curriculum (Harris, 1996, p. 20). Despite the fact that opinion polls suggest that few parents will actually make use of this right (Allen, 1987) the Circular suggests that the provision has implications for all pupils, as it advises that spontaneous discussion and honest answering of questions outside of the sex education curricula should be restricted 'where they involve pupils whose parents have withdrawn them from sex education' (Paragraph 30). Additionally the Circular states that:

> The prime responsibility for bringing up children rests with parents . . . the teaching offered by schools should be complementary and supportive to the role of parents, and should have regard to parents' views about its content and presentation. *The more successful schools are in achieving this, the less the likelihood that parents will wish to exercise their right of withdrawal.* (Paragraph 7, my emphasis)

Interpreted in this way, the provision is likely to lead to caution by governors in designing sex education programmes, with homosexuality being one of the most likely topics for exclusion on the basis of it being one of the subjects most likely to offend at least some parents.

Underlying this calculation is the identification of parents as a group whose collective knowledge is perceived as being highly reluctant to accept child sexuality and especially homosexuality, particularly with regard to their own children. This calculation is problematic, as it relies on a monolithic conceptualization of parents; a number of recent incidents indicate that newly empowered parents sometimes act in opposition to government policy.[8]

However parents choose to exercise their influence, and even if many choose not to, their role as 'consumers' marks a significant shift in the nature of the provision of education services. Barron and Scott comment that 'redefining the citizen as an economic actor, tends to threaten the universality and uniformity of service provision and hence to diminish social "rights" ' and that in effect 'wants' replace 'needs' (1992, pp. 527, 544). The result is that the question whether or not children, and in particular young lesbians and gays, might benefit from the inclusion of homosexuality in sex education lessons is replaced by the question whether or not parents want homosexuality to be included.

Some parents may of course support the inclusion of homosexuality. The Circular appears to recognize the possibility that some parents may lead 'immoral' lifestyles or be 'irresponsible' in some way and consequently suggests that parental opinions should not be treated with equal respect. Under the heading 'A Moral Framework for Sex Education' it states, ambiguously, that 'teachers should help pupils, whatever their circumstances, to raise their sights' (Paragraph 8).

Government 'guidance': repression and invisibility

On devising the sex education curriculum, governors are guided not only by parents but also by the Circular which provides an interpretation of the requirement that sex education be taught within the context of 'moral considerations and the value of family life' (Section 403(1)) and makes reference to homosexuality.

Section 403(1) was described by Kenneth Baker as 'a clear signal reinforcing the institution of marriage as the foundation of a healthy family life and the very bedrock of our civilization' (quoted in Durham,

1991, p. 107). However, the provision is clearly open to a far broader interpretation and in keeping with the provision, 'pupils could be encouraged to look at the value of a variety of family arrangements, including lesbian families, single parent families and extended families' (Melia, 1989, p. 220). Nevertheless, the Circular hints at the intended interpretation in its advice that sex education should be 'set within a clear framework of values and an awareness of the law on sexual behaviour', and that 'pupils should accordingly be encouraged to appreciate the value of stable married and family life' and 'should be enabled to recognize the physical, emotional and moral implications and risks of certain types of behaviour' (Paragraph 8). The emphasis on marriage and the criminal law precludes a positive approach towards homosexuality or other alternatives to heterosexual married life.

In contrast to 'parent power', the advice contained in the Circular represents an explicit attempt at centralized regulation of the content of the curriculum. This repressive technique of control reflects the influence of neo-conservativism with its emphasis on authority, discipline and hierarchy. Significantly within this discourse, in contrast to neo-liberalism, a strong centralized state is unproblematic and less importance is attached to individual freedom. It is because children and adolescents are not sexual citizens, and hence are forbidden sexual freedom by contemporary legal and moral norms, that the neo-conservative discourse, with its emphasis on sexual repression and prohibitions, has had far greater influence in sex education, at least within the classroom, than it currently has in matters affecting adult sexuality.

In connection with homosexuality, a repressive approach was clearly apparent in the 1987 government circular, *Sex Education at School* (November 1987), which adopted almost identical language to that of Section 28 (Paragraph 22). However, the approach in the current 1994 circular differs strikingly to the extent that there is now no specific advice to governors as to how the subject should be addressed. Indeed, apart from the restating of Section 28, the word 'homosexual' itself is avoided. Referring to the criminal law, it states in the final paragraph under the heading 'Other Indecent Assault' that:

> It is an offence to commit buggery with a human being or an animal. This does not apply where two men over the age of 21

> consensually commit buggery in private.... Gross indecency between men is an offence unless the act is committed in private and both parties consent and have attained the age of 21 years.[9] (Annex B)

While the removal of the explicitly restrictive approach may encourage some governors to be more flexible in their approach, the more likely outcome is a continuation of the present situation in which the subject is simply avoided (Rudyat, Ryan and Speed, 1992).

Individual advice outside the classroom

A pastoral role for teachers?

The Circular advises that:

> Good teachers have always taken a pastoral interest in the welfare and well-being of pupils ... this function *should never trespass on the proper exercise of parental rights and responsibilities*. (Paragraph 38; my emphasis)

The language used here, in particular the words 'trespass' and 'rights', suggests that caution by teachers is required not on the basis of the interests of the child, but that to act in any other way would be an unacceptable interference with the proprietorial rights of parents over children. This restricted role for teachers is reinforced by paragraphs 39 and 40 of the Circular, which suggest that advice to under-age pupils on such matters as contraception 'without parental consent or knowledge would be an inappropriate exercise of a teacher's professional duties'; that pupils have no right to confidentiality in their communications with teachers about sexual matters; and that such advice may be unlawful. The message from the Circular that 'teachers are not health professionals' (Paragraph 39) is significant because it suggests that the decision in the case of *Gillick* v. *West Norfolk Area Health Authority* ([1985] 3 All ER 402), which enables doctors to give contraceptive advice to under-age girls without parental knowledge or consent, does not apply to teachers. This results in uncertainty for teachers as to the extent to which they can take a 'pastoral interest' in their pupils (Lenderyou, 1994, p. 141). It also represents an attempt to 'coerce schools and teachers into accepting a policy on individual advice that has no legal foundation' (Blair and Furniss, 1995, p. 198).

While in the context of individual advice no explicit reference is made in the Circular to homosexuality, this policy has serious implications for gay and lesbian pupils, particularly as teachers are often considered to be more approachable than parents by pupils wishing to discuss their sexuality. Furthermore, because sexual activity under the age of sixteen is illegal, teachers will, understandably, be extremely reluctant to offer advice to most male pupils about safer sex practices. Consequently in this area, as within the classroom, the implication is that teachers should subjugate their perception of the needs of their pupils to the wishes of parents.

The uses of 'health'

Outside of the classroom the Circular introduces new actors into the structure. Paragraph 40 advises teachers approached on matters of personal sexual behaviour, in particular when a pupil 'has embarked on or is contemplating, a course of conduct which is likely to place him or her at moral or physical risk or in breach of the law', to 'wherever possible, encourage the pupil to seek advice ... from the relevant health service professional ... and the Head Teacher should arrange for the pupil to be counselled'. 'Health' has become a key word in sex education, to the extent that it is now frequently referred to as 'health education' by both sex educators themselves and within government departments. The substitution of the word 'health' for 'sex' and the suggested role of health professionals and counsellors has a number of implications and meanings.

Most significant is the acceptance within the context of a pupil/health professional relationship of the fact that a pupil may be sexually active – a possibility that is either ignored or is at least highly problematic within the classroom and within the pupil/teacher relationship. The discrepancy in the position of pupils in the locations of 'health' and 'education' demonstrates how children as legal objects are constructed in ways that often conflict in order to enable conflicting practices or expertise to operate simultaneously (Moran, 1986, p. 84; O'Donovan, 1993, p. 91). In the health context the child is constructed in law as a patient, independent and potentially (homo)sexual, while in the education context the child is a pupil, dependent, non-sexual and heterosexual on obtaining adulthood. The former construction brings the advantages of access to practical advice about sexual behaviour, sexuality and, of particular importance for young gay men, information about HIV/AIDS.

The involvement of health service professionals and counsellors in sex education has increased considerably in recent years, partly as a result of the restrictions placed on teachers to provide these services in the context of sex education. However, the extent to which pupils are encouraged to use such services, or indeed made aware of their availability, is dependent on the attitude of school governors towards them and there exists a wide diversity of provision (Denman *et al.*, 1996).

Furthermore it is important to remember that the Circular does not envisage these services being provided to all pupils, but only to those who as a result of their sexual behaviour are 'at moral or physical risk or in breach of the law'. This has the effect of marginalizing those pupils and problematizes their sexuality to the extent that a homosexual pupil is perceived as having a moral, health or legal problem as opposed to a right to information. While it is undeniable that a gay man under sixteen has a legal problem, the same cannot be said for his health or morals. In this way the health programme operates in a converse way to the construction of 'biology' within the National Curriculum. Biology, considered essential for all pupils, refers to sex which is 'natural', 'functional', 'moral' and 'legal' and consequently excludes any practical advice to children and any mention of homosexuality. In contrast the health programme, restricted to a minority of pupils, is associated with illness, illegality and immorality – a construction that implicitly reinforces negative problematizations of homosexuality. While the discourse of health is used to legitimize the provision of practical sex education, it simultaneously reinforces the norm of the child as ideally non-sexual and heterosexual on reaching adulthood.

Though health professionals have a significant role within the legal structure, no definition is provided for the terms 'health professional' or 'counsellor', nor is there any indication as to what type of advice and information they should provide. This is significant because while pupils are independent of their parents in this location, they are not autonomous. The introduction of health professionals reflects a welfare approach in that the focus is on the interests of the child rather than the parents, but the definition, or diagnosis, of the child's problems or interests are determined by the professional, who constructs the child in accordance with the expertise and 'knowledge' of his or her profession. Furthermore, recognition of a child's sexual activity in this location legitimizes for health professionals a degree of surveillance far greater than that permitted to teachers and in many cases greater than that available to parents. Consequently in this location, while a child's sexual activity is to a certain extent decriminalized, it is at the same time pathologized through the medical gaze of the health professionals.

This has particular significance for homosexual pupils, as attitudes towards homosexuality vary widely amongst, and indeed within, the different health professions (Gordon, 1994) and consequently it is unclear as to how a homosexual pupil referred to such a professional will be 'treated'.

'Health', like biology, can serve a political purpose with an explicitly normalizing intent. Furthermore, the utilization of the 'neutral language of science' within the health discourse serves to depoliticize the debate; in this way the scientific claim to truth conceals the discursive construction of knowledge and consequently conceals the exercise of power (Foucault, 1979).

Conclusions and strategies for resistance

The legal structure of sex education operates in such a way as to severely undermine the possibility of homosexuality being either mentioned at all or dealt with in a positive and open manner. As this chapter has demonstrated, this is achieved not so much by repressive and explicitly negative provisions such as Section 28, but by the use of more subtle and less visible techniques. This consequently challenges traditional political methods of resistance. For whereas the openly repressive and authoritarian nature of Section 28 resulted in unprecedented activism from the lesbian and gay community and, similarly, pressure groups such as Stonewall made representations to the government in connection with the openly negative 1987 circular, the present structure, by operating on a more localized terrain and through agents independent of the state, undermines these paths. However, this does not foreclose the possibility of resistance – rather it requires new strategies.

The identification of parents as consumers has a significant effect on strategies for challenging sex education programmes, as the individualization of service provision ensures that 'collective protest is displaced by individual complaint' (Barron and Scott, 1992, p. 544). This restricts the possibility of a collective debate and decision being made as to the role, if any, that sex education might take in challenging homophobia and significantly excludes from consideration the opinions of people who are not parents of children of school age and children themselves. In developing strategies on a localized terrain to encourage parents to demand a more open and pluralistic sex education, it is important to recognize that the broad term 'homophobia' does not adequately acknowledge the variety of reasons behind the problematization of homosexuality (Cooper, 1994: 161). Significantly the concerns of many parents are quite distinct from the calculations of the 'religious' right; consequently local resistance will have to challenge a variety of fears and constructions of homosexuality.

An alternative strategy is to make governors aware of the experiences of pupils who identify as lesbian and gay. This approach, which is adopted by the Sex Education Forum, makes use of recent research that revealed that many lesbian and gay men felt unsupported by the school sex education they received and experienced isolation during their time at school (Stonewall, 1994), and notes that disturbing rates of suicide and mental health problems can arise from such isolation (Sex Education Forum, 1994, p. 21). The references to the health of young lesbians and gays represents a welfarist approach, as it enables the Forum to suggest a type of sex education that it believes to be in the best interests of these pupils.

The Sex Education Forum also reminds governors of their general duty, under Section 351 of the Education Act 1996, to 'prepare *all* people for the responsibilities and opportunities of adult life' (1994, p. 55). The suggestion that governors are failing in their statutory duty by not openly addressing homosexuality in the curriculum represents an attempt to assert a right of lesbians and gays to be acknowledged within the system. This strategic movement away from challenging prohibitions towards claiming protection reflects a more general shift in lesbian and gay activist engagement with the law (Herman, 1994).

While these rights and welfarist strategies are pragmatic and successfully identify points of instability within the legal and health discourses, they are not unproblematic (Herman, 1994; Lehring, 1997). Both strategies imply that lesbian and gay pupils are a clearly identifiable minority and have particular needs and interests. While increasing numbers of young people do identify themselves as lesbian or gay and, particularly in the context of safer sex information, they clearly have special needs (Watney, 1994; p. 268), this approach could potentially lead to a situation in which only those pupils who identify themselves, or are identified by others, as lesbian or gay receive such information. This would reinforce the marginalization and problematization of those pupils and would restrict the possibility of all pupils having access to information about (homo)sexuality and safer sex information.

More problematically, while the assertion of lesbian and gay identities does not in itself represent an essentialist stance on sexuality, there is a possibility that reliance on the existence of such identities as the basis for the claiming of rights in sex education could lead to the characterization of those identities within the classroom not so much as 'necessary fictions' (Weeks, 1991, p. 98) but as biological facts. A strategic essentialist approach has politically expedient consequences, in that a belief in the immutability of sexuality strengthens the claim for rights and implicitly counters fears that homosexuality can be promoted through education. Similarly it would enable homosexuality to be categorized as natural, which would validate its inclusion in the privileged location of biology in the National Curriculum.

However, sex education is not simply a means to provide young people with information about sex, it is crucially a site for the production of knowledge about sex and sexuality. Consequently, while adopting an essentialist stance has pragmatic advantages and positive lesbian and gay identities have proved politically effective and individually empowering, particularly in challenging societal and familial opposition, upholding this position within the sphere of education as a fixed truth denies young people, regardless of their sexuality, the opportunity, and more importantly the encouragement, to think beyond these constructions and to develop and experiment with new sexual identities and forms of relationships. Put simply, a progressive sex education is not necessarily less normative than a repressive one (Foucault, 1979). The real challenge, and one that requires the translation of radical or queer approaches towards sexuality into effective political strategies (Wilson, 1997), is to imagine a programme for sex education that enables young people to appreciate the uses of current adult sexualities and identities but at the same time prepares them for a future of uncertainties and disorder.

Notes

1. Section 28(1) states that 'a local authority shall not (a) intentionally promote homosexuality or publish material with the intention of promoting homosexuality; (b) promote the teaching in any maintained school of the acceptance of homosexuality as a pretend family relationship'.
2. Section 28 refers only to the actions of local education authorities and not to school governors, who are responsible for the provision of sex education. However, notwithstanding its symbolic effect, there is indeed evidence that it has an inhibitory effect on teachers and governors (Colvin and Hawksley, 1989, pp. 44, 52, 54; Meredith, 1992, p. 27).
3. 'Traditionalists' is used here to refer to a broad group of right-wing religious and conservative pressure groups, politicians and writers.
4. This Act consolidates the provisions formerly in the Education (No. 2) Act 1986, the Education Reform Act 1988 and the Education Act 1993.
5. The compulsory provision was introduced by the Education Act 1993. Secondary school education commences for children at the age of eleven.
6. The circular has been criticized for 'failing to distinguish where it is offering an interpretation of the law (however slanted) from the places where it merely offers a statement of the Secretary of State's view of good practice' (Blair and Furniss, 1995, p. 198).
7. Education (National Curriculum) (Attainment Targets and Programmes of Study in Science) Order 1991, SI 1991\2897.
8. Particularly relevant in this context is the incident concerning Jane Brown, the Head Teacher portrayed by the media as a 'dangerous politically-correct lesbian' for refusing tickets for a performance of *Romeo and Juliet*, who was supported both by parents and governors (Sanderson, 1995, pp. 79–84; Cooper, 1997).
9. The Criminal Justice Act 1994 subsequently lowered the age of consent for homosexual activity to eighteen and decriminalized the act of consensual buggery between human beings. Following the vote in the House of Commons in June 1998 the age of consent for homosexual activity will be reduced to sixteen in the near future.

References

Allen, I. (1987) *Education in Sex and Personal Relationships*. London: Policy Studies Institute.

Barron, A. (1996) 'The governance of schooling: genealogies of control and empowerment in the reform of public education', *Studies in Law, Politics and Society*, **15**, 167–204.

Barron, A. and Scott, C. (1992) 'The Citizen's Charter programme', *Modern Law Review*, **55**, 526–46.

Bash, L. and Coulby, D. (eds) (1989) *The Education Reform Act: Competition and Control*. London: Cassell.

Bell, V. (1993) 'Governing childhood: neo-liberalism and the law', *Economy and Society*, **22** (3), 590.

Blair, A. and Furniss, C. (1995) 'Sex, lies and DFE Circular 5/94: the limits of sex education', *Education and the Law*, 7 (4), 197–202.

Burchell, G., Gordon, C. and Miller, P. (eds) (1991) *The Foucault Effect: Studies in Governmentality*. Hemel Hempstead: Harvester Wheatsheaf.

Colvin, M. and Hawksley, J. (1989) *Section 28: A Practical Guide to the Law and Its Implications*. London: NCCL.

Cooper, D. (1994) *Sexing the City: Lesbian and Gay Politics within the Activist State*. London: Rivers Oram Press.

Cooper, D. (1997) 'Governance troubles: school authority, gender and space', *British Journal of Sociology of Education* 18, 501–17.

Dean, M. (1994) *Critical and Effective Histories: Foucault's Methods and Historical Sociology*. London: Routledge.

Denman, S., Pearson, J., Davis, P. and Moody, D. (1996) 'A survey of HIV- and AIDS-related knowledge, beliefs and attitudes among 14-year-olds in Nottinghamshire', *Educational Research*, **38** (1), 93–9.

Durham, M. (1991) *Sex and Politics: The Family and Morality in the Thatcher Years*. London: Macmillan.

Foucault, M. (1979) *The History of Sexuality*, Vol. 1. London: Allen Lane.

Freeman, M. (1985) 'Towards a critical theory of family law', *Current Legal Problems*, **38**, 153–85.

Gordon, P. (1994) 'The contribution of sexology to contemporary sexuality education', *Sexual and Marital Therapy*, **9** (2), 171–80.

Harris, N. (1993) *Law and Education: Regulation, Consumerism and the Education System*. London: Sweet and Maxwell.

Harris, N. (ed.) (1996) *Sex Education and the Law*. London: National Children's Bureau.

Herman, D. (1994) *Rights of Passage: Struggles for Lesbian and Gay Legal Equality*. Toronto: University of Toronto Press.

Lehring, G. (1997) 'Essentialism and the political articulation of identity', in S. Phelan (ed.), *Playing with Fire: Queer Politics, Queer Theories*. New York: Routledge.

Lenderyou, G. (1994) 'Sex education: a school-based perspective', *Sexual and Marital Therapy*, **9** (2), 127–44.

Melia, J. (1989) 'Sex education in school: keeping to the "norm" ', in C. Jones and P. Mahoney (eds), *Learning Our Lines: Sexuality and Social Control in Education*. London: The Women's Press.

Meredith, P. (1992) *Government, Schools and the Law*. London: Routledge.

Miller, P. and Rose, N. (1992) 'Political power beyond the state; problematics of government', *British Journal of Sociology*, **43** (2), 173–205.

Moran, L. (1986) 'A reading in sexual politics and law: Gillick v. Norfolk and Wisbech Area Health Authority', *Liverpool Law Review*, **8** (1), 83–94.

O'Donovan, K. (1985) *Sexual Divisions in Law*. London: Weidenfeld and Nicholson.

O'Donovan, K. (1993) *Family Law Matters*. London: Pluto Press.

Powell, V. (1996) 'Who's afraid of Section 28?', *Gay Times*, April, p. 25.

Quicke, J. (1988) 'The "New Right" and education', *British Journal of Education Studies*, **36** (1), 5–20.

Rudyat, I., Ryan and Speed (1992) *Today's Young Adults – 16 to 19-year-olds Look at Diet, Alcohol, Smoking, Drugs and Sexual Behaviour*. London: Health Education Association.

Sanderson, T. (1995) *Mediawatch*. London: Cassell.

Sex Education Forum (1994) *Developing and Reviewing a School Sex Education Policy: Positive Strategy*. London: National Children's Bureau.

Stonewall (1994) *Arrested Development*. London: Stonewall.

Thomson, R. (1993) 'Unholy alliances: the recent politics of sex education', in J. Bristow and A. Wilson (eds), *Activating Theory: Lesbian, Gay, Bisexual Politics*. London: Lawrence and Wishart.

Thomson, R. (1994) 'Prevention, promotion and adolescent sexuality: the politics of school sex education in England and Wales', *Sexual and Marital Therapy*, 9 (2), 115–26.

Watney, S. (1994) *Practices of Freedom*. London: Rivers Oram Press.

Weeks, J. (1991) *Against Nature*. London: Rivers Oram Press.

Wilson, A. (1997) 'Somewhere over the rainbow: queer translating', in S. Phelan (ed.), *Playing with Fire: Queer Politics, Queer Theories*. New York: Routledge.

8

What's in a Name: Naming Legal Needs in AIDS Service Organizations

Petra Wilson

Introduction

After only a brief period of time spent as a volunteer worker in an HIV advice agency, it became clear to me that a great many of the people living with the human immunodeficiency virus (HIV) in the United Kingdom suffer injustice and discrimination at the hands of employers, landlords, health care providers, relatives and other people in general. As a lawyer, I saw this discrimination as the source of potential disputes suitable for resolution by law, and so began to explore the reported case law for the legal resolutions to the problems that presented themselves on a weekly, if not daily, basis.

The case law for which I was looking was, however, almost non-existent. A June 1990 trawl of Lexis, a legal data base, showed eighteen decided court cases to that date in which HIV had been an issue in any way,[1] while my latest trawl in 1996 showed only ten more.

The fact that very few cases could be found was not entirely surprising, since a vast body of academic writing over the past twenty years has shown that a considerable gap exists between the number of possible and actual legal claimants.[2] It is of course impossible to provide an overview of the huge literature that was produced here. Constraints of space allow me to hint at it only through one quotation:

> what is injurious depends on current and ever changing estimations of what enhances or impairs health, happiness, character and other desired states. Knowledge and ideology constantly send new

> currents through this vast ocean . . . characterisation of an event as a grievance will depend on the cognitive repertoire with which society supplies the injured person and his idiosyncratic adaptation of it. (Galanter, 1983, p. 13)

In this brief quotation one can begin to see the common threads found in the studies of access to law and unmet legal need: financial factors; knowledge and understanding of the institutions and organizations; personal, popular and idiosyncratic beliefs; and institutional factors.

In this chapter I wish to look at only one small aspect of the many issues that can influence use of legal services by people affected by HIV. Readers should note that this is only one narrow perspective and one that does not consider at all the issue of financial and other personal inhibitors to the use of law. My focus is on the early stages of the establishment of an HIV advice organization, and I draw particularly on the work of Mather and Yngvesson (1980) and Santos (1977), who argue convincingly that any audience, no matter how informal, will necessarily be a transformative influence as a story is told and re-told to suit the particular audience. Accordingly, it seemed worthwhile to explore the transformative effect of third parties who claimed that they did not have their own agenda for translating the client's story into any particular form of need.

The larger study I conducted therefore posed the question: why do so few people affected by HIV use formal legal dispute resolution to counter the acts of discrimination and injustice they experience? It sought to answer that question by examining closely the way in which people affected by HIV use advice services, in order to test the hypothesis that law is not a useful tool in addressing the needs arising from such experiences. Readers should not, however, accept without question the validity of the assumptions in that central research question. The question in itself suggests several assumptions and ideas about use of law generally. First, it begs the question: what does it mean to *use* law?[3] Second, it suggests that using law is good, and that a failure to use it will amount to some sort of unmet need. It would seem to reject the idea that failure to use the law may be an informed and rational decision, and it could be argued that it is no more than legal hegemony to ask why legal solutions are not used. While that criticism is accepted and should be borne in mind by the reader, for the purposes of the larger study it was necessary to accept the use of law as a given good in order to explore more deeply the hypothesis that legal and para-legal advisors are highly significant information and image brokers for the law and thus their impact on legal claim-making should be considered.

In this chapter I wish to draw only on a small part of that study, focusing on the impact of the political perspective of the advice agency on the construction of legal needs by the client. I use some of the data collected as part of the larger study to examine the idea that some agencies, although anxious to meet the needs of people affected by HIV, unwittingly obfuscate their clients' legal needs.

Here, however, I must add a further caveat. The social and medical phenomenon of HIV has been dominated by the social construction of homosexuality, sexually transmitted diseases and drug use. In an exploration of the use of law by people affected by HIV, it is important to remain conscious of the baggage those three phenomena bring with them. It is without a doubt that gay and lesbian identity and political activism formed a very significant part of the definition of needs discussed below. It would have been possible to write solely about the role of gay and lesbian politics in AIDS service organization; here, however, the aim is to look at the picture through the depoliticized lens presented by the respondents. For although none of the 43 respondents used in this discussion denied the role of lesbian and gay polices in their own identification, all maintained that when dealing with clients, whatever their sexuality, such issues should be kept distant from their advice as far as possible.

Fieldwork

Data were collected using three methods: complete participation, complete observation and interviews. The discussion in this chapter draws almost exclusively on data gathered in the course of in-depth, open-ended interviews with 43 advice workers in 26 agencies in three cities in England. It should be noted that data reported in this chapter were not collected in London. Although informants in London were used in other parts of the study, it was decided that London should not be used as a study site when investigating access to legal advice. London offers people affected by HIV so much in terms of general and specialist advice that a study conducted there would produce a picture that could not be generalized to other areas of the country.

The interviews used in this chapter were conducted in cities that were chosen to provide as representative a sample of service providers and users as possible; accordingly the sample was taken from a metropolitan city, an urban area with a high gay population, and a city with a high ethnic population. It was hoped that in this way any significant factors affecting service users who belonged to the particular group's provider, would become evident.

However, the typology described was not used in an exclusive way; the categories cannot realistically be used in any form of closed typology, since any service user or provider may have membership of any combinations of the categorization; a user could be labelled, for example, as a gay drug user or black gay man. The categories served a purpose therefore only in ensuring that as inclusive as possible a range of HIV service providers could be researched. They were significant only in recruitment of service providers, not service users. Once the cities had been chosen, as many as possible of the service providers operating in each city were recruited on to the study. The providers taking part in the study therefore include members of voluntary, statutory and private sector agencies. The term 'service provider' is construed very broadly to include any agency that would advise a person affected by HIV on an issue related to their HIV status.

My analysis then draws on this data to explore the impact of the early socio-political alignments of a help agency on its eventual clients. It is based on the idea that in order to understand the role of AIDS service organizations in transforming the claims of people affected by HIV, it is necessary to consider the way in which such organizations understand their clients' needs, and to examine the way in which a given AIDS service organizes itself to meet those needs.

Defining needs in an AIDS service organization

On a purely logical basis, clients can only use the services that the agency provides. However, on a more significant level, the way in which the agencies define and interpret the needs of its prospective clients will have a significant bearing on the way in which the services are used, and perhaps more importantly on the way in which demands are made. Described in this way, it can be seen that the social reality of the client exists in a paradoxical relationship with the social reality of the provider.

Both are keys in the construction of the other's reality, and yet each believes that their perceived reality exists independently of either's construction (Berger and Luckman, 1967).

The definition of need in an HIV agency is therefore one of the key components in what Berger and Luckman describe as the 'internalisation moment' in the construction of a person's social reality. An internalization moment occurs when the patterns and values that have become dominant in an institution in which one is involved are learned and assimilated into one's own construction of reality (Doyal and Gough, 1991). It may be argued, therefore, that the way in which agencies define the needs of clients can have two significant effects: first, it will affect the type of service providers sought, and second, it will shape the way in which the service providers understand and respond to the client's needs.

In order to explore this hypothesis, information was sought from the respondents on the aims of the agency, the perceptions of clients and their needs, and the training of the service providers. Questions to elucidate these issues were asked, both orally in the interviews, and in analysis of the interview data.

Defining the aims of the organizations

The stated primary aim of all the agencies interviewed was, without exception, to support people affected by HIV and their carers. A second main aim of most organizations was to undertake health education work, within both the client group and the wider community. The origins of these aims are easily understood by looking again at the motivations of the original agency members: the interactionist response to a given state in their lifeworld. Yet, as described above, to understand these reasons more fully it is important to look at the way in which the actors of the group gave meaning to their action, that is, how they themselves interpreted their desire to 'support people with HIV' or 'to educate the community away from fear and stigmatization of HIV and AIDS'.

One way to do this is to look again at the expressed motivations of the service providers. Interviews established that the prime motivation of most of the voluntary and statutory service providers was a sense of crisis, a sense that a great need existed and that nothing was being done to meet that need:

> XXX was formed 5 or so years ago as a purely voluntary AIDS agency. It was set up in response to a talk by someone from the THT [Terrence Higgins Trust] which was given at a local gay club. After it a group of people got together and said 'we have got to do something about this, we have got to provide information and support'. They then went to a training course and set up a one night a week helpline which is the backbone of the operation.

In examining the way in which the specific needs of clients were conceptualized out of that feeling of a generalized need, it is useful to look at the motivations in service provision, that is to look at the way in which the providers conceived of an ideal mode of service provision.

In a study of the functioning of Frontliners, an organization established 'to provide support for people with AIDS by people with AIDS' (Moreland and Legg, 1991) and a similar evaluation of the Landmark Trust, 'a non-institutional service centre for people living with HIV and AIDS' (Gatter, 1993), the desire that the services should be consumer driven is highly evident. The extent of this commitment is evident even in the labels that the service organizers chose to attach to their organizations: services *for* people living with AIDS supplied *by* people living with AIDS; and a *non-institutional* service centre. It is clear that the service providers did not want to seem to be setting themselves up as an organization where the needs of clients would be predefined by the service supplier.

A commitment to consumer-led demand is equally evident in the current study and can be typified by the emphatic statement of one of the service organizers that they did not want to be seen as ' "professional talk", we are just not willing to say to people "right, this is what we do and this is what you need" '.

Most of the agencies, both in this study and in those carried out by Moreland and Legg (1991), Gatter (1993), Sharma, Sexton and Davis Smith (1991) and the Hull–York Research Team (1993), who between them interviewed a total of 156 AIDS service organizations, indicate that one of the main measures by which the service providers seek to maintain a consumer-led service, is to ensure that people affected by the virus remain key members of the organization, as well as clients: that is, that people affected by HIV are also service providers and have a voice in the organization of service provision. This intention was voiced by several of the service providers in this study, who pointed out that people directly affected by HIV must always have 'a majority say' on service provision:

> When we set up this as our main motivation, to supply a service that was led by people directly affected, at the time that was because people had bad feelings about other organizations that had not really been in touch with what users wanted and needed.

Other service providers stressed their commitment to user participation by citing a clause in their constitution requiring a minimum percentage of HIV-positive workers, while another cited a requirement that each worker had to have an HIV-positive shadow on whom he or she could call for expert advice.

It would seem, then, that the ideal model of service provision, at least in the voluntary sector, is one that represents a simple response to the needs the clients themselves expressed, not an assessment of need by an expert. It is easy to understand why this model of 'grass roots service provision from within the community' (Patton, 1990) should be so attractive to the voluntary organizations working in this area. Presenting oneself as part of the community, as 'one of us', represents a non-threatening image and one that should therefore be more attractive to potential clients. Furthermore, being part of the community was a simple reality for many of the agencies, since they grew as a result of the impact of HIV and AIDS on the immediately affected community.

The impact of the non-directive model

One way of understanding the way in which an organization conceptualizes and anticipates client need is to look at the way in which service providers are recruited. It is suggested that in the recruitment of both paid and voluntary workers, the people within an organization charged with staff recruitment and development will look for certain qualities. It is further suggested that in the recruitment of paid staff certain sorts of qualification will be sought, while in voluntary staff specific packages of training will be offered to ensure that volunteers are able to provide the sort of services that providers anticipate they will require when working within the organization. In looking closely at these requirements, it is therefore possible to gather some understanding of the extent to which clients' needs are anticipated by service providers.

The most significant issue in looking at the qualifications paid workers brought with them into HIV and AIDS work, is that none of the qualifications stand out as common among the employees. Their experience is distributed more or less evenly across health care work (including health education, nursing and GU medicine), teaching, social work, counselling (including clinical psychology), welfare rights (including debt and housing work) and law.

It is interesting to note that the sample of providers included six solicitors, two barristers and two law graduates, amounting to a total of ten people trained in legal issues out of a total sample of 26. A further significant issue is that only five organizations reported that they sent their paid staff on HIV-specific training courses, such as those run by the Terrence Higgins Trust or the National AIDS Counselling Training Unit (NACTU), again indicating that they did not perceive of the needs of people with HIV as a highly differentiated form of need.

It would seem, therefore, that no specific qualities are looked for in paid workers, and that at least to this extent it would seem that the organizations do not have any particular client needs in mind when appointing paid staff. The employees themselves reported an entry in AIDS advice work through personal commitment and tangential involvement in the field at the time at which the 'crisis' first became evident. Note the comments made by four different paid workers in four different AIDS service organizations:

> I was already working on a health education project, when the AIDS co-ordinator job was advertised. I was already involved in a Switchboard initiative so I applied for the job.

> neither XX or I have any background in this sort of work, we got into this because we were already involved on the voluntary side.

> my background is in the voluntary sector, in homelessness work ... but I was already involved, well, just because most gay men who cared and were sufficiently out were involved at the beginning, so I didn't really need any special training.

> I worked in the drug rehab sector, but I got involved in this through work I had done in New York. I came back eighteen

> months ago and just needed to get involved here, after my experiences over there I felt I had something to offer.

It would seem that paid workers work from a base of personal commitment in much the same way as voluntary workers seem to have been motivated through a sense of personal commitment, as argued in the studies of Moreland and Legg (1991) and Sharma, Sexton and Davis Smith (1991).

In voluntary staff, however, the pattern of training is somewhat different. All organizations using voluntary staff reported some sort of training for them, although the duration of the training volunteers received varied greatly, ranging from periods of one weekend to thirteen weeks of training.

When asked on what issues the training of volunteers concentrated, the most significant issue was that specific needs were not highlighted, that is, volunteers were not trained to spot particular types of needs and respond to them accordingly. The single most common issue in training was to do with attitudes, as illustrated by one respondent:

> volunteers are interviewed by two or three people and we ask things like: What is the biggest social problem today? What is it like to be gay? Put yourself in the position of a black person, put yourself in the position of a person with HIV, what are the problems they are experiencing? We ask questions like that so that we can see if they can empathize. We grill them on equal opportunities and impartiality so it's not about experience, but about attitudes.

It is evident that at least as far as training is concerned, the AIDS service organizations studied did not have any preconceived ideas about the needs of clients, and thus far they seemed to be true to their intention not to define the needs of their clients.

Conclusions

This brief discussion has explored the extent to which service providers are key actors in what Felstiner, Abel and Sarat (1980–81) have labelled the first transformative stage of dispute resolution: the naming stage, during which the perceived injurious experience of the client is named in a way that makes it amenable to solution. It would seem that in the HIV and AIDS advice setting, service providers are keenly aware of their transformational potential, and are anxious not to be manipulative in defining the needs of their clients. This desire would seem to be carried through in the training, where the attitude of the providers appears to be a more important issue than their skill or training.

It may be suggested that because the organizations were initially developed in a time of 'crisis management', the founding members came often from the affected communities and were driven by a desire simply to help and support those immediately affected (Berridge, 1996). In this study, one impact of that location of service within the affected communities was identified. It would seem to have engendered a belief that the key to good service provision is empathy rather than expertise, and service provision should be directed as far as possible by people with HIV.

It may also be suggested that the historical location of AIDS service organizations within an established environment of caring professions is significant in understanding the way in which the organizations have developed. The rich literature on professionalization in the caring professions has alerted many service providers that expertise of any sort in a field can lead to an atmosphere of 'occupational closure' in which the service providers 'aim for an occupational monopoly over the provision of certain skills and competencies in a market for services' (Witz, 1992, p. 49). Witz argues that such closure will occur when any service provision organization is set up. She argues further that two particular strategies will be mobilized to produce such closure and thereby to ensure market survival. Exclusionary strategies, which seek to name the provider as the only legitimate owner of a particular skill; and demarcational strategies, in which the provider seeks to locate his or her position as valuable and unique within an existing market of service provision in the given field.

Witz (1992) argues that the concept of exclusionary and demarcational strategies is useful particularly in understanding the relationship between obstetricians and midwives in the health service, in which midwives seek to maintain authority by establishing a personal relationship with clients that cannot be undermined by the hierarchical dominance of the obstetrician with the hospital setting. In the voluntary sector of AIDS service organizations, similar tactics of exclusion and demarcation are made on the basis of a special perspective on client need. Just as the male obstetrician cannot deny that a female midwife will have access to a sort of information that he cannot obtain, so the generic social worker will have to accept that the gay male volunteer has an expertise that is not available to an 'outsider'. Thus it may be argued that AIDS service providers have been keen to avoid the labelling of client's needs, since in maintaining that an ability to empathize is all-important, they can retain their position in the provider's market.

Having thus considered some of the historical factors that may have had a bearing on the way in which AIDS service organizations were developed, it is somewhat easier to understand, and interpret, the apparent reluctance of the service providers to define the needs of their clients. It may be argued that the reluctance to name is borne essentially of a political commitment to a re-evaluation of the helping professions in which the client is perceived as an active and positive force within the helping process, rather than as the recipient of some sort of beneficence. It is suggested, however, that in the practice of making the client the key actor in the definition of a need, and of casting the provider in an empathetic rather then expert role, the AIDS service providers have sought also to gain territorial purchase on the wider service provision community. By emphasizing the need to understand HIV and AIDS from within the affected community, providers both in the statutory and voluntary sector have achieved a form of professional closure. The result of such closure would seem to be that the needs, while not named in terms of a conventional professional expertise, are nevertheless named. They are named, in effect, by not being named: defined as needs that can become evident once the client feels sufficiently secure within an environment of support. It is not suggested that service providers intentionally manipulate clients so that they seek only the sort of empathetic and supportive service they offer, but it is suggested that this orientation will necessarily have an effect on the way in which clients choose services once in contact with an organization.

Notes

1. The search was for cases in which AIDS or HIV was a significant characteristic of one of the parties. The count therefore included cases where one or more of the parties was alleged or established to have HIV infection. In some cases HIV was relevant only in so far as the defendant's medical condition was pertinent to sentencing (*R* v. *Moore* [1991]), while in other cases the real or alleged infection was the central issue in the case. Such cases would include *X* v. *Y* (1988) in which it was decided that it

was not in the public interest for the HIV status of medical doctors to be published in a newspaper, or *Buck* v. *Letchworth Palace* (1987) in which a man was dismissed because his colleagues refused to work with him because they believed him to be HIV-positive.

2. Three special issues of the *Law and Society Review* provide a comprehensive starting point in this area: *Litigation and Dispute Processing* (1974, 9, nos. 1 and 2), *Delivery of Legal Services* (1976, **11**, no. 2) and *Dispute Processing and Civil Litigation* (1980–81, **15**, nos. 3 and 4). The three editions together contain some of the most influential papers in this area of scholarship. They introduce, for example, Galanter's (1974) typology of litigants as 'one-shooters' and 'repeat players', and Felstiner, Abel and Sarat's (1980–81) model of the transformation of an injurious experience to a dispute through the three key stages of naming, blaming and claiming. A useful overview is provided by Russell Smith and Sally Lloyd-Bostock's annotated bibliography: *Why People Go to Law*, Oxford: Centre for Socio-Legal Studies, (1990).
3. The question, what does it mean to use law, is an extremely complex question, which would in itself be worthy of a doctoral thesis. In seeking to answer the question one would have to examine at length the way in which people are 'using' law simply because they are conscious of its existence. It could be argued that in adhering to the rules of law one is 'using' law. However, this examination is not attempted in this study. Here the expression 'using law' is used to cover only situations in which people seek to use the services of a solicitor to begin proceedings against another. It includes therefore cases in which a settlement is reached without court action.

References

Berger, P. and Luckman, T. (1967) *The Social Construction of Reality*. London: Penguin.

Berridge, V. (1996) *The Making of Policy 1981–1994*. Oxford: Oxford University Press.

Doyal, L. and Gough, I. (1991) *A Theory of Human Need*. London: Macmillan.

Felstiner, W., Abel, R. and Sarat, A. (1980–81) 'The emergence and transformation of disputes: naming, blaming, claiming', *Law and Society Review*, **15**, 631.

Galanter, M. (1983) 'Why the "haves" come out ahead: speculations on the limits of legal change', *Law Society Review*, **9**, 95.

Gatter, P. (1993) 'Anthropology and the culture of HIV? AIDS service organisations', in P. Aggleton, P. Davis and G. Hart (eds), *AIDS: Facing the Second Decade*. London: Falmer.

The Hull-York Research Team (Tolley, K., Maynard, A. and Robinson, D.) (1993) *Social Care and HIV-AIDS*. London: HMSO.

Mather, L. and Yngvesson, B. (1980) 'Language, audience and the transformation of disputes', *Law and Society Review*, **15**, 775.

Moreland, L. and Legg, S. (1991) *Managing and Funding AIDS Organisations: Experience from the Closure of Frontliners*. London: Compass Partnership.

Patton, C. (1990) *Inventing AIDS*. London: Routledge.

Santos, B. de S. (1977) 'The law of the oppressed', *Journal of Law and Society*, **12**.

Sharma, S., Sexton, S., and Davis Smith, J. (1991) *Volunteering in HIV and AIDS Organisations: A Report of a Survey*. Berkhampstead: The Volunteer Centre.

Witz, A. (1992) *Professions and Patriarchy*. London: Routledge.

9

The Netherlands: Front Runners in Anti-discrimination Laws

Martin Moerings

Recent changes in the criminal and civil law, which seek to render illegal discrimination based upon a person's sexual orientation, place the Netherlands both at the forefront of law reform and in a unique situation in Europe. This chapter undertakes a critical analysis of those developments, placing them within the context of Dutch society and its tolerance towards homosexuality.

Tolerance towards homosexuality

In Dutch society, tolerance has increased enormously in the last fifteen to twenty years. For example, in 1968, 64 per cent of the population believed that homosexuals should be able to live the way they themselves wanted. By 1991 that figure had risen to 95 per cent. But being left free to live any way they want is not the same as having equal rights. For example, while in 1991 93 per cent accepted the right of lesbian and gay couples to inherit from each other, only 47 per cent believed that they should be allowed to adopt children. These reservations with respect to adoption are undoubtedly based on the idea that children should be able to grow up in a family with a father and mother.

While the Netherlands has a reputation of long tolerance towards homosexuals, this did not become manifest until the end of the 1960s. Those were the years when leaders of the gay movement and a number of important social workers began to emphasize that homosexuals are 'gewoon hetzelfde' ('just like anyone else') (Sengers, 1971), differing only in their sexual preference. This idea was also predominant within COC, the Dutch organization for the integration of homosexuals that was, for many years, their mouthpiece. Integration in society was its aim: not to be different, because one was gay, but to be part of society – an emphasis on being identical, not unique. During that period there was a preference for the term 'homophiliac', rather than 'homosexual', in order to demonstrate that what was at stake was not merely sexuality, but love and affection for a person of the same sex.

During the 1970s, reaction to this approach set in, starting in certain student circles. A number of radical gay groups appeared, with names like 'red gays', for whom homosexuality also had political significance. Here homosexuality meant more than that one's choice of sexual partner differs from that of heterosexuals (Warmerdam, 1991). The more moderate COC also swapped integration for emancipation, changing the emphasis to the uniqueness of one's development and identity as a homosexual and one's specific position in society – in which, for example, marriage need not be copied as a way of giving shape to a relationship.

During the past ten to fifteen years, the gay movement in the Netherlands, in so far as it has ever been possible to speak of a united front, has fragmented. The approach adopted is more pragmatic. In most sectors of society gay groups have arisen taking a pragmatic stand in their fight for their own specific interest in their own field (Schedler, 1992). Most political parties have their own gay groups. There are groups within the trade unions, including the union of government employees. Within the army there is the foundation for homosexuality and armed forces. Their is a national group of lesbian doctors. These are just a few examples. Only industry and commerce have lagged behind and, as far as I know, have no gay groups. To this extent, the emancipation, acceptance and furthering of the interests of homosexuals in the Netherlands is relative, although in comparison with most, if not all, countries it may seem remarkable.

I wish to avoid giving the impression that the relatively favourable position of homosexuals is entirely due to their own effort. It is fairer to say that they were active on a modest scale, providing the public with information, lobbying by their leaders and later through large demonstrations by groups of homosexual men and lesbian women. Such action needs a fertile soil in which to flourish (van Stolk, 1991). During the 1960s a number of leading figures in the field of public morals were instrumental in influencing thinking about sexuality in general, such as on the use of contraceptives and abortion and also on homosexuality. They were able to lift homosexuality from the sphere of sinfulness and perversity, at first via sickness and deviance, and later by regarding it as a variation of sexuality. These men and women brought their influence to bear on the moral climate and created an openness that allowed homosexuals to speak and be heard.

It is characteristic of Dutch society that it remains open to moderate action groups in general, listens to them, takes them in and, in doing so, manages to neutralize them to a certain extent.

Tolerance and the law

The cultural climate of Dutch society in general, certainly in the eyes of foreigners, appears tolerant. The scope of that tolerance is strongly determined by recognition of the citizen's right to autonomy. At the same time, this is also a restriction, for individuals may not exercise their own right at the expense of others. In general, the government is reluctant to legislate in the field of (sexual) morals. If citizens in their private lives, voluntarily and on the basis of mutual consent, engage in sexual activity, this is not regarded as a matter for interference by the state. Unlike in England, sado-masochist activities to which those concerned agree, are not prohibited. Sexual contacts between adults and young people between twelve and sixteen years of age are allowed, on the condition that the young person consents. Prosecution takes place on the basis of complaints only. Both the young person involved and the parents have the right to lodge a complaint. A problem remains as to what action the public prosecutor should take if the young person has consented to the contact, but the parents have complained to the authorities. The legislature does not act as the keeper of sexual morals in the private sphere and is reluctant to interfere in it.

There are, however, limits and the authorities do indeed act if social or public order is threatened. Even in this respect the Dutch take a distinctive approach. For example, a bill is currently before parliament (1997) that proposes to legalize brothels, provided they comply with certain conditions. The city of Amsterdam has started to issue licences to brothel-keepers under the condition that they provide sufficiently large rooms and do not force prostitutes to work without condoms. Prostitution is also allowed in public places, such as isolated factory areas. These are adapted by the authorities for that purpose. There is room for the women to take a break, for example, in a bus; visitors park their cars between hoardings; condoms are available. There are even special facilities for customers arriving by bicycle.

Anti-discrimination provisions

With respect to the law, I want to focus upon those laws that address the matter of discrimination. If the government steps aside where people enjoy sexual pleasures with mutual consent, the next step seems fairly obvious, namely that the citizens who want to prevent their fellow citizens from doing so should be subject to the law. This may be regulated by way of the criminal law to be found in the criminal code (in which the Netherlands, Sweden and some other countries have taken the lead) and in civil law, which in the Netherlands is to be found in the General Equal Treatment Act (de Algemene Wet Gelijke Behandeling).

Although the criminal law aims to deter discrimination against gays and lesbians, many situations experienced by the victims as discrimination remain outside the scope of the law because the legal provisions have the nature of a compromise and require very specific conditions. When acts do come within the criminal law, even though the criminal justice authorities are taking discrimination ever more seriously, there are still factors that make enforcement very difficult (Moerings, 1997).

Discrimination is now prohibited by way of various provisions within the criminal code. It is an offence under section 137(d) of the code to incite publicly, for example via the distribution of pamphlets, hatred, discrimination, or violent acts against persons because of their homosexual preference. An example might be: 'It's about time that homosexuals in cruising areas whose filthy acts drive mothers with children out of parks were taught a good lesson.' Under this provision it does not matter whether or not the 'inciter' has actually been successful through the distribution of his or her pamphlet.

Participation in or support of activities aimed at discriminating against people because of their homosexual preference is also prohibited in section 137(e). Participation in a demonstration aimed at incitement to hatred of gays is also prohibited. Anyone who provides financial support for such activities while staying out of sight is also liable to punishment.

The most important provisions are those which penalize insults in public and prohibit discrimination in the workplace. It is an offence to utter insults intentionally, either verbally or in writing, in public against a group of people because of their homosexual preference (section 137(c)). You may not call someone a 'filthy queer' in public. Remarks made in newspapers and books and radio and television messages are always 'public'. An insult in a personal letter stating: 'They should have gassed all of you during the war' does not fall under this provision. The general insult provision, found in section 266, which has been in force for some time, does not require a public insult. This is actually a complaint-based offence: prosecution can only take place after a complaint has been filed by the person insulted. In the new section 137(c) the circle of people who may turn to the police has been expanded considerably. Although the actual 'victim' may not have felt himself insulted, an insulting remark may be a reason for an organization, such as COC, to report it to the police.

This new section requires the *intention* to insult. In the past, in cases of racial discrimination, it had often been argued that there was no intention to insult because no one knew that such a remark would be insulting to a certain group of people. But the courts have rejected this argument. If one knowingly takes the risk that a remark might be insulting, intention is present (doctrine of recklessness). What is relevant is whether a remark like 'filthy queer' can be considered insulting to homosexuals in general. The penalty the courts may impose for violation is imprisonment for up to one year or a fine not exceeding 10,000 guilders (about £4000). However, the court seldom imposes the maximum penalty. It usually imposes far less.

The other important provision is section 429 quarter, which prohibits discrimination in the exercise of one's office, profession or business. Neither public officials nor private employers and institutions may discriminate. For example, an employer may not reject an applicant because of his or her homosexual preference and a housing association is also not allowed to refuse homosexual tenants. A bank may not refuse a permanent position to an employee for making known the fact that he is homosexual, for example by wearing a pink triangle, the symbol of the gay movement. This section is aimed at the exercise of a profession, so a private landlord who wants to rent a room may refuse to rent it to a lesbian or a gay man. This is an example of an instance where the government remains in the background where private matters are concerned. This offence is categorized as a misdemeanour. In this instance intention or guilt need not be proved. For the perpetrator to be liable to punishment it is not required that his purpose was to discriminate. Indirect discrimination also falls within the scope of this section, as the Supreme Court has ruled in cases of racial discrimination.

The section covers both direct and indirect discrimination. If someone is not allowed to rent a certain house or apartment because he is gay, then he is a victim of direct discrimination. Indirect discrimination occurs when a certain requirement is made that seems neutral, but leads indirectly to discrimination and when such a requirement cannot be justified (is not justifiable). For example, a job advertisement for bulb peelers that specifies fluency in Dutch as a requirement may seem like a neutral requirement, but leads to indirect discrimination of ethnic minorities, which cannot be justified: fluency in Dutch is not necessary for an adequate fulfilment of the job. An example of indirect discrimination against gays would be an insurance company that refused to insure people who are HIV-positive. This policy affects homosexual men in particular, but may be justifiable objectively because of the increased insurance risk. Or suppose that a housing association in a certain neighbourhood will only rent houses to families with children because this provides a friendly atmosphere. The result is that homosexuals are indirect victims of this policy, without there being a clear objective justification for this.

Discrimination on the grounds of section 429 quarter carries a lighter penalty than breach of the above-mentioned criminal provisions. The sentence is at most two months' detention or a fine of up to 10,000 guilders. As far as I have been able to ascertain, since its introduction no one has yet been criminally convicted of discrimination on the ground of homosexuality. Several reports filed by the public prosecutor have been dismissed for various reasons. The following are examples of cases brought under this provision.

The first relates to two young men sunbathing in the dunes at Zandvoort, an area that is known as a meeting place for homosexuals. One was naked, the other wore bathing trunks. They were startled by a policeman on horseback who galloped towards them and fired a battery of curses at them, including 'get out of here, you dirty sods'. Then, with his horse, he forced them into thorny bushes. The two young men filed a report against the policeman. This complaint did not lead to prosecution. The police officer was reprimanded by his superior and received a mark on his conduct record. This will, for the time being, probably cost him promotion and perhaps be more effective than a small fine.

A second case refers to a police report made against an elected public official in Zwolle, who had uttered discriminatory remarks against homosexuals outside the council meeting. The public prosecutor found that proof of discrimination could be furnished. However, he decided to settle the matter with an oral warning, because the municipal council had condemned the remark in public.

To date, the criminal court has not yet had to give an interpretation of the concept of gay discrimination. When this does happen, it is likely that the court will be guided by the anti-discrimination provisions that are found in the General Equal Treatment Act. This will ensure that what is allowed under the civil law will not be unlawful via criminal law. This was the reasoning of the former Minister of Justice.

There is some evidence that the provisions of the criminal law that forbid discrimination against gays appear to defeat their purpose. Either they are not enforced or discrimination against gays does not occur (any more) in the tolerant country of the Netherlands – though the latter is certainly not true. One aspect of criminally relevant discrimination that does not fit neatly into anti-discrimination law is that which is accompanied by violence.

Anti-gay violence

'Queer bashing' in the Netherlands usually occurs in parks or at parking places along the motorways. Men who use these places to make homosexual contacts are beaten up and sometimes robbed. These acts of violence are often performed by groups of adolescents. The groups are often formed *ad hoc* in cafes or other public meeting places, where the collective idea takes root to 'go out and scare some queers, to hunt them down, scare the shit out of them', beat them up and take their money. The violence is directed towards gays, not only because they are an easy prey at badly lit parking spots or in parks, but also because such groups 'hate' gays 'like hell', an aversion that is reinforced in the macho cultures of the group. Such groups are prepared and able to be violent on a scale that individuals acting alone would never dare. Their aversion to gays is pronounced, and they assume that other people share it and they are suprised to be locked up by the police for it. The police should really be agreeing with them (Boogaard and van Stolk, 1992).

This is a matter of trying to change the mentality of these young people, but also of their parents: 'We once threw a queer naked into the canal', the father of a young 'queer-basher' said. 'If we manage to convey an image of queer-bashing as a cowardly act, not a prank, by a group of boys attacking one man and if that image were to take hold, there would be very little honour in it any more' (Boogaard and van Stolk, 1992).

'Queer-bashers' are prosecuted for grievous bodily harm or public violence. There is no special provision in the Criminal Code against 'queer-bashing'. The anti-gay nature of the act is not important when it comes to evidence of the offence. In order to achieve a change in mentality among the (potential) perpetrators, we might do well to emphasize the anti-gay nature of such violence in court. But this has its disadvantages. Both trial dossier and court procedure would then confront the victim with his homosexual contacts. Many are not prepared to 'come out' in this way, especially if they are married men who restrict their gay activities to evenings out in the park. Every now and then, a 'queer-basher' is arrested who wants to come clean and who, for pragmatic reasons, admits to having robbed and threatened scores of men. The victims have not reported the violence to the police. In order to amass enough evidence, the police advertise in the local press for victims to come forward: 'discretion guaranteed'. The result is often less than encouraging.

Whether or not a victim will dare go to the police, depends very much on the climate in the police department: whether it gives an impression of 'it's their own fault' or whether victims are taken seriously. During the past ten years, police culture has changed considerably, and for the better. In some towns, the police recruit new personnel through the gay press. In Rotterdam, two officers – one gay, one straight – have been assigned to keep an eye on gay meeting places. Their task is to prevent violence from occurring and to persuade victims to make a report to the police. Some colleagues, however, have ambivalent views about this project and the straight member of the team has now stopped his work. The heads of the prosecution service (the procurators-general) have developed a policy in which discrimination, not only against gays, is taken ever more seriously. They have produced a directive requiring the public prosecutors and the police to take an active stand against discrimination (Richtlijn Discriminatiezaken, 1 September 1993). As a result, all reported crimes and complaints must be duly recorded and the police are to look out for discriminatory features of cases, even if those concerned have not recognized them as such. Prosecution is the rule, because of its exemplary effect. In court, the prosecutor is to stress the discriminatory background of a case and to ask for more severe penalties because of it. Judges have absolute discretion in sentencing, but there have been examples in which the sentence passed was more severe than usual because of the anti-gay nature of the offence. As yet, no criminal sentences have been passed in cases involving discrimination against gays, but the penalties for such offences as causing grievous bodily harm and public violence do take the nature of the case into account.

Civil law: the General Equal Treatment Act

Civil legislation has also been enacted in order to take note of and combat discrimination. On 1 September 1994 the General Equal Treatment Act came into force. The Equal Treatment Commission, an independent, professional organization, reviews the complaints it receives to see if the regulations on equal treatment have been violated. It deals with unequal treatment involving religion, personal convictions and views, political orientation, race, gender, nationality, marital status and sexual preference (homo- or heterosexual preference; paedophilia is excluded). It is forbidden to treat people differently on these eight grounds of discrimination in working relationships between employers and employees. Unequal treatment is forbidden in any area that is related to work, from job advertisements to actual employment. These regulations also apply to people in the professions, such as lawyers, civil law notaries and doctors. It is also forbidden to discriminate in offering goods and services such as taking out insurance policies, renting houses, or opening bank accounts.

Not all forms of discrimination fall within the scope of this Act. In this respect this new legislation is a typical example of the Dutch policy of accommodation and political compromise. A debate went on for almost ten years before the Christian Democrats were willing to let the Act pass, with some important exceptions. One area exempt from its provisions is the Church. On the grounds of religious freedom, priests and ministers may preach family values from the pulpit, may label homosexuals as sinners and may portray homosexuality as a sickness. Such statements may only be made during church services and not outside them.[1]

Under certain circumstances exceptions are also made for Christian schools. Debates on this issue in particular have been going on for years both in and out of parliament. Christian Democrats are holding fast to their demand that schools should be able to bar homosexual teachers and students from their school on religious grounds. The compromise reached is that such schools may bar gay teachers if this is necessary for fulfilment of their functions. This means that a distinction may be made between gay teachers who teach physics and those who teach religion or social studies. The latter may be barred if they express their feelings at school, such as by kissing their partner in public or wearing a pink triangle, thereby identifying themselves with a group that does not recognize marriage as the cornerstone of society. However, a teacher may never be rejected solely because he or she *is* homosexual, if he or she has not expressed this in any way.

Neither does the private domain of the family fall within the scope of the General Equal Treatment Act. This is not so much as a result of compromise, but due more to the reserved role that government plays in private life. Parents are free to deny the homosexual preference of their child or, even worse, to throw their child out of the house for being gay or lesbian. Nor does the Act concern itself with the internal functioning of private associations. Closed clubs may be exclusively aimed at gays or lesbians. If they are heterosexual clubs they may refuse to allow two men or two women to dance with each other. The situation is different when associations open themselves to the public, such as the student association that operates a discotheque in order to better its financial position, to which non-members are also admitted. They may not maintain their exclusively heterosexual orientation there.

The Equal Treatment Commission

The Commission deals with complaints about 'direct' as well as 'indirect' discrimination under the Act. Anyone who feels that he or she is being treated unequally may request a decision from the Commission in his or her case. As an individual, you may submit a request only if you yourself have suffered some disadvantage. If you prefer not to file a complaint yourself, you may ask someone else to do so as your representative, for example a family member, a friend, and also a pressure group such as COC. Pressure groups may also file complaints to the Commission independently. However, they can only file complaints if they are organizations or societies that were officially founded to promote the interests of the people to whom the regulations on equal treatment apply.

The Commission will question the complaining party and the person or organization that is allegedly discriminating. Third parties have a duty to participate at the request of the Commission. Failure to participate gives rise to a criminal offence. It could be said that the Commission is like a judicial organization. However, one important difference is that the Commission itself searches for the information that it feels it needs. The Commission's decision is not legally binding. It cannot force the party who is found guilty of discrimination to co-operate with its decision. However, often after the decision has been made, the Commission may talk to representatives of the organization in which the case occurred, hoping that good communication will help to prevent unequal treatment in the future.

The Commission seeks to influence the mentality of society by making statements in individual cases, but also by exposing structural inequality. For this purpose it can conduct research on its own initiative and does not just have to wait until a complaint has been submitted. A topic being focused upon at present is the artificial insemination and *in vitro* fertilization of lesbian women: to what extent should a distinction be made between married women and women who have a different form of cohabitation in respect of access to these methods?

In gay and lesbian circles, the Commission is viewed with a certain amount of scepticism because up to now it has made too few significant statements, owing to the many exceptions that the law allows. The Commission makes many more positive statements – but also receives many more complaints – with regard to the distinction according to sex and civil status. This often involves unequal employment opportunities and unequal remuneration and chances of promotion in the workplace. Here, too, the evidence of unequal treatment is easier to produce than in homosexual cases where, for instance, the employer can fairly easily hide behind arguments which have nothing to do with sexual orientation.

Up to now (spring 1997) the Commission has received fourteen complaints about sexual preference discrimination. Complaints usually concern the exclusion of the homosexual partner from the survivor's pension. Unfortunately, the Commission was unable to pronounce that the rules on pensions amount to discriminatory treatment of partners in homosexual relations – although this is the case – and that the rules should be adapted. The rules on pensions are not (yet) covered by the Equal Treatment Act.[2]

The Commission pronounced in favour of an employee of the Dutch Rail Company (Nederlandse Spoorwegen). His partner was not offered the free rail services abroad that are available to married couples. The Commission found that this amounts to discrimination on the basis of marital status. Unmarried partners in heterosexual relationships are also excluded from the facilities concerned (Oordeel Commissie Gelijke Behandeling, Judgment of the Equal Treatment Commission 96–52).

Another positive decision was given on a request from the dance world: are they allowed to deny couples of the same sex access to dance competitions? Dancing schools defend the distinction with an appeal to the sexually determined roles of the partners: a typically female and male role. The Commission sought extensive information from representatives of the dance world and came to the conclusion that at dance competitions, the jury should only take account of technical dance criteria. The Commission does not consider direct discrimination on the basis of sex to be permitted and concludes furthermore that especially homosexual men and lesbian women are affected by this distinction because they would want to dance with partners of the same sex. This also results in an indirect distinction being made on the basis of sexual preference. It is striking that during the handling of this case the dance world emphasized that homosexuals were not excluded at all. On the contrary, the dance couples of opposite sexes included many homosexual men. In the comments that later appeared in the press it was stated frankly that a homosexual appearance of two men or two women was an obstacle to admittance to dance competitions, which makes it clear (once again) that legal and social reality do not have to coincide.

The crop of complaints about gay discrimination two years after introduction of the Act is smaller than expected. Various factors might explain this: few people know about the Commission; people hesitate to complain because the Commission cannot give binding decisions; gay discrimination might not be so serious after all.

Marriage, also for gays?

If laws are being enacted that aim at stamping out unequal treatment in everyday life, at the same time some laws still exist that are in themselves discriminatory. The most obvious example is the law on marriage, which allows only persons of the opposite sex to marry and therefore restricts the legal effects of marriage, such as the right to inherit and the opportunity to adopt children, to married heterosexuals.

Meanwhile, a large majority of the population is of the opinion that gay partners should have the same rights of inheritance as married couples (95 per cent). The population is, however, less keen to allow homosexuals the opportunity to adopt children; just less than half are in favour (47 per cent) (Sociaal en Cultureel Rapport, 1992). This has resulted in the law on Partner Registration (1 January 1998). This is another example of Dutch negotiation. This law makes it possible for couples of the same sex to be officially registered and to acquire the same rights and duties in a number of areas as married people. They may inherit from each other and have the right to a dependent's pension, but they also have a mutual duty to maintenance. The most important difference between registered partnership and marriage lies in the field of parenthood. A same sex couple cannot adopt a child. This reflects, as seen, the wishes of the small majority of the population if a married woman gives birth to a child, her husband is automatically the father, but if a lesbian woman does her female partner cannot, in law, be the other parent. In other words, by law on Partner Registration, partners of the same sex cannot both be parents.

The legislation on registration has not gone far enough for the liking of the Second Chamber of Parliament. It found that marriage as such, with all of its legal effects, should be open to homosexual couples (81 to 60 votes). A committee was appointed to look into the advantages and disadvantages of such a course. Those who oppose it regard the right of marriage for homosexuals as, among other things, a subversion of our culture. However, gay marriage signifies a departure from an ideology that regards the purpose of marriage as procreation.

Conclusion

Criminal and civil anti-discrimination laws make clear that discrimination against homosexuals is recognized and refuted by the Dutch government – although only up to a point. The fact that these laws are a compromise is probably the most important reason why the number of cases reported to the police and complaints filed have remained few in number. The chances that the result would be favourable are, given the exceptions for which the law provides, smallest in those situations where discrimination is most likely to occur. Moreover, discrimination, for example in job applications or in promotion, is difficult to prove. Employers are able, quite easily, to hide behind socially and legally acceptable excuses. At the same time, homosexual men and women engage in a form of self-selection by staying away from the sectors where discrimination is most likely to occur. In any event, the Netherlands, and especially its cities, provide relatively wide opportunities for living according to one's own sexual preference.

Notes

1. Not all church congregations are eager to use this freedom. There are tolerant Christian movements, within both the Catholic and Protestant churches, for whom a homosexual pastor is not a problem and who are willing to sanctify a homosexual relationship in a church service.
2. There are pension funds that provide pensions for the surviving partner from a homosexual relationship. The Pension Fund for Government Employees will, in future, pay a pension to partners in homosexual relationships.

References

Boogaard, H. van den and van Stolk, B. (1992) 'Potenrammers: vandalisme tegen mensen', in J. Fiselier and F. Strijbosch (eds), *Cultuur en Delict*. Den Haag: Vuga.

Moerings, M. (1997) 'The Netherlands', in D. J. West and R. Green (eds), *Sociolegal Control of Homosexuality: A Multi-nation Comparison*. New York: Plenum Press, pp. 299–312.

Schedler, P. E.(1992) *Buitenstaanders binnenshuis, vrouwen en homo's in organisaties*. Rijksuniversiteit Leiden, DSWO Press.

Sengers, W. J. (1971) *Gewoon hetzelfde: een visie op vragen rond de homofilie*. Bussum: Brand.

Sociaal en cultureel rapport (1992) Den Haag: Sociaal en Cultureel Planbureau Rijswijk.

Stolk, B. van (1991) *Eigenwaarde als groepsbelang, sociologische studies naar de dynamiek van zelfwaardering*. Bohn Stafleu van Loghum.

Warmerdam, H. (1991) 'Guerrillero's tegen normaliteit. De radicale homobeweging in Nederland 1975–1980', in I. C. Meijer, J. W. Duyvendak and M. P. N. van Kerkhof (eds), *Over normaal gesproken*. Amsterdam: Schorer.

10

Gay and Lesbian Sexualities in South Africa: From Outlawed to Constitutionally Protected

Ronald Louw

Introduction

From 1948 to 1993 the apartheid policy of the National Party government in South Africa sought to radically reorganize social relations among people in both the public and private domains, from geographically relocating citizens on the basis of imposed racial classifications to determining with whom they could have sexual intercourse.[1] Various state apparatuses were at the disposal of the government to impose its policy, ranging from torture and judicial killings to state-controlled media propaganda. However, the implementation of apartheid was resisted by many on whom the policy was imposed. Resistance varied from armed insurrection to non-violent protest. A thread that ran throughout the implementation of apartheid was the use of the law as a means of repression and social regulation. But the law's terrain was also a contested one, for it was also a site of resistance and struggle. This contested role of oppression and challenge of the law within complex and fluid social relations are examined in this chapter, particularly the liberatory and formative role the law has played and will continue to play in sexual politics in South Africa since 1994.

The received common law in South Africa, Roman-Dutch in origin, criminalized homosexual conduct, which today consists of the offences of sodomy and unnatural acts.[2] The apartheid government enshrined and extended the common law, principally via the Sexual Offences Act of 1957. In section 14 the heterosexual age of consent[3] was set at sixteen years while that of homosexuals (both gays and lesbians) was set at nineteen years (Isaacs and McKendrick, 1992; Louw, 1994). Most peculiar of all was the provision contained in Section 20A which made it a crime for two men at a party to commit an act which was 'calculated to stimulate sexual passion or give sexual gratification', where a party was defined as being an occasion where more than two persons were present. The provision was inserted after police raided a party of over 350 homosexual men and women in Johannesburg in 1966 and sought legislative assistance in curbing what was portrayed in the media as a dangerous social vice (Cameron, 1994). Finally, sodomy was classified as a Schedule 1 offence in terms of the Criminal Procedure Act of 1977, which permitted the killing, in certain circumstances, of sodomites or suspected sodomites.[4] In private law, to name just some instances, there was no recognition of same-sex domestic partnerships (Cameron, 1994, p. 97), no extension of partnership benefits in employment, discrimination against gays in the military,[5] and informal reports of police harassment of gay men (Gevisser and Cameron, 1994). Allied to the law was a significant degree of social intolerance, which contributed to this oppression. Despite this, homosexual expressions were not entirely suppressed. Pockets of resistance took various forms, perhaps most publicly by the 'moffie[6] queens' who led the annual new year Coon Carnival by sections of the Cape 'coloured' population though the streets of Cape Town (Chetty, 1994, p. 115). Generally, however, expressions of same-sex desire in South Africa have remained private and hidden, but with significant variations along, particularly, racial lines. De Vos comments:

> This makes it difficult, probably impossible, to talk of homosexual identity in South Africa as a monolithic, describable, stable concept. Most probably different homosexual identities were and still are produced by a unique set of power relations and apparatus in the context of colonialism, capitalist development and racial domination. (De Vos, 1996, p. 274)

After years of political struggle, when finally the apartheid government collapsed, South Africa adopted a negotiated constitution[7] with a Constitutional Court having the power of legislative review, and explicitly prohibited discrimination on the ground of sexual orientation. Central to the constitution is subsection 8(2) of the equality clause in the chapter on Fundamental Rights:

> No person shall be unfairly discriminated against, directly or indirectly, and, without derogating from the generality of this provision, on one or more of the following grounds in particular: race, gender, sex, ethnic or social origin, colour, sexual orientation, age, disability, religion, conscience, belief, culture or language.

The constitution was the first in the world that explicitly prohibited discrimination against gays and lesbians. Furthermore, in the post-April 1994 period the country has, amongst others, a President who openly supports gay and lesbian equality[8] and a respected Supreme Court Judge, Edwin Cameron, who has a history of gay and lesbian activism and was also shortlisted for appointment to the bench of the Constitutional Court.

Processes of resistance and change

The question I want to explore in this chapter is: 'What complex of social forces brought about this change for gays and lesbians from being policed and outlawed to being guaranteed constitutional equality?' In suggesting an answer, it needs to be appreciated that to date (July 1997) the change is not as radical as it appears. First, prior to the adoption of the constitution, gay and lesbian organizations and lobbying groups had been gradually gathering strength and asserting their rights to equality in the context of a broader political struggle that was striving for inclusivity and the establishment of a human rights culture. Second, in terms of the law, the lives of gays and lesbians have not changed substantially, as all the crimes and various forms of discrimination enumerated above remain part of the law. These two points need to be elaborated upon.

For decades prior to 1994, gays and lesbians, principally in the white community, sporadically organized themselves into various groupings. These provided largely for social gatherings and were avowedly apolitical organizations. In reality they represented a conservative mindset whose members were more concerned with their own immediate social needs than in locating the gay and lesbian struggle within the broader political struggle for liberation. An early exception to this was the Law Reform Movement, which developed a public profile. In 1968 the government proposed draconian anti-gay legislation, which prompted a number of gay professionals to organize themselves into raising money to retain attorneys to make submissions to the government's Select Committee on the legislation (Gevisser, 1994, p. 32). But having achieved their objective, the group disbanded (money that it raised which remained unused was kept in trust and eventually made available to the National Coalition for Gay and Lesbian Equality). It was only by the mid-1980s that the first overtly political gay and lesbian organizations began to emerge. In Cape Town a number of activists formed Lesbians and Gays Against Oppression (LAGO) before changing to the Organization for Lesbian and Gay Activists (OLGA), with the specific aim of being a lesbian and gay organization opposed to apartheid (Fine and Nicol, 1994, p. 270). Significantly, they were accepted as an affiliate member organization of the United Democratic Front (UDF), a broad anti-apartheid alliance that was widely perceived as the unofficial internal wing of the then banned African National Congress (ANC) and the South African Communist Party. In the face of increasing government oppression, the UDF established the broadest possible anti-apartheid front including widely divergent organizations. It was this politically inclusive policy that provided the opportunity for the admission of OLGA to the UDF and so placed gay and lesbian rights on the public agenda and integral to the human rights struggle. After its unbanning, OLGA lobbied the ANC, which resulted in the inclusion of sexual orientation as a ground of non-discrimination in the ANC's draft Bill of Rights. OLGA also initiated the drafting of a Lesbian, Gay and Bisexual Rights Charter, which was nationally endorsed on 11 December 1993 (Fine and Nicol, 1994, p. 274). Although OLGA had a high profile, it was restricted to a small number of people who were almost exclusively white (Toms, 1995).[9]

However, in the former southern Transvaal province[10] and economic heartland of South Africa, the first mass-based African gay and lesbian organization was established: the Gay and Lesbian Organization of the Witwatersrand (GLOW). While initially based in Johannesburg's black dormitory town of Soweto, GLOW spread to other larger urban areas in the province. Although its policy was one of non-racialism, because it organized in the African townships, its membership was principally African. (It is only with the establishment of the National Coalition for

Gay and Lesbian Equality that significant interaction between racially based organizations has occurred.) The public profile of its leader, Simon Nkoli, contributed significantly to its growth and influence. Nkoli had been one of the accused in the notorious Delmas Treason Trial, one of the attempts of the collapsing apartheid regime to crush political dissent. The trial lasted four years, but after conviction all the accused were acquitted by the Appellate Division (*S* v. *Malindi*, 1990 and Davis, 1990). During the trial Nkoli openly declared his homosexuality to his fellow accused (two of whom are now provincial premiers). While this initially caused much dissent among the accused, he was eventually supported by his co-accused and the ANC in his stand (Nkoli, 1995, p. 249). GLOW remains the single largest organization mobilizing African gays and lesbians.

The early 1990s also saw a change in attitudes within the law. In the courts there was a growing realization that gay men, particularly in respect of sodomy, should no longer be criminalized for their sexual conduct. In the 1990 case of *S* v. *M* an appeal court held that:

> The majority of people, who have normal heterosexual relationships, may find acts of sodomy unacceptable and reprehensible. We cannot close our eyes, however, to the fact that society accepts that there are individuals who have homosexual tendencies and who form intimate relationships with those of their own sex. It has to be taken into account that homosexuality is more openly discussed and written about. It is common knowledge that so-called gay clubs are formed, where homosexuals openly meet and have social intercourse. If that is accepted by society, even with reluctance or distaste, it is also a factor that has to be taken into account by the courts when sentence is considered. Whether homosexual conduct between consenting males in private ought still to be punishable has been the subject of considerable debate, especially since 1967, when homosexual acts in private between consenting males above the age of 21 were legalised in England.

Subsequently in the 1995 case of *S* v. *H*, the Cape Supreme Court explicitly criticized the criminalization of sodomy[11] and, after quoting extensively with approval from the dissenting judgments of Justices Blackmun and Stevens in the United States Supreme Court case of *Bowers* v. *Hardwick*, held that:

> Whilst immutability of homosexual orientation would make the

> criminalization of adult, private, consensual homosexual acts even more undesirable, this does not detract from the broader and more fundamental consideration, already alluded to, that principles of equality, privacy, autonomy and the absence of public harm militate strongly against criminal proscription of such acts.

Furthermore, while legal academics had occasionally criticized the criminalization of homosexual conduct (Van Niekerk, 1970 and Labuschagne, 1986), it was only with the publication of Cameron's (1993) article 'Sexual Orientation and the Constitution: A Test Case for Human Rights' in the prestigious *South African Law Journal* that gay and lesbian debate publicly and forcefully emerged in legal discourse.[12]

Constitutional protection

Before proceeding to the second point raised above, namely the fact that legally little has changed for gays and lesbians and the consequent challenges that the gay and lesbian movement now faces, it is useful to consider the immediate history of the inclusion of the sexual orientation provision into the constitution. Once the National Party government had acknowledged the failure of apartheid and negotiations began for the drafting of a new constitution, the majority of South Africans were opposed to unfair discrimination. Cheryl Carolous, executive member of the ANC and Deputy Cabinet Minister, stated: 'For the same reasons that I oppose racism and sexism I oppose homophobia' (quoted in *Equality*, 1995, 4). While the full implications of the commitment to non-discrimination in respect of gays and lesbians had probably not been realized, the foundation had been laid for the gay and lesbian lobby to ensure their protection in the constitution. Significantly all the major parties to the negotiations prohibited discrimination against gays and lesbians in their constitutional proposals. The proposals of the ANC, the Inkatha Freedom Party and the Democratic Party specifically referred to sexual orientation, while that of the National Party referred only to natural characteristics. However, during the months of negotiations, the equality clause went through six revisions in which the sexual orientation provision was at times dropped when the clause was drafted generally rather than specifically (Botha and Cameron, 1995, p. 282).

The protection afforded by the equality clause in the interim constitution was, however, not the end of the constitutional struggle for the gay and lesbian lobby. The final constitution was drafted over a period of two years by the Constitutional Assembly (consisting of the 400 elected members of the House of Assembly and the 90 nominated members of the Senate) and approved by Parliament on 8 May 1996. In order to produce the draft, the Constitutional Assembly established a number of Theme Committees and sub-committees, each dealing with specific aspects of the constitution. Theme Committee Four that oversaw the drafting of the Bill of Rights and its sub-committee that dealt with the equality clause proposed retention of the sexual orientation provision in the final constitution and furthermore extended its application to private persons as well as the state. In drafting its proposal, all the major parties advocated retention. However, the African Christian Democratic Party (ACDP), represented by only two members in the House of Assembly, was vociferous in its objection to the provision. Along with a loosely aligned religious right, which is, presently, at best an informal alliance of conservatives representing both Christian and Muslim religions and incorporating various language and racial groups, it was able to mobilize public resistance to the retention of the provision. Its condemnation of homosexuality was coupled with the emotive and popular condemnation of abortion and the recent abolition by the Constitutional Court of the death penalty in *S* v. *Makwanyana* (1995). On the other hand, the former leader of the influential Church of the Province of Southern Africa and Nobel peace laureate, Archbishop Desmond Tutu, came out in support of the retention of the provision. In a written submission to Theme Committee Four, Archbishop Tutu wrote:

> Within the Church of Christ, and indeed amongst adherents of other faiths, there is much debate and differences of opinion on the question of homosexuality. The theological issues are complex and far from resolved. It is indisputable, however, that people's sexual nature is fundamental to their humanity.
>
> The apartheid regime enacted laws upon the religious convictions of a minority of the country's population, laws which denied gay and lesbian people their basic human rights and reduced them to social outcasts and criminals in the land of their birth. These laws are still on the Statute books awaiting your decision whether or not to include gay and lesbian people in the 'Rainbow People' of

> South Africa. It would be a sad day for South Africa if any individual or group of law-abiding citizens in South Africa were to find that the final constitution did not guarantee their fundamental human right to a sexual life, whether heterosexual or homosexual.
>
> I would urge you strongly to include the sexual orientation clause in the final constitution.[13]

In terms of the interim constitution, the final constitution has to be ratified by the Constitutional Court as being in accordance with the constitutional principles enumerated in a schedule to the interim constitution. The Constitutional Court has refused ratification principally on the issues of provincial government powers, local government and industrial bargaining provisions. Although the constitution has been referred back to the Constitutional Assembly for redrafting, it is anticipated that the proposed equality clause will remain intact.

National mobilization

Constitutional protection guaranteeing equality to gays and lesbians cannot be expected by itself to produce any desired changes. This is not to deny the importance of the constitutional protection. Although no existing laws discriminating against gays and lesbians have changed, discrimination on the basis of sexual orientation has been prohibited in three recent statutes: the Electoral Act of 1993, the Promotion of National Unity and Reconciliation Act and the Labour Relations Acts of 1995. Furthermore, it has had a perceptible influence on the lives of gays and lesbians in making them more publicly confident in their lives and their sexual orientation.[14] The non-discrimination provision is only a first but necessary step towards freedom from discrimination. The challenge that now faces a gay and lesbian movement is to give the constitutional guarantee a content that makes it meaningful. How gays and lesbians approach the constitutional protection will impact significantly on sexual politics in South Africa and a future gay and lesbian identity. The potential exists to place gay and lesbian politics within a broader political discourse of equality and inform not only how gays and lesbians see themselves but how they are seen (De Vos, 1996).

The first step towards achieving this was the establishment of the

National Coalition for Gay and Lesbian Equality which, on 3 December 1994, brought together for the first time in South African history 43 gay and lesbian organizations representing almost all such organizations in the country. At the launch of the National Coalition three main objectives were set. First, a campaign would be launched at retaining the sexual orientation clause in the final constitution. Second, the National Coalition would seek the decriminalization of same-sex sexual acts and challenge other forms of discrimination against gays and lesbians. Finally the National Coalition would raise funds for the development and training of especially African and lesbian leaders within gay and lesbian organizations.

With regard to the first objective (retaining the sexual orientation provision), much has in effect been achieved as outlined above. The National Coalition, funded largely by international donors, employed a national lobbyist and a number of provincial coalitions were established[15] to develop popular support for the retention of the sexual orientation provision. The National Coalition's campaign of lobbying and petitioning various sectors of South African society brought about for the first time in South Africa an emerging gay and lesbian 'movement' when people of different colours and political persuasions embarked jointly on the campaign. Possible tensions beneath the surface of unity, which may emerge in certain circumstances, should not be ignored. Such tensions may be racial, political or between gay men and lesbians. At the first national lesbian conference held in 1995 the latter tension emerged, but not sufficiently to disrupt the unity established by the formation of the National Coalition.

With regard to the second objective, a specific programme of action was outlined that recognized the need to establish an ordering of strategic priorities, with less contentious actions being approached initially.[16] In order to systematically direct the campaign, it was also agreed that all litigation should be co-ordinated through the National Coalition. In adopting this strategy, the National Coalition expressly drew on the successes of earlier similarly structured campaigns such as the decade-long successful End Conscription Campaign and the more protracted workers' rights movement.

Arguably the third objective, specifically the training of an African leadership, with the implied need to organize within the African community, presents the most complex challenge to the National Coalition. As indicated above, De Vos argues that given South Africa's history, it is not possible to talk of one sexual identity. Nor are these fixed, but instead are constantly being re-examined and reconstructed. This is also true among Africans. Dunton and Palmberg (1996, pp. 19–20) raise the point in the following comment:

> Can we realistically talk about an African homosexual community? Do the individuals whose lives are discussed in the previous section form a community of African gays and lesbians? Do they think of themselves as members of a homosexual community? Perhaps we should talk, less categorically, about men who love men and women who love women, a phrase that we deliberately introduced above. By this expression we want to include men and women who have a sexual preference for members of the same sex, and men and women who occasionally and voluntarily engage in same-sex sexual acts, but who nevertheless do not consider themselves members of a homosexual community. . . . The question to face is whether the idea of a gay and lesbian community is a Eurocentric phenomenon.

An important issue now in South Africa is how these identities are to be shaped by gays and lesbians and by 'men who love men and women who love women'. It seems probable (and perhaps unquestioned?) that a Western construction of gay and lesbian identity is being pursued.

The legal process must impact on this project. In the pre-constitutional sodomy case of *S* v. *H* (1995), American jurisprudence in respect of gay and lesbian politics was significantly relied upon by the court. By adopting its particular programme of action, the National Coalition is asserting that same-sex politics is to be advanced and shaped within a public framework of an essentially Western, rights-based constitutional discourse. However, this is not exclusive to gay and lesbian politics. Current debate in South Africa on issues as diverse as abortion and land reform are all taking place within such a discourse. To disengage gay and lesbian politics from this historical process is unlikely, whether desirable or not. The majority of South Africans have endorsed, albeit symbolically by voting in the first democratic elections in the country's history, a Western constitutional dispensation, as South Africa's constitution relies heavily on German and Canadian jurisprudence.

With this backdrop, a number of factors that may inform the National

Coalition's objective of training an African leadership need to be delineated. First, open acknowledgement of homosexuality amongst many Africans remains taboo. Instead, where it occurs, it is often kept hidden. Nkoli comments: 'African communities have always evaded the issue of homosexuality and have never talked about it but that does not mean that it has never existed' (Nkoli, 1995). Many African gay men relate the fact that their families are aware of their homosexuality, and may even tacitly support it, or at least be sympathetic, but will not acknowledge it publicly. It may still be expected that a homosexual child will marry and have children (Louw, 1995b). In fact many do so and then continue to live homosexual lives hidden from those immediately around them. Dunton and Palmberg (1996, p. 20) argue that a culture of silence exists in African societies with regard to homosexuality and questions of sexuality are not debated openly.

Second, despite the existence of organizations such as GLOW and ABIGALE (the Western Cape-based Association of Bisexuals, Gays and Lesbians), which have worked specifically within the black communities, black gays and lesbians, particularly Africans, are still largely unorganized. Prior to 1994, Africans had been subjected to brutal racist oppression such that 'to many blacks, a concern by blacks in gay affairs seems frivolous, irrelevant and divisive' (Dowie quoted in Gevisser, 1994, p. 56). Now that the struggle against legalized apartheid has been won, and that constitutional litigation may bring about a different form of struggle, new organizational possibilities exist that might need to be explored.

Finally, it is widely considered that homosexuality is un-African, that it did not exist prior to European colonization, and that it was an import from the West (Dunton and Palmberg, 1996). These views have been expressed by some prominent leaders. In 1987, two senior officials in the ANC's London office, Ruth Mompati and Solly Smith, attacked the gay liberation movement (*Equality*, 1995 and Fine and Nicol, 1994, p. 270).[17] Bennie Alexander, Secretary-General of the Pan Africanist Congress, has also repeatedly condemned homosexuality as being un-African. In Winnie Mandela's trial, on a charge of kidnapping, Holmes (1994, p. 292) argues that her defence 'codified homosexuality as sexual abuse, and characterised homosexual practice as a white, colonising depredation of heterosexual black culture'. More recently, in August 1995, President Robert Mugabe of Zimbabwe spoke out virulently against gay and lesbian equality in Zimbabwe, forcing the closure of the book stall of the Gays and Lesbian of Zimbabwe (GALZ) at the annual Zimbabwe International Book Fair, and compared gays and lesbians to dogs and pigs.[10] When he thereafter visited South Africa in September, he was met by a 400-strong contingent of protesting gays and lesbians at the airport. Nkoli (1995), who was among the protesters, stated: 'I had to show him that all the comments he made about homosexuality being a "Western disease" were not true.' At the 1996 Book Fair Mugabe again expressed similar views. While being denied by African gays and lesbians, the 'un-African' argument is also challenged by studies of homosexuality in South African prisons (Haysom, 1981) and in the gold and diamond mine labour compounds (Moodie, 1988). While some have held that these studies are indicative only of 'forced' situational homosexuality, Achmat (1993, p. 105) has argued that the disruption of African social relations by colonialism, capitalism and urbanization 'created new forms of disciplined and useful bodies – new pleasures and desires'. It is such ruptures that question the stability of culture and create new opportunities for political intervention.

Conclusion

The inclusion of sexual orientation as a protected ground in the constitution and the inevitable litigation (whether initiated by the National Coalition or otherwise) and parliamentary reform, will impact on gay and lesbian identity formation in South Africa. Sexuality will more than ever before become a public issue. Whether this shift into the more public domain will result in substantive equality and greater acceptance and freedom for gays and lesbians remains to be seen. Initial indications are that such a shift is taking place (De Vos, 1996, p. 290). Nevertheless, the next few years will be decisive ones in directing the gay and lesbian movement and in forming gay and lesbian politics and identity in South Africa.

Notes

1. See generally the Group Areas and the Population Registration Acts of 1950 and the Sexual Offences Act of 1957. Section 16 of the latter prohibited sexual intercourse between people of different racial classifications. (See also note 4.)

2. Sodomy is defined as unlawful and intentional sexual intercourse *per anum* between human males: Burchell and Milton, 1991, p. 571. Snyman (1995, p. 340) argues that the offences of sodomy and bestiality are two separate crimes distinct from unnatural sexual offences and that an accused may still in addition be convicted for committing a vaguely defined unnatural sexual offence. See also *S* v. *V* (1967) and *S* v. *M* (1979). See De Vos (1996, p. 274–81) for earlier criminal acts and a history of criminalization.
3. Strictly speaking, the term 'age of consent' only applies to heterosexual sex, but it has been colloquially applied in respect of homosexual sex as well.
4. Section 49(2) of the Criminal Procedure Act 51 of 1977 justifies the killing of a person who flees arrest and who cannot otherwise be apprehended. The offences for which the section is applicable are considered among the most serious in South African law and are listed in a schedule to the Act. They include treason, sedition, public violence, murder, culpable homicide, rape, indecent assault, bestiality, robbery, kidnapping, childstealing, assault when a dangerous wound is inflicted, arson, malicious injury to property, housebreaking, theft, and fraud.
5. Gay men in the South African Defence Force have been treated variously from benign tolerance to being subjected to drug therapy and psychiatric treatment. The official SADF position as stated in 1993 was that gays should not be discriminated against but should be offered rehabilitation facilities! The African National Congress's position has been more tolerant and there is recognition of the role gay soldiers played in the liberation struggle while fighting for Umkhonto weSizwe, the armed wing of the ANC (Louw, 1995a).
6. The term 'moffie' is used variously in South Africa to refer to male homosexuals, effeminate men and transvestites. Its earliest recorded use is probably 1929. Initially the term was particularly derogatory, but it has more recently been appropriated by the gay community, thereby stripping it of its derogatory connotation (De Waal, 1994).
7. The Constitution of the Republic of South Africa Act 200 of 1993, referred to as the interim constitution, has a limit of five years during which time the Constitutional Assembly has to draft a final constitution. The rights contained in Chapter 3 are subject to the general limitation provision of section 33, which stipulates that the limitation should be reasonable and justifiable in an open and democratic society and not negate the essential content of the right.
8. At his first public address after his release from 27 years imprisonment, Nelson Mandela outlined his vision of a new society in which he included non-discrimination on the grounds of sexual orientation. More recently President Mandela gave support to British gay activist Sir Ian McKellan while on a fund-raising tour for the National Coalition for Gay and Lesbian Equality and representatives of the National Coalition.
9. Toms went on to achieve international fame when he was sentenced to three years' imprisonment for refusing to serve in South Africa's apartheid Defence Force. See *S* v. *Toms* (1989) and *S* v. *Toms; S* v. *Bruce* (1990).
10. The region is now named the province of Gauteng (place of gold). It is geographically the smallest but wealthiest and most urbanized of the nine provinces incorporating the city of Johannesburg and many of the country's gold mines.
11. The accused had been convicted of sodomy in a lower court and had been sentenced to twelve months' imprisonment wholly suspended. The matter had been heard prior to the introduction of the interim constitution and thus the review court had

no power to strike down the offence. It was accordingly only concerned with the appropriateness of the sentence. As the accused had pleaded guilty, there was little evidence led at the trial. However, for purposes of sentence the review court accepted that this was a case of a private (near a public road but not at a place where the public could reasonably have observed the conduct) homosexual act between two consenting adult men. The sentence was altered to a caution and discharge, the lightest possible sentence in South African law. See also Louw (1994).

12. Subsequently the same journal published an article by Lind (1995) on sexual orientation and family law.
13. Similar support has been expressed by the Revd Mogoba, Bishop of the Methodist Church of Southern Africa who, in his submission to the constitutional Assembly expressly distanced his church from the ACDP (Letter dated 8 June 1995). All submissions made to the constitutional Assembly are available on the World Wide Web site http://www.constitution.org.za/.
14. One of the many examples is that of Dr Helen de Pinho who, in her submission to the Constitutional Assembly, wrote: 'As a lesbian, the interim constitution has provided me and my partner of many years standing, an opportunity to live our lives honestly and openly in the knowledge that our rights to equality and non discrimination in South Africa are guaranteed' (23 May 1995, http://www.constitution.org.za/).
15. Gauteng, Western Cape, Eastern Cape, Free State and KwaZulu-Natal (representing five out of the nine provinces but including almost all the major South African cities and a majority of the population).
16. The programme of action agreed upon was as follows:
    1. The abolition of the common law prohibition on sodomy;
    2. The abolition of Section 20A of the Sexual Offences of 1957;
    3. To challenge the ban on recruitment of gays and lesbians into the South African Defence Force;
    4. To challenge the discriminatory ages of consent;
    5. To challenge the requirement in the Human Tissue Act 65 of 1983 where a woman requires her husband's consent prior to artificial insemination;
    6. To challenge discrimination against gays and lesbians in adoption of children;
    7. To obtain partnership benefits such as medical aid and pension in employment;
    8. To obtain partnership benefits with regard to immigration and naturalization;
    9. To obtain access to state-owned media; and
    10. To obtain recognition for permanent institutionalized gay and lesbian unions.

    (Minutes of the First National Gay and Lesbian Legal and Human Rights Conference (3 December 1994) at 6/7).
17. At the International Conference on Children, Repression and the Law in Apartheid South Africa held in Harare from 24 to 27 September 1987 Mompati again indicated, in response to a question from gay and anti-apartheid activist and conscientious objector Ivan Toms, that gays and lesbians would not be protected in a post-apartheid South Africa. However, after intervention from South African Communist Party leader Joe Slovo, Mompati privately apologised to Toms (1995) explaining that her position was a result of ignorance rather than homophobia.

18. See for example 'Gays worse than dogs and pigs – Mugabe' in *The Citizen*, Johannesburg, 12 August 1995; 'Gays are perverts who have no rights, says Mugabe' in *The Citizen*, Johannesburg, 2 August 1995; 'Mugabe calls for global organisation against gays' in *Business Day*, Johannesburg, 17 August 1995. Numerous other newspaper articles, comments and cartoons appeared in the South African press critical of Mugabe's stance. See also Dunton and Palmberg, 1996.

References

Achmat, Z. (1993) ' "Apostles of civilised vice": "immoral practices" and "unnatural vice" in South African prisons and compounds, 1890–1920', *Social Dynamics*, **19**, 92.

Botha, K. and Cameron, E. (1995) 'Sexual orientation', *South African Human Rights Yearbook 1994*, **5**, p. 281.

Burchell, J. and Milton, J. (1991) *Principles of Criminal Law*. Cape Town: Juta.

Cameron, E. (1993) 'Sexual orientation and the Constitution: a test case for human rights', *South African Law Journal*, **110**, 450.

Cameron, E. (1994) ' "Unapprehended felons": gays and lesbians and the law in South Africa', in M. Gevisser and E. Cameron (eds), *Defiant Desire: Gay and Lesbian Lives in South Africa*. Johannesburg: Raven Press.

Chetty, D. R. (1994) 'A drag at Madame Costello's: Cape moffie life and the popular press in the 1950s and 1960s', in M. Gevisser and E. Cameron (eds), *Defiant Desire: Gay and Lesbian Lives in South Africa*. Johannesburg: Raven Press.

Davis, D. M. (1990) 'The Delmas trial and the danger of political trials for the legitimacy of the legal system', *South African Journal on Human Rights*, **6**, 79.

Dunton, C. and Palmberg, M. (1996) *Human Rights and Homosexuality in Southern Africa*. Uppsala: Nordiska Afrikainstitutet.

Fine, D. and Nicol, J. (1994) 'The lavender lobby: working for lesbian and gay rights within the liberation movement', in M. Gevisser and E. Cameron (eds), *Defiant Desire: Gay and Lesbian Lives in South Africa*. Johannesburg: Raven Press.

Gevisser, M. (1994) 'A different fight for freedom: a history of South African lesbian and gay organisations from the 1950s to 1990s', in M. Gevisser and E. Cameron (eds), *Defiant Desire: Gay and Lesbian Lives in South Africa*. Johannesburg: Raven Press.

Gevisser, M. and Cameron, E. (eds) (1994) *Defiant Desire: Gay and Lesbian Lives in South Africa*. Johannesburg: Raven Press.

Haysom, N. (1981) *Towards an Understanding of Prison Gangs*. Cape Town: Institute of Criminology, University of Cape Town.

Holmes, R. (1994) ' "White rapists made coloureds (and homosexuals)": the Winnie Mandela trial and the politics of race and sexuality', in M. Gevisser and E. Cameron (eds), *Defiant Desire: Gay and Lesbian Lives in South Africa*. Johannesburg: Raven Press.

Isaacs, G. and McKendrick, B. (1992) *Male Homosexuality in South Africa*. Cape Town: Oxford University Press.

Labuschagne, J. M. T. (1986) 'Dekriminalisie van homo- en soofilia', *Tydskrif vir Regwetenskap*, **11**, 167.

Lind, C. (1995) 'Sexual orientation, family law and the transitional Constitution', *South African Law Journal*, **112**, 481.

Louw, R. (1994) 'Homosexuality and the age of consent', *South African Journal on Criminal Justice*, **10**, 132.

Louw, R. (1995a) 'Conscription', *South African Human Rights Yearbook 1994*, 5, p. 33.

Louw, R. (1995b) 'The emergence of a black gay political identity in Durban', paper presented at the Gay and Lesbian Colloquium, Cape Town.

Moodie, T. D. (1988) 'Migrancy and male sexuality on the South African gold mines', *Journal of Southern African Studies*, **14** (2), 228.

Van Niekerk, B. (1970) 'The "third sex" Act', *South African Law Journal*, **87**, 129.

Nkoli, S. (1994) 'Wardrobes: coming out as a black gay activist in South Africa', in M. Gevisser and E. Cameron (eds), *Defiant Desire: Gay and Lesbian Lives in South Africa*. Johannesburg: Raven Press.

Nkoli, S. (1995) *The Saturday Paper* (Durban), 5 September 1995, p. 5.

Snyman, C. R. (1995) *Criminal Law* (3rd edn). Durban: Butterworths.

Toms, I. (1995) personal communication with the author.

De Vos, P. (1996)'On the legal construction of gay and lesbian identity and South Africa's transitional Constitution', *South African Journal on Human Rights*, **12**, 265.

De Waal, S. (1994) 'Etymological note: on "moffie" ', in M. Gevisser and E. Cameron (eds), *Defiant Desire: Gay and Lesbian Lives in South Africa*. Johannesburg: Raven Press.

Reported cases

United States of America

Bowers v. *Hardwick* 478 US 186 (1986).

South Africa

S v.C 1983 (4) SA 361 (T).
S v.C 1987 (2) SA 76 (W).
S v. *H* 1995 (1) SA 120 (C).
S v. *M* 1979 (2) SA 167.
S v. *M* 1990 (2) SACR 509 (E).
S v. *Makwanyana* 1995 (6) BCLR 665.
S v. *Malindi* 1990 (1) SA 962 (A).
S v.*Toms* 1989 (2) SA 567 (C).
S v.*Toms; S* v. *Bruce* 1990 (2) SA 802 (A).
S v.*V* 1967 (2) SA 17 (E).

11

Piecemeal to Equality: Scottish Gay Law Reform

Brian Dempsey

General legal writing often assumes that there is one 'British' legal system, and lesbian and gay writers often ignore entirely, or relegate to an appendix, the experiences of their Scottish 'brothers and sisters'.[1] A clear example of this marginalization is found in an article titled 'Lesbian and Gay Rights Campaigning' (1995), written by Anya Palmer, deputy director of the English group Stonewall, a well-resourced organization that claims to know something about lesbian and gay rights. In her article, Palmer tells us, for example, that gay male sex was decriminalised in Britain in 1967 (1995, p. 34). This is to confuse Britain with England and Wales. Then, writing of the failure of the 1994 campaign for an equal age of consent, Palmer takes comfort that the vote at least allowed activists to see which MPs took what position: 'For twenty-seven years MPs have not had to make a stand on lesbian and gay issues' (*ibid.*, p. 40). Yet on the evening of 22 July 1980 the proposed decriminalization of gay male sex in Scotland was debated in the House of Commons for 90 minutes. Thereafter 283 MPs voted on the matter, 203 in support of reform and 80 against (*Hansard*, House of Commons, 22/7/80, Vol. 989, col. 322). Similarly, experience of oppression and resistance in the North of Ireland, the Isle of Man and the Channel Islands are also made invisible.

Reasons for this marginalization are not difficult to discover. England has been the dominant economic and political force in the United Kingdom and English nationalism, conscious or otherwise, finds its place in all walks of life. Scotland has its own legal system, yet it does not have its own legislature. The focus of power, and therefore of law reform, has been and remains in London. This latter point, at least, may be about to change.

Palmer's erroneous statements, based one might hope upon ignorance, not only serve to deny Scottish lesbians and gay men our history, but also falsify British history as a whole. This chapter seeks to provide information on the situation in Scotland and to encourage writers and activists to acknowledge that they cannot simply reduce the United Kingdom to the English experience and treat it as the common experience of people in Britain. Further, to ignore our experiences will leave important lessons unlearned.

Background to reform

Unlike the position in England, sodomy, like many areas of Scots criminal law, remains a common law offence, consisting of and limited to anal penetration between two male persons (Gordon, 1978, p. 894). Prosecutions appear to have been rare, with Hume claiming, in the last few years of the eighteenth century, that there were only two cases in the records. In 1570 John Swan and John Litster were convicted 'of the wild, filthie, execrabill, detestabill, and unnatural sin of sodomy, otherwise named bougarie', and in 1630 Michael Erskine was convicted of 'diverse points of witchcraft and filthy sodomy' (Hume, 1797, Vol. 1, p. 469). The punishment in each case was strangulation at the stake followed by burning of the bodies. It was not until 1887 that the death penalty for sodomy was abolished in Scotland (by s.56 of the Criminal Procedure (Scotland) Act 1887), some 27 years later than in England.

However, the notorious 'Labouchere amendment', which introduced the crime of gross indecency (s.11, Criminal Law Amendment Act 1885, later re-enacted as s.7 of the Sexual Offences (Scotland) Act 1976) did extend to Scotland,[2] and was used, along with the Scottish common law offence of shameless indecency (McLaughlan, 1934) as the primary legal weapon for the punishment of male same-sex acts. The protean nature of the latter offence, which established that '[a]ll shamelessly indecent conduct is criminal', gave very great discretion to the court.[3]

The Wolfenden Report of 1957 (Wolfenden, 1957) recommended reform of the law in Scotland as well as in England and Wales. However, many of the concerns that prompted the setting-up of the Wolfenden Committee were particular to England. This is especially true of the public and press reaction to the Montagu trial in 1954, the concerns over homosexuals as spies and the instigation of high-profile homophobic campaigns by the Metropolitan Police (Weeks, 1977, p. 159, ch. 14). Further, as Wolfenden would note, the different criminal procedure in Scotland resulted in fewer (arguably more appropriate) prosecutions and greater consistency in sentencing than in England (Wolfenden, 1957, pp. 50–52). Prosecutions in England for 'homosexual offences' had more than trebled between 1945 and 1955 (from 782 to 2504 prosecutions) (*ibid.*, p. 131), whereas in Scotland the number of prosecutions was declining and reached a low of 71 in 1956 (*ibid.*, p. 141). These factors led to a situation where the 'problems' of homosexual activity and its policing were perceived as being predominantly 'English'.

Only one member of Wolfenden's Committee dissented and rejected any decriminalization of gay male sex (*ibid.*, p. 117). That the dissenter was also the only Scot on the committee, James Adair OBE, was an unfortunate portent of what was to come. A former Procurator Fiscal (a local public prosecutor), Adair's opposition was based on his perception of the 'best interests of the community' and the moral fabric of society. His outdated and fundamentally prejudiced approach was to be quoted with approval in parliamentary debates whenever proposals were brought forward to change the law in Scotland.

All of the Bills that sought to enact the reforms contained in the Wolfenden Report, from 1962 through to 1967, restricted themselves to England and Wales. The reasons for this were many. Scots law, unlike English, had not been consolidated in this area. The Church of Scotland, unlike the Church of England, flatly opposed the Wolfenden Report in the years 1957–68. There was also the absence of a Scottish organization like the (English) Homosexual Law Reform Society to lobby for change.

The accusation was repeatedly raised that the true reason for Scotland's exclusion was that Scottish Labour MPs would rally to defeat reform if it extended there. Reform would then have failed entirely. One of the loudest opponents of reform, Tory Sir Cyril Osborne, went further and suggested that the second reading of Humphrey Berkeley's Sexual Offences Bill 1965 was being held on a Friday afternoon in the knowledge that Scottish MPs would be travelling home to their constituencies. He bemoaned the absence of those 'good Scottish Socialist Calvinistic MPs' (*Hansard*, House of Commons, 11/2/66, Vol. 724, col. 833).[4] The image here is of a morally conservative, austere Protestant Scots MP of working-class origin in contrast perhaps to the moral laxity of London and 'worldly', less simplistic MPs in general. A similar point was made in 1967 when, during passage of Leo Abse's Bill on a Monday, Ray Mawby, an English Tory, accused the sponsors of knowing that if they included Scotland then 'all Scottish Members would descend in their wrath and vote solidly against the Bill' (*Hansard*, House of Commons, 3/7/67, Vol. 749, col. 1514).[5]

This exclusion allowed opponents of reform to fantasize, for the sake of mischief and confusion, about great difficulties in store for the police and for the public. Mawby raised, to some hilarity and barracking, the problem of the London to Edinburgh night sleeper – two men might be acting within the law up to the border, he said, but then be at danger of arrest as they enter Scotland. A heckler called out that a conductor shouting 'Stop at Carlisle' might have provided the solution (*Hansard*, House of Commons, 3/7/67, Vol. 749, col. 1449).

Extending reform to Scotland

> As has been said before, there are as many variations of homosexuality as there are colours in the rainbow. They range from the mentally ill through the compulsive lecher to the decadent pervert. (Scots Peer Lord Ferrier, *Hansard*, House of Lords, 10/5/77, Vol. 383, col. 170)

The first campaign group for homosexual rights in Scotland, the Scottish Minorities Group (SMG) was formed in early 1969 (Dempsey, 1995). Under two further names, Scottish Homosexual Rights Groups (SHRG) and Outright Scotland,[6] this organization has remained the sole national, lesbian, gay, and latterly bisexual, rights group in Scotland.

Although, as noted above, the situation regarding prosecutions was less prone to abuse than had been the case in England,[7] the struggle for extension of law reform, and the political and social changes that this would reflect, was to be a central item on SMG's political agenda. Fear of the law, whether implemented or not, often meant denial of services to lesbians and gay men, from newspapers refusing to run advertisements for gay flatshares to victims of extortion being unable to approach the police.

SMG's law reform campaign had two approaches, first to say that no matter what you might think about the merits of homosexual activity, it was unjust and contradictory to have a fundamentally different legal situation in Scotland from England and Wales. A significant number of MPs and Peers would be swayed by this approach and their votes would prove crucial to the success of the campaign. The second approach, naturally favoured by SMG, was to argue that homosexual men and women should receive equality of treatment before the law. This approach essentially sought the extension of the 1967 Act with a reduced age of gay male consent equal to that of heterosexual consent.

In 1971 SMG targeted bodies such as the Scottish Council for Civil Liberties (SCCL), seeking support for a campaign to introduce legislation, and began work on drafting a Sexual Offences (Scotland) Bill. This Bill would extend the terms of the 1967 Act to Scotland with one significant alteration, that is an age of consent at eighteen. The Bill followed the 1967 Act by specifically excluding the Armed Forces from its scope and used the offensive legal term 'defectives' when excluding people with learning disabilities from the right to give consent.

Reaction to the draft Bill was mixed. Lord Arran, who had played a key role in winning reform in England, wrote supportively to SMG and undertook to find a Scottish Peer to sponsor it. He indicated, however, that any reduction in the age of consent from 21 might ruin its chances. The unlamented Nicholas Fairbairn QC (later MP and Solicitor General)[8] argued that as no prosecutions were being pursued in Scotland that would not have been competent in England, then no attempt should be made to change the law.

Letters were sent by SMG to all Scottish Peers and MPs and several meetings were held at Westminster. Standard letters were drawn up for SMG members and others to send to their MPs calling on them to support a change in the law. SMG secured the active support of a few Members and two of these, Robin Cook and David Steel, were to become vice-presidents of the group. In addition to this active support, many MPs and Peers were to write to SMG over the years pledging their votes for law reform.

Then, in 1976, the Labour Government re-enacted the Labouchere amendment as section 7 of the Sexual Offences (Scotland) Act. The re-enactment of this reactionary 1885 law almost ten years after it had been partially repealed in England was seen by campaigners as a dangerous retrograde step. Despite the Bill being presented as a consolidation measure, its contents not to be amended during its passage through Parliament, a number of MPs, including Conservative Malcolm Rifkind, attempted to exclude this provision from the Bill (*Hansard*, House of Commons, 3/11/76, Vol. 918, col. 1570–84).[9]

From 1971, the Crown Office (responsible for the prosecution of crime in Scotland) had a policy of non-prosecution of offences when these fell within the terms of the English reforms, a policy publicly acknowledged in 1973. Even in debates during the passage of the 1976 Bill the Lord Advocate stated that re-enactment of the law posed no threat as it would not be implemented in practice. While everyone conceded that the Lord Advocate had the power to shape prosecution policy, such a blatant disregard for the will of Parliament was rightly highlighted as an absurdity (*Hansard*, House of Commons, Vol. 918, cols. 140–6). Though the fears of activists that re-enactment would bring renewed prosecutions of consenting acts in private were to prove unfounded, they did act as a spur to efforts for reform.

It should be noted that the failure of reform was not always based upon anti-gay prejudice. Robin Cook's 1978 private Member's Bill, based on the 1967 Act, highlighted a mundane difficulty faced in getting legislation through Parliament: that any Bill could become the victim of an inter-party squabble. In this case a Tory MP shouted 'object' at first reading not because he did object but because a Labour MP had objected to a previous Tory Bill. That Labour MP had only objected because a Tory had objected to his Bill![10]

Robin Cook's successful 'last minute' amendment to the Criminal Justice (Scotland) Bill in 1980 brought the law on homosexual activity in Scotland into line with the provisions of the 1967 Act in England (*Hansard*, House of Commons, 22/7/80, Vol. 989, cols. 283–322). In debate, accusations were made of bad faith on Cook's part. One Peer complained of the tactic of introducing such an amendment into a Bill at such a late stage, perhaps unaware that Labouchere had done just the same thing in introducing gross indecency into the law in 1885. A more reasonable complaint was that Cook's amendment was, in effect, an entire Bill in itself (*Hansard*, House of Lords, 21/10/80, Vol. 413, col. 1817).

An amendment was inserted in the House of Lords to make it plain that acts other than in private would remain an offence. It was suggested that

Cook had been seeking to introduce less restrictive provisions into Scots law by leaving out a restriction on the presence of more than two people (*Hansard*, House of Lords, 21/10/80, Vol. 413, col. 1812 *et seq.*). This amendment followed an unfortunate article in *Gay News* under the title 'MPs Pass "Orgy law"' (*Gay News*, 1980, No. 197, p. 1).

Countering the objection that, as there had been no prosecutions in ten years in Scotland that would not have been competent in England, the law did not have to be changed, Labour's Bruce Millan stated 'I am all in favour of the Crown Office and the Lord Advocate having a certain amount of discretion in prosecution policy. . . . But to say that, regardless of the circumstances, there is an offence still on the statute book that will not be prosecuted goes well beyond any legitimate discretion of any Lord Advocate' (*Hansard*, House of Commons, Vol. 989, col. 307).

Extending reform to Scotland had proved to be slow work for SMG. During the course of its ten-year campaign many thousands of letters had been written to MPs and Peers, and dozens of supportive parliamentarians had been approached by correspondence and at meetings. Support had been won from numerous trade union branches, trades councils, the Scottish Trade Union Council (STUC) and the civil liberties group, SCCL. Although SMG and its successor, SHRG, had produced several draft bills, including the 1975 Draft Sexual Offences Bill in conjunction with England's Campaign for Homosexual Equality (CHE) and the 1979 Draft Bill to Amend the Sexual Offences (Scotland) Act 1976, not one of these was taken up by a Peer or MP and won. They did, however, play an important role in focusing efforts for reform and setting out the demands of lesbians and gay men, especially as both the 1975 and 1979 Bills sought an age of consent at sixteen.

Two other aspects of SHRG's work should be mentioned here. First, in January 1979 three members of SHRG raised an action at the European Court against the British government alleging breaches of Articles 8 and 14 of the ECHR (Dempsey, 1995). The case was dropped when it became clear that Cook's reform would be successful.

Then, in August 1979, John Saunders was sacked from his job as handyman at a youth camp in Aberfoyle, north of Glasgow (Saunders, 1980). Though at the Employment Appeal Tribunal (EAT) it was successfully argued that gay men posed no greater 'risk' to children than heterosexual men 'nevertheless [the EAT] held that because others believe homosexuals are a "risk" to children, this view may be held by a "reasonable" employer' (Employment Protection Appeal, 1980). The campaign in support of employment rights for lesbians and gay men brought together SHRG, CHE, the Northern Ireland Gay Rights Association, the Scottish and the 'National' Council for Civil Liberties and won support from many trade union branches in both Scotland and England. Scores of MPs expressed their support for a change in the law to protect lesbian and gay workers and the case generated coverage in the Scottish and British press, which tended towards neutral reporting of the facts.

It is striking that the Saunders campaign managed to attracted such wide support outside of Scotland. Though this was in part founded upon the merits of the case, it is significant that the outcome of the case, with its resultant judicial authority for irrational and homophobic employment practices, was always going to have an impact on industrial tribunal cases in England and Wales and not just in Scotland. Yet, despite failure in the courts, this blatant denial of justice highlighted the insidious effect of continued criminalization and was a spur to the work that would lead to limited decriminalization (Jeffery-Poulter, 1991, p. 143).

Since Cook's amendment was passed (as s.80 of the Criminal Justice (Scotland) Act 1980), there has been little sustained law reform work. SHRG lost membership as the main cohesive influence, total criminalization of gay male sex, had been removed. It also lost members as decriminalization allowed the commercial scene to offer rather more attractive meeting places than SHRG's somewhat dated discos. It is perhaps understandable that law reform activity should have diminished during the 1980s, when a great deal of energy was, of course, taken up with surviving the attacks of the Thatcher years and dealing with the impact of AIDS.

In the years following 1980 the high points of political activism, in Scotland as in England, were to be the Lesbians and Gays Support the Miners campaign and the strong reaction against 'Section 28'. One recent success for Scottish activists was the inclusion of shameless indecency within the terms of the decriminalization enacted in 1980, which meant that the theoretical risk of being prosecuted for consenting, private, sexual activity between two men aged eighteen or more was removed (s.148 of the Criminal Justice and Public Order Act 1994).

Towards *A Claim of Right*

In the wake of the election of a new Labour government, and pending a referendum, the chances of some form of devolved Scottish Parliament appear to have increased. The powers of that body will no doubt be the subject of fierce dispute, but it is certain that the establishment of a Scottish legislature would present new opportunities for lesbian and gay activists – no longer would Scottish law reform be dependent on the actions of a Parliament in England.

In their various ways, the major political players in Scotland, Labour, the Liberal-Democrats and the SNP, all support the principle of a Bill or Charter of Rights. The aim for each, at least as publicly stated, is for a modern, open society based on equality of opportunity and recognition (even celebration) of difference. With 74 per cent of all Scottish MPs – and 92 per cent of Scots Labour MPs – voting for equality in the 1994 age of consent vote (Clark and Dunphy, 1995, p. 92), it would seem that support for lesbian and gay rights by the STUC and others over recent years has ensured that those 'good, Scottish, Socialist Calvinistic' homophobes of the 1960s remain firmly in the past. Another recent example of the readiness to address our rights can be found in the Liberal-Democrat's Home Rule (Scotland) Bill 1995 (Bill 34, Session 1994/95). In the schedule titled 'The Charter of Rights and Freedoms', discrimination against homosexuals (*sic*) would be unlawful (Schedule 3, para. 57).[11] The Bill was defeated for reasons unrelated to its provisions on lesbian and gay rights. Given this political support, it is likely that any new Parliament would seek to entrench some form of protection for human rights.[12]

The central issue on Outright's political agenda is, therefore, ensuring that we are expressly included in the provisions of any rights document enacted or endorsed by the new body. Our document, *A Claim of Right* (Outright, 1996), sets out this demand, which will be achieved through inclusion of our draft 'Equality Article' which guarantees equal protection of the law 'without discrimination on any ground such as actual or perceived . . . sexual identity or orientation'. Based on the SCCL's *Bill of Rights for Scotland* (SCCL, 1992), this short document is being widely distributed among the lesbian and gay community and to MPs, MEPs, trade unions, and other political and community groups. Even in the event that Scotland is denied a legislature by Westminster, *A Claim of*

Right forms a focus for a valuable discussion of the principle of equality of treatment. This concern for the principle of equality will de-centre gay men's issues and make our work more relevant to the concerns of lesbians and transgendered and transsexual people. We shall also be able to link our struggle for rights to those of other marginalized groups in society.

While an examination of the effectiveness of human rights law in protecting lesbians, gay men and other minorities lies outside the scope of this chapter (see Waaldijk and Clapham, 1993 and Wintermute, 1995), some general points might be made. Despite undoubted limitations, straightforward incorporation of the European Convention on Human Rights would constitute a gain for people in Scotland. The most striking limitation is, for us, the fact that Article 14 of the ECHR omits mention of 'sexual orientation'. We would hope that the discussion generated by *A Claim of Right* would ensure augmentation of the ECHR in this respect should it be incorporated into Scots law (Wintermute, 1995).

Conflict of (claimed) rights complicates matters and experience of the fight for recognition of our rights in other countries shows that there are likely to be a number of disputes with other groups over the extent and interpretation of any rights legislation. Stychin (1995, ch. 4) has described the homophobic tactics and impact of the victorious campaign by pro-censorship feminist's in the battle over interpretation of Canada's 1982 *Charter of Rights and Freedoms* (Butler, 1992). Lesbians and gay activists in Scotland and the UK will have to become conversant with a fundamentally new type of rights politics.

Building upon the principle of equality, Outright is seeking to generate discussion on the substance of lesbian and gay political demands. Detailed demands, many of which can be achieved without constitutional change, covering such areas as education, employment and criminal law reform, need to be explored and developed. Contentious issues in lesbian and gay politics must be addressed. The divisions raised by simplistic equality arguments in the 'gays in the military' campaign must be acknowledged (Tatchell, 1995). Similar disputes are likely on the question of whether we should seek the right to marry 'just like heterosexuals', or rather seek the ending of the special status granted to marriage, with its resultant marginalization of people who do not live in a couple relationship and continued oppression of women and young people. This process of clarification and discussion will be of value regardless of any political manoeuvres on devolution. The setting up of a Scottish Parliament will not see the conclusion of our struggle. It will mean the opening of a new, challenging and immensely exciting political battle for our human rights.

Lesbians and gay men in Scotland have a firm base of law reform experience on which to continue the struggle for our rights. From lagging behind reform in England, we may soon be in a position to lead the way. 'Scottish' may, in terms of sexual citizenship and law reform, come to imply visibility, progress and openness rather than invisibility and backward-looking religious moral proscription.

Acknowledgement

My thanks to Dr Simon Taylor, the late Ian Dunn and the editors of this volume for comments on a draft of this essay. Responsibility is mine alone.

Notes

1. Exceptions to this trend include Jeffery-Poulter (1991) and Weeks (1977).
2. The first reference to its use in Scotland is a case of 8 June 1886, *A. Clark & J. Bendall* v. *Stuart*, 1 White 191, an appeal against conviction on a technicality.
3. Until the Criminal Justice (Scotland) Act 1980 was amended to include shameless indecency in 1994 (by means of s.148 of the Criminal Justice and Public Order Act 1994), all forms of sexual activity between men, whether in public or private, could, in theory, have been prosecuted.
4. Berkeley himself confirmed this to David Steel MP (*Hansard*, House of Commons, 22/7/80, Vol. 989, col. 290).
5. David Steel MP stated that it was 'surely a fallacy that Scots MPs were not there on Mondays'.
6. Outright Scotland can be contacted at 58A Broughton Street, Edinburgh, EH1 3SA.
7. At the second reading of the Earl of Arran's 1965 Sexual Offences Bill, the Earl of Dundee stated that there had not been a single prosecution in Scotland arising out of a blackmail prosecution, nor for offences more than twelve months old (unless aggravated), all due to the policy of the Crown Office – why could such a directive not be introduced in England? (*Hansard*, House of Lords, 12/5/65, Vol. 266, cols. 90–1).
8. Fairbairn was to end his days as a rather pathetic though highly offensive homophobe, calling for the recriminalization of male same-sex acts. See for example *Hansard*, House of Commons, 21/2/94, Vol. 238, col. 98.
9. Despite this principled stand in 1976, Rifkind was to oppose decriminalization in 1980, by which time he was a junior Minister in the Scottish Office. He lost his seat in Parliament in the 1997 elections.

10. Correspondence between Robin Cook and Ian Dunn, 14 April 1978 and 21 April 1978.
11. Interestingly paragraph 47 of this schedule would have had the effect of recognizing marriages between parties of the same sex.
12. Scottish law, containing elements of both the common law and civil traditions, has greater authority for entrenchment of legislation than does English law. The most commonly cited authority is *obiter dictum* of Lord President Cooper in (MacCormick, 1953), 'The principle of the unlimited sovereignty of Parliament is a distinctly English principle which has no counterpart in Scottish constitutional law', *per* Lord Cooper at 411.

References

Butler (1992) *R v.* Butler (1992), 89 DLR (4th) 449.

Clark, I. and Dunphy, R. (1995) 'The effect of parliamentary lobbying on Scottish MPs in the age of consent debate', *Scottish Affairs*, **10**, Winter.

Dempsey, B. (1995) *Thon Wey*. Edinburgh: USG.

Employment Protection Appeal (1980) *Saunders Case Bulletin No. 1*. Edinburgh: Employment Protection Appeal *et al.*

Gordon, G. H. (1978) *The Criminal Law of Scotland*, 2nd edn. Edinburgh: W. Green.

Hume, D. (1797) *Commentaries on the Law of Scotland Respecting the Description and Punishment of Crimes*, reprinted 1986. Edinburgh: Butterworth.

Jeffery-Poulter, S. (1991) *Peers, Queers and Commons*. London: Routledge.

MacCormick (1953) *MacCormick* v. *HMA* 1953 SC 396.

McLaughlan (1934) *McLaughlan* v. *Boyd* 1934 JC 19.

Outright (1996) *A Claim of Right*. Edinburgh: Outright.

Palmer, A. (1995) 'Lesbian and gay rights campaigning', in A. R Wilson (ed.), *A Simple Matter of Justice?* London: Cassell.

Saunders (1980) *Saunders* v. *Scottish National Camps Association Ltd* (1980) IRLR 174.

Saunders (1981) *Saunders* v. *Scottish National Camps Association Ltd* (1981) IRLR 277.

SCCL (1992) *A Bill of Rights for Scotland*. Glasgow: SCCL.

Stychin, C. F. (1995) *Law's Desire*. London: Routledge.

Tatchell, P. (1995) *We Don't Want to March Straight*. London: Cassell.

Waaldijk, K. and Clapham, A. (eds) (1993) *Homosexuality: A European Community Issue*. London: Nijhoff.

Weeks, J. (1977) *Coming Out*. London: Quartet.

Wintermute, R. (1995) *Sexual Orientation and Human Rights*. Cambridge: Clarendon.

Wolfenden, J. (1957) *Report of the Departmental Committee on Homosexual Offences and Prostitution*, Cmnd 247. London: HMSO.

12

Intimate Queer Celluloid: *Heavenly Creatures* and Criminal Law

Elena Loizidou

> Strangely, the foreigner lives within us: he is the hidden face of our identity, the space that wrecks our abode, the time in which understanding and affinity founder. By recognising him within ourselves, we are spared detesting him in himself. A symptom that precisely turns 'we' into a problem, perhaps makes it impossible. The foreigner comes in when the consciousness of my difference arises, and he disappears when we all acknowledge ourselves as foreigners, unamenable to bonds and communities. (Kristeva, 1991, p. 1)

Before . . .

Heavenly Creatures (1994), a film directed by Peter Jackson, is about a passionate friendship. Peter Jackson paints a picture of the 'true' story of a New Zealander, Pauline Parker, and Juliet Hulme, from England. The protagonists meet at a girls' school in Christchurch, New Zealand, in 1952. The school becomes the space where their dreams and fantasies[1] meet. Their friendship is built around their shared love for Biggles books, the singer Mario Lanza and James Mason films. They find themselves in each other. Their world seems to become one. Even more, their shared world becomes blurred with the world of 'reality'. Their shared world becomes one of fantasy, a world that dictates their existence until they have to face the limits of their fantasies. At this point their world of fantasy is transformed into a world of nightmare, but alas, a world still of shared nightmare. Their fantasy world is transformed into a nightmare by their parents, who want them to be separated, to be taken apart. The experience of the limits (social and symbolic) represented in the limits of their shared fantasies, dreams and laughter prompts the girls to murder, or, as they say, to 'remove' Pauline's mother. Pauline's mother was regarded by both as the obstacle to their eternal love and life together. The girls are arrested, convicted of murder and sentenced to life imprisonment. The defence makes a plea of insanity, which fails. Just before the credits appear on screen, a sentence stands before our eyes: 'It was a condition of their release that they never meet again.' It seems that the final sentence of the law is to continue forever; they are condemned to an eternal separation. The following analysis will seek to examine this enforced separation. It will become the mirror that functions as a screen (Copjec, 1995, p. 16), reaching into the unconscious of the criminal justice system and enabling us to read how the criminal justice system arrives at its decisions.

Intertextual legal studies

Intertextual legal studies have been on the increase during the 1990s in Britain. A number of books have put criminal law into a philosophical, historical and sociological context.[2] These important scholarly approaches have opened up the textuality of criminal law to its surrounding context, enabling us to see not only that criminal law is not an autonomous text, but also that criminal law's denial of interdependence in fact leads to various miscarriages of justice.

This chapter aims to supplement this movement in a different way. My aim is to examine (criminal) law without privileging the legal text (case law, statutes, judicial sentence). The privileged text of law is an authoritative voice. By way of this voice of law, identity is inscribed. The identity of the voice of law is here referred to in the masculine. This use of 'he' or 'his' as a reference to the voice of the privileged text is not a reference to any biological masculinity, but rather it refers to a more general idiom of one particular voice that represents itself in universal constructs and invents the category of the Other without taking into account the voice of the Other. The use of 'he' or 'his' is important not only because it is part of a feminist strategy, but also because through analysis one can see that the stable and inventive 'he' is not only unstable, but also has the characteristics that it attributes to the Other, to the Other that it constructs as an outsider or as a foreigner to its textuality. The use of it within this text aims at showing this (Moi, 1990).

For years we have believed in his voice; in a voice that was telling us that he is a supreme authority and an autonomous system. Along with sustaining his supreme authority, we sustained his authority of definition, an authority that pins down his own boundaries (criminal law as a rational realm that delivers objective justice) and the boundaries of the bodies (compare Goodrich, 1990, ch. 3; Moran, 1996) that come to law (as outsiders, as irrational, as criminal) and are silenced and ultimately punished through law. This process of passivity, of accepting his word as authority, has distracted our gaze from the processes that he uses to define the bodies that come to it.

By using *Heavenly Creatures* I want to supplement the intertextual work that has been done in criminal law in a different way. I want to use this cinematic text to shed some light on the processes that criminal law uses to define the bodies that come to it. Here, criminal law (case law and statute, sentencing) will have to face the word of an image that is outside (Rush, McVeigh and Young, forthcoming, ch. 8) its boundaries. It will have to face the image that he constructs as being outside his own domain. This means that for a while law will have to become the object of gazing, his textual authority will have to be silenced, he will have to listen to his story being said otherwise. Through the story of the Other he will face the structure of his illogic; he will thus face the same silencing that he has imposed upon the Other.

In this chapter criminal law will be read as a process that constructs law as a regulatory agent in society. This will be traced through the unconscious of the film's textualities. In more psychoanalytic terms, criminal law will be read as the symbolic that regulates, censors and deprives the Other of 'the imaginary domain' (Cornell, 1995). The terms 'symbolic' and 'imaginary' are borrowed from Lacan's psychoanalytic vocabulary. The symbolic is not understood here to mean icons or symbols, but rather is taken to mean signifiers (Blonsky, 1980). Signifiers are differential elements that have no meaning in themselves, but acquire meaning through their mutual processes or relations. Through these relations they form a closed system. Law (signifier, word) could be said to be that which resides in the symbolic, for his signifiers are words that can have no meaning or no one meaning in themselves but rather acquire meaning through their relation with other words. Furthermore law or legal have no meaning in themselves but rather acquire meaning through their relation with what is not law, what is illegal. The imaginary according to Lacan (1992) is the realm of images, whether unconscious or conscious. The imaginary is the pre-Oedipal, or pre-symbolic face where the subject cannot differentiate itself. For Kristeva (Moi, 1990, pp. 164–5) the imaginary (which Kristeva calls the semiotic) is the stage where the pre-Oedipal subject is linked to the mother. The passage to the symbolic (the law) will necessitate that this pre-Oedipal subject identify either with the Law of the Father[3] or with the Mother. If identification with the Law of the Father does not happen, then the subject will remain marginal, or put Otherwise, it will never feel part of the symbolic.

Outside in

My analysis involves a double process. On the one hand the outside, the cinematic text, will challenge the orthodox story about criminal law (criminal law as a set of rules that are applied in a courtroom in offering justice to victims of crime). On the other hand the text of *Heavenly Creatures* (the characters, the inside) will be presented as carrying along an unconscious metaphor, the metaphor of law. In this way the outside/inside dichotomy will be presented as problematic. The inside/outside dichotomy that is used by criminal law or the law in a more general sense to set itself apart and to privilege itself as an authoritative voice, will appear merely phantasmatic[4] (Douzinas, Goodrich and Hachamovitch, 1994, pp. 35–68). The film as law's unconscious becomes the domain that unveils this phantasmatic image of criminal law. It is important to raise this issue of the phantasmatic or the blurring of the inside/outside dichotomy not only for the sake of raising an issue of movable boundaries (of boundaries in flight), but also to raise this issue in relation to the effect of these mobile boundaries. The blurred boundary, the imaginary or phantasmatic allows one to see that the 'deviant', the 'outsider' (Camus, 1983), the 'queer' are not so far away. The 'foreigner' is within the criminal law. By subjecting the 'foreigner' to a definition that constructs him as the 'outsider', 'deviant' or 'queer', I will argue, law carries out one of its gross injustices.

Criminal law in its metaphorical sense creates the category of the criminal, the matricide in the particular case of this film. The murder is constructed or invented by the symbolic, which is unable to recognize, respect and ultimately let the imaginary be. In more legal terms the symbolic or law is unable to understand the realm of intimacy and imagination, is unable to grasp something beyond the realm of a Cartesian subject (Descartes, 1968, pp. 102–12). Law's inability to understand the imaginary forces him to construct the other as an 'outsider' as a 'foreigner', or as 'queer'.

'Queer'

The word 'queer' here is used in a different sense from that used by academics and activists who are implicated in 'queer politics'. Here, it is used to mean the world of intimacy and imagination. This world is considered here as a highly volatile world, a world of moment and instability. In some ways the word 'queer' is used as a metaphor for the temporality and singularity of the life of a subject. This world is considered here as the opposite of the world of the symbolic and its institutions, which recognize the subject in terms of its memory, understanding and knowledge. Stychin (1995) gives us a multiplicity of contexts where the word 'queer' is used. One of the ways he uses the term or he tells us that the term is being used is the following:

> Queer signifies a more fluid conception of subjectivity, a 'new elasticity in the meanings of lesbian and gay' in which the fixity of sexual identity is loosened. It also thereby challenges the coherence of the subject and, in so doing, it simultaneously underscores the exclusions that the closure of identity categories inevitably brings. (Stychin, 1995, p. 141)

Although in some ways the above seems to resemble the way that I have chosen to use the word 'queer', it is in many ways different. Stychin constructs the 'queer' as a floating signifier, as a political transgressor of identities, as an anti-essentialist term. Nevertheless the quotation suggests otherwise. Stychin's definition does not evade the essence of sexuality (gay, lesbian). It does not evade categorization (reference to identity) and it establishes the floating 'signifier' as a new signifier of sexual identity (by the mere fact that he does not escape from the discourse of a sexual identity). His subject is still a sexual subject. He innovatively constructs a new sexual subject, the 'queer' that is not static, that in its movement, in its act, destabilizes the dichotomy of deviant and legal and constructs the 'queerness' of law. In its polemic it seems to deny difference. For example, Stychin is strongly sceptical of the bisexual, which he explains in the following terms.

> However, I am sceptical whether bisexuality as an identity or, for that matter, 'queer' sexual practices engaged in by those who would not (or could not) define themselves as lesbian or gay, necessarily are of particular political importance. That is, I question whether such practices and identities are likely to interrupt the constitution of sexual and gender categories by revealing their contingency and social constructedness. (Stychin, 1995, p. 153)

Ironically Stychin creates a category of closure. Thereby he creates this new identity and new boundaries. He is transgressive, but not enough. His new categorization establishes a new law. 'Queer' is law. The subject if it is to be legitimate, must fall within the bounds of the identical: to have the sexual identity of 'gay or lesbian', to be out and not silent. What Stychin does is to formulate his own symbolic, his own public domain, thereby denying once more the imaginary domain and its emotional, intimate, private body.

Butler (1993, pp. 223–42) in her chapter 'Critically Queer' questions the way that the word 'queer' is used by gay political and academic activists, as a transgressive signifier, in other words as a signifier that re-reads or undoes the way that the word has been used. The word has been used traditionally to signify a 'pathologised sexuality' (*ibid.*, p. 223). Butler questions the affirmative use of the word by pointing out that if such political practices or rather performances are stripped of their historicity and their own exclusionary practices, then such performances are counter-productive to the issues that they tend to mobilize. Butler characteristically states:

> As much as identity terms must be used, as much as 'outness' is to be affirmed, these same notions must become subject to a critique of the exclusionary operations of their own production: For whom is outness a historically available and affordable option? Is there an unmarked class character to the demand of universal 'outness'? Who is represented by which use of the term, and who is excluded?
> Who is represented by *which* use of the term, and who is excluded?

> For whom does the term present an impossible conflict between racial, ethnic, or religious affiliation and sexual politics? What kinds of policies are enabled by what kind of usages, and which are backgrounded or erased from view? In this sense, the genealogical critique of the queer subject will be central to queer politics to the extent that it constitutes a self-critical dimension within activism, a persistent reminder to take the time to consider the exclusionary force of one of activism's most treasured contemporary premises. (Butler, 1993, p. 227)

Butler's perspective on queer politics forms a powerful critique for academic writings that are uncritically exclusive. Stychin's critique of the bisexual comes within the parameters of her critique. He rejects the bisexual as a constitutive member of the 'queer' category but his rejection, or should I say his scepticism, is not formulated in any analytical or deconstructive manner. He suggests that such an 'identity' does not contribute to the interruption of gender or sexual construction, but at no point does he analyse his reasoning: he does not offer us a reason for his exclusion. This uncritical scepticism limits an otherwise potentially powerful critique of gender and sexual constructionism.

By taking Butler's criticisms seriously, I would like to turn the debate on 'queer' politics to a different (dis)orientation. I would like to engage with the term in a way that has not yet been marked, in a way that does not invoke the politics of visibility and 'outing', but rather in a way that invokes the other of these politics, silence. Silence here would become the constitutive idiom of the subject, rather than visibility. The word 'queer'[5] then, as it will be used here by myself, does not invoke any reference to sexual identity.

It rather invokes, and provokes a different reading of law and its subjects. The subject is not only a cognitive or a sexual body. The subject is a body with emotions, with inarticulate emotions, sentiments and desires. These inarticulate emotions, desires and sentiments, these movements that cannot be trapped in one realm, form actions, or rather they trigger a movement within the subject. These movements or actions are embedded with emotions and float within the imaginary domain. The symbolic appears unable to feel them. If it is to feel them, it needs to formulate them into a voice, and even more to translate them into its own voice. This ultimately means that the symbolic is not feeling the subject as the subject: it means that the law gives a voice to the subject; the law invents the subject.

The imaginary and its 'queer' moments refer to the movements of intimacy, emotion, and as it appears in *Heavenly Creatures*, love. These movements are read as being censored by the symbolic. They are read as excesses that the symbolic cuts off, sacrifices and denies in its attempt to secure its own domain, and ultimately its own re-productivity. They are also read as effective resistances, as moments where the symbolic becomes what it censors. It becomes the 'outsider', the 'queer', the 'foreigner', the 'emotional body'. Ultimately they are read as strategic singularities that indicate that if they are to affect the symbolic they are to stay unnamed, unidentifiable, ' ... being such as it is' (Agamben, 1993, p. 1).

... the ...

> Memory's images, once they are fixed in words, are erased. (Calvino, 1974, p. 69)

What follows forms the theoretical frame through which I am going to analyse the film. Its content and posititioning might sound irrelevant, but it is *the* frame not only of the stories but also the stories that law says. In addressing the frame, one also addresses consciously the fact that anything we (law) write about is a story.

Calvino's quotation is of importance to the analysis of the story. The quotation comes from *Invisible Cities*, a book about travelling stories narrated to Kublai Khan by Marco Polo. Marco Polo travels. On his return home, he tells the stories about the places he has visited to the Great Khan. The Khan listens to the stories and imagines them. Most of the times the image of the cities becomes different in his eyes when compared to the eyes of Marco Polo. Consider, for example, Marco Polo's narration of his visit to Venice and the response given by Kublai Khan.

> 'You leave there and ride for three days between the northeast and east-by-northeast winds ...'. Marco resumed enumerating names and customs and wares of a great number of lands. His repertory could be called inexhaustible, but now he was the one who had to give in. Dawn had broken when he said: 'Sire, now I have told you

> about all the cities I know.' 'There is still one of which you never speak.' Marco Polo bowed his head. 'Venice,' the Khan said. Marco smiled. 'What else do you believe I have been talking to you about?' The emperor did not turn a hair. 'And yet I have never heard you mention that name.' (Calvino, 1974, pp. 68–9)

One of the reasons for this non-convergence of the image and the voice is given by the quotation. Calvino tells us that memory's images, once they are fixed in words, are erased. The story telling of cities, the experience of cities, once put into words erases the city, erases the images that enter into the mind of the subject that visited the city. If one takes up a Lacanian (Lacan, 1990; Rush, McVeigh and Young, forthcoming) frame of analysis one notes that there is no other subject but a speaking subject. Lacan tells us that one's existence is reiterated through one's language, in his attempt to kill any romantic notion of an original self prior to language, an existence prior to language (Moi, 1990, p. 148). He goes on to tell us that the metaphor, the substitution of one word for another annihilates (*ibid.*, p. 158) the first signifier (graphical representation, word). The substitution of the signifier seen (the city visited) for the spoken signifier (the city described in words) is done through the process of metaphorization that in some way or another erases the first or substitutes it with the second. In this sense Lacan's analysis of language agrees with the quotation from Calvino. But let me return to Calvino and the importance of the quotation for my analysis.

Calvino sees the world of words as a world of erasure, as a world that eludes the images of memory, the sensation of memory. The 'original' image is eluded because it is put into logos, into reason. How? To speak of a memory, to speak of an image that resides in memory, requires a question. The question forces you to answer for that image – the answer has to be given in language. Language pre-exists you according to Lacan, and this language resides in logos.

The explanation given above is important for the analysis of the cinematic text, *Heavenly Creatures*, and the representation of criminal law that emerges from it. While law (and criminal law in particular) sees itself as a set of coherent and rational rules, law fails to see that there is no correspondence between the justice that it promises (for the attribution of responsibility is an attribution of justice since an event occurred outside the courtroom, outside the law, and thus triggered a disturbance that needs to be retrieved) and the justice that delivers. In other words, law claims that the redress of the imbalance that occurred outside ought to be judged objectively within law. This objective judgment promises somehow a listening ear and a talking subject. It promises that the voice that will be reaching the ear of law will not meet with any interference and will not be extracted with force from the speaking subject, from the subject that is under judgment. This is the 'nature', after all, of objective judgment, judgment based upon the spoken words of the Other and not judgment based upon the world of the judge. If the judgment delivered is based upon the spoken wor(l)d of the judge (the representative of law or the author of law), then justice becomes a force of law[6] and not the end of law. In this event one can conclude that justice is not delivered, or rather that a particular form of justice is delivered, law as justice. Here the particular Other that is judged gets eluded, she becomes invisible in the eyes of law, her voice is not heard, just merely erased and substituted by his voice. Law denies the occurrence of such an event. Law continues to claim that justice is delivered in the name of the Other, in the words of the Other and according to an objective application of the rules.

Heavenly Creatures

The cinematic representation *Heavenly Creatures* shows the criminal law as a process obsessed with confessions. Through the confession, law puts memory's images into words. It is to this process of confession that eludes the subject as an emotional body and reconstitutes that subject as a legal mind that reasons, that I now want to turn. This processes of translation, which comes about through confession, allows criminal law to punish the Other that comes to it. What can be inferred from the analysis above is that the world of silent memory, a memory that is not articulated in words, resides in the realm of fantasy, emotions or the imaginary. It belongs to the realm of fantasy because according to Lacan the only subject that exists is the speaking subject, and it belongs to the realm of emotions because emotions are directly opposite to reason (Descartes, 1968, p. 105). In other words, silenced memory carries with it certain ingredients (emotions, fantasy) that cannot be translated into legal language, into what I call his language. Silence thus becomes the moment, the 'queer' moment that interrupts the legal process. Law consequently cannot cope with this moment of silent memory. It cannot because language[7] or putting memory's images into words is what sustains its sovereignty. After all, it needs a speaking subject to pass on his judgment. Silent memory is something intimate, sacred to the otherwise speaking subject; it somehow represents her private or imaginary realm. Law on the other hand demands to make it public so as to translate it into his words and redeem her from her sins, through punishment. I will show through the film how law demands confessions and how he deals with those that refuse to give in to his demands.

Law as a metaphor resides in the symbolic order – the order that demands confessions, in contrast to the characters of the film that seem to reside in the imaginary domain. The differential relationship between the legal and the illegal puts law in the symbolic order over against the imaginary domain, creating law as a subject but also law as a closed system. Law's demand for confessions or unsilencing forms an integral part of its process of differentiation and definition that positions him within the symbolic.

It is my contention that the two main characters of the film (Pauline and Juliet) confront this tension between their imaginary existence (a sensational, image oriented, intimate, undifferentiated relationship) and the symbolic which demands that they confess (and thus mark their entry into language and law). Their resistance to confession signifies perhaps an unconscious 'realization' that if they are to confess they are to escape from the realm of the imaginary or semiotic. Their resistance to confession which is symbolized through the crime of matricide, is also significant for another reason. It signifies that if one is to become a legal subject, if one is to enter the symbolic in some way or another, one has to face a violence, the violence of law or the violence of the symbolic. I will now pursue these points by way of a more detailed analysis of two scenes from the film that portray the suspension between the imaginary and the symbolic, the 'queer' suspension if you will.

Crime: Scene 1

Juliet Hulme's father, Dr Henry Rainsford Hulme, who was the rector of Canterbury University College, Christchurch, becomes sceptical of the intimacy of Juliet's and Pauline's friendship. He sees the friendship of the girls as problematic when on the return from the sanitarium where Juliet was staying as a result of having tuberculosis, he sees the two girls holding hands in the car. Dr Hulme then visits Pauline's parents and brings to their attention that the friendship is rather unwholesome. He blames Pauline for this unwholesome friendship. Dr Hulme acts as the symbolic here in differentiating between what is permissible in the girls' friendship and what is not. He then gives them the address and name of a doctor who can actually deal with the 'problem' that he sees Pauline developing. As it happens, Pauline's mother takes her to the doctor. Pauline's encounter with the doctor is of significance. The doctor begins the examination by asking Pauline a series of questions that will lead him to his diagnosis and eventually his cure. The doctor first asks Pauline whether she likes girls. She answers 'No'. He then asks her whether she likes Juliet. She answers 'Yes'. These are the only two questions that the doctor asks Pauline with regard to liking girls. From this the doctor concludes that Pauline is suffering from homosexuality. He believes that she really should have other friends and should not be hanging around only with Juliet, and that in the future there might be a cure for this disease.

The doctor in this scene can be read as a metaphor of law. He performs some of the attributes of the institution of law, such as questioning, reliance on previous cases and delivering judgment. As a metaphor of law and ultimately as the symbolic, the doctor takes it upon himself to question Pauline. His questions are indirect. Indirect questioning falls within the parameters of the laws of evidence (Keane, 1989, pp. 106–7). Leading questions such as 'Are you in love with Juliet?' would not have been acceptable in a court because they would have been considered as attempts to feed words into the mouth of the witness or the person in question. Nevertheless the indirect nature of the question forces the person under question to confess and it allows the inquirer to construct the confession in a way that feeds words into her mouth. For example, Pauline had offered monosyllabic answers to the doctor. The nature of her answers indicate that she did not want to put her memory images into words, that she did not want to share 'their' world with the doctor. This is symbolized when at the end of the conversation with the doctor she imagines that one of her heroes plunges a knife through him. This fantasy image symbolizes her desire to kill the law of the father and remains in her undifferentiated intimate world of the imaginary.

The symbolic, as we can observe from the film, cannot cope with this resistance to confession, with this keeping the private to the private. The symbolic cannot cope with her monosyllabic answers, which are almost synonymous with silence. Silence cannot give a conclusion, a judgment, for the doctor, therefore he has to use the nature of his questions and Pauline's monosyllabic answers to conclude what he has already prejudged. Here we see the application of deductive reasoning. Her answer to the first question in combination with her second answer allows the doctor to deduce that Pauline does not like all girls but she does like Juliet, therefore, she has formed a passionate liaison with Juliet which can only be defined as homosexuality.

In this scene the doctor as a metaphor of law and as representative of the symbolic, is obsessed with the word 'homosexuality' and the meaning of that word. The symbolic as such is uninterested in the privacy of the subject. The symbolic is uninterested in interpreting the desire of the subject for silence. Such desire, such silence, become meaningless for the symbolic. Since it translates as meaningless it is then described or vomited out, as deviant, as homosexual, as foreign, as 'queer', as imaginary. While law translates the Other into the categories of the 'outlaw', it simultaneously involves itself in a process where it defines itself, where it sets up its own boundaries and creates food for its body to live. These boundaries construct the 'outlaw' as a healthy body. They also construct law as a healthy body (symbolized by the doctor in the film). This healthy body is also presented as a body that through its judgment can cure the 'outlaw', as a body that does not fall within its parameters.

What is interesting in this scene is how Pauline perceives the symbolic or the law. Pauline's resistance, Pauline's monosyllabic answers or non-answers, signify a reluctance to give in to this world of identity, signification and rationality. It furthermore 'reveals' an unconscious realization that the symbolic will be unable to feel the women's world of imagination, love, intimacy, or as they name it, their 'fourth world'. This unconscious realization is symbolized in the film with the phantasmatic murder of the doctor by a clay statue, which signifies even more Pauline's desire to kill the symbolic and the Law of the Father – the law that differentiates, categorizes and cognitively understands the subject.

Crime: Scene 2

The second scene that I want to focus on elaborates on the above. In particular it deals with the issue of how the subject deals with the censorship of its silence. The second scene consists of the murder or the sacrifice of the mother. This develops into a story of separation: a story where families (families being here metaphors of law or the symbolic) act to separate the two girls, Pauline and Juliet.

Pauline and Juliet want to live together. When Juliet finds that she has to leave New Zealand for South Africa she wants to take Pauline with her. Pauline cannot go, not only because her parents (especially her mother) will not let her go, but also because she does not have a passport (her pass to an 'independent' legal subjectivity and escape). Once more Pauline and Juliet find that the symbolic cannot allow them to live their fantasies: to let them be; to let them dwell in their own private teenage world. The symbolic once more wants them to confess their fantasies, to make them speak their fantasies in words so as to elude them, kill them. Once they confess to their sin, the symbolic will allow them to walk free, but separately from that sin or that crime, since the symbolic would have punished them (by separating them, by uttering a sentence upon them) and thus welcome them to his world. In this way the symbolic or the law will be able to exert its authority or even more to identify itself through this violent demand. Somehow, though, the girls refuse to give in. They refuse to confess their dreams, they refuse to be separated. Their refusal to confess and enter the symbolic is supplemented with their attempt to fight the cause of their problem. Pauline sees her mother as the problem to their togetherness. Since this miserable woman (as Juliet calls her) is set up by the girls as their obstacle, they decide to 'remove' her. The image of the mother here becomes something more than the traditional image of a caring mother, the mother that the child is linked to in Kristeva's semiotic or the imaginary. The mother in their eyes here becomes the symbolic that wants to castrate them (by demanding their separation).

Pauline's mother seems to be the one that acts as the Father but as a castrated Father because she has no other language than the Father's language. This is well evidenced in a scene in the film. The day after Pauline was caught by her father sleeping with their male lodger, her mother shouts at her that she has broken her father's heart with her immoral acts. Her mother talks of the 'pain' that Pauline's act caused in the Name of the Father. There is perhaps another reason for Pauline's mother being the obstacle. Pauline's mother is a woman, sharing the same genitals as her daughter. This biological fact raises an expectation for Pauline, an unconscious expectation perhaps, that she would allow her to be with her dream companion. These two moments make it apparent that

Pauline's mother is twice castrated; first by virtue of her nature and second, culturally.

The mother is a woman who has been subjugated to the laws of the symbolic and she thus lives to conserve the Law of the Father. It is for this reason that Pauline consciously or unconsciously punishes her mother. Betrayed by the one from whom she was expecting understanding, she decides to remove the betrayal, to remove the pain of the betrayal, to remove it in order not to confess. Little did she know that the woman she was accusing was not the cause of her pain, the cause of the betrayal. Little did Pauline and Juliet know that the symbolic (the law) does not allow any act or removal, any 'queer' moment, beyond its territoriality. It does not allow any moment beyond itself because their act of removal is a demonstration of individual territoriality, beyond the symbolic and thus an act that threatens both the symbolic and the law that resides within it. Little did Pauline know that her mother was only an agent of this symbolic. Little did they know that their act (like her answer to the doctor) will be translated into a confession and thereby named a crime and the signature for their eternal separation.

The murmur of violence

Every discourse among interlocutors is a struggle against outsiders, those who emit interference and equivocation, who have an interest in that communication, who have an interest that the communication not take place. But to the extent that communication does take place and the statements are established as true, it designates outsiders as not making sense, as being mystified, mad or brutish, and it hands them over to violence (Lingis, 1994, p. 135).

So the law once more forcefully gains its confession, once more forcefully strips the individuals of their dreams, their fantasies, their togetherness. Law demands confessions. Law wants us to strip off our skins, to tell our stories. Law appears here to be similar to the man that Irigaray describes in the following terms: 'Such is the failure of the Man who does not make his own boundary out of the skin of the other. He is turned back to the other side of his limit' (Irigaray, 1991, p. 36). A limited man. This law is not only the institutional law, this law is the law of the text, the law of our textuality and our existence within this textuality. This law, as it appears from the analysis of the two scenes, wants us to tell our stories, to share our fantasies so as to name them, to translate them, to paint them in its own language. This means that the Other that faces the law sheds its skin in order not only for law to judge him or her but also for law to construct its territory so as to build its fortress, so as to protect its empire. In the meantime, however, in this legal process of the symbolic Pauline and Juliet are sentenced not only to prison but to eternal separation. Law keeps the dreamers apart, it keeps them beyond of the symbolic, the imaginary moment, away afar from its land, from the land of its reasonable territory.

The silence, the 'queer', the resistance of Pauline and Juliet, however, interrupted the pure image of law, of justice through law. The scenes that have been analysed in this chapter painted the blood stains of the processes that law takes up in legitimizing his authority and simultaneously categorizing the subject. Silence interferes in this process, it shakes up its foundations and 'reveals' at last the unjust mechanisms of law. Silence also attempts to disengage through resistance from the current mechanisms of the symbolic. Silence recognizes the uniqueness of the Other, in the sense that images, emotions, and moments that the Other experiences are part of her private archive, part of her unspoken memory, and that any translation, any confession would denigrate her uniqueness into sameness. Silence effectively resists the symbolic, even if the symbolic translates her into a guilty actor. It effectively resists the symbolic since it does not participate in its logocentric processes of identification, categorization and ultimately sameness.

If law is to alter his violent image, perhaps law has to stop resisting. Perhaps law has to stop thinking that it is making conscious decisions, perhaps law has to pause and listen to those voices that refuse to speak, to those voices that still dream. Perhaps, though, silence is not what law is afraid of. Perhaps it is what silence reminds law of that terrorizes its existence. Silence perhaps symbolizes for law the Other of life, death. If silence ultimately interrupts law's immortality, then perhaps law's violence symbolizes a desperate man's attempt to sustain his empire through the death of the Other. *Heavenly Creatures*, though filtered through that law, is inescapable from his death. Law's conscious representation of himself as the messenger of justice, as different from the violent 'outlaw', is dead. If law has lost his essence, if he is just a persona, then perhaps he needs to reconsider what silence is murmuring for; unique, 'queer' reflexivity.

Notes

1. Their world of fantasy is represented in the film with visual references to a princess, castles and the unicorn.
2. See the works of Lacey, Wells and Meure (1990), Norrie (1993), Clarkson and Keating (1994), Stanley (1996). The attempt here is to widen the context by reading a cinematic construction of criminal law.
3. Note here that the Law of the Father ought not to be read literally, in other words the Father is not somebody who is a man, the gender does not matter. Somebody gets to be the Father when that somebody appropriates the symbolic language of the Father, a language or voice that forces the Other to be outside the symbolic. See Moi (1990, ch. 8).
4. The phantasmatic derives from the word fantasia, which as a philosophical term has different meanings. In Aristotle, fantasia is the process by which the image is presented to us; this process does not belong to the space of intellect or to the space of sensation. Fantasia is rather suspended between the world of intellect and the world of sensation. This suspension creates a movement and through movement fantasia is affected (Aristotle, 1957; Douzinas, Goodrich and Hachamovitch, 1994).
5. For a critical reading of 'queer' see also Grosz, 1995, ch. 13.
6. For an elaborate and philosophical discussion of the force of law see Cornell, Rosenfield and Carlson, 1992, ch. 1. In his celebrated essay Derrida analyses Benjamins' 'Critique of Violence' and draws our attention to the fact that law or *droit* has two idioms, a foundational and a conservationist one. Both of these idioms, he says, are founded on violence. Both idioms present themselves as being part of, or an integral part of, the social contract of democracy. Nevertheless none of these idioms claim that they are founded on or involve violence. This amnesia of *droit* constitutes the violence, because it signifies the 'passage from presence to representation' (Cornell, Rosenfield and Carlson, 1992, p. 47).
7. 'Legal Language thus explicitly served the exclusory function of keeping the law within the legal institution and subject to the singular techniques of its interpretive tradition. . . . The language of the law is the language of memory, of memorials and monuments, according to Davies and so appropriately shrouded in a documentary language never intended for human speech or the corruption of popular use' (Goodrich, 1990, pp. 88–9).

References

Agamben, G. (1993) *The Coming Communities*. Minnesota: University of Minnesota Press.

Aristotle (1957) *On the Soul*. London: Harvard University Press.

Blonsky, M. (1980) *On Signs*. London: Routledge.

Butler, J. (1993) *Bodies That Matter*. London: Routledge.

Calvino, I. (1974) *Invisible Cities*. London: Picador.

Camus, A. (1983) *The Outsider*. London: Penguin.

Clarkson, M. V. C. and Keating, M. H. (1994) *Criminal Law: Text and Materials*. London: Sweet & Maxwell.

Copjec, J. (1995) *Read My Desire: Lacon against the Historicists*. Cambridge, MA: MIT Press.

Cornell, D., Rosenfeld, M. and Carlson, G. D. (eds) (1992) *Deconstruction and the Possibility of Justice*. London: Routledge.
Cornell, D. (1995) *The Imaginary Domain*. London: Routledge.
Grosz, E. (1995) *Space, Time and Perversion*. London: Routledge.
Descartes, R. (1968) *Discourse on Method and the Meditations*. London: Penguin.
Douzinas, C., Goodrich, P. and Hachamovitch, Y. (eds) (1994) *Politics, Postmodernity and Critical Legal Studies*. London: Routledge.
Goodrich, P. (1990) *Languages of Law*. London: Weidenfeld and Nicholson.
Irigaray, L. (1991) *Marine Lover of Friedrich Nietzsche*. New York: Columbia University Press.
Jackson, P. (director; 1995) *Heavenly Creatures*.
Keane, A. (1989) *The Modern Law of Evidence*. London: Butterworths.
Kristeva, J. (1991) *Strangers to Ourselves*. New York: Harvester Wheatsheaf.
Lacan, J. (1990) *Television*. New York and London: W. W. Norton & Company.
Lacan, J. (1992) *Ecrits*. London: Routledge.
Lacey, N., Wells, C. and Meure, D. (1990) *Reconstructing Criminal Law*. London: Weidenfeld and Nicholson.
Lingis, A. (1994) *The Community of Those who Have Nothing in Common*. Bloomington: Indiana University Press.
Moi, T. (1990) *Sexual/Textual Politics*. London: Routledge.
Moran, L. (1996) *The Homosexual(ity) of Law*. London: Routledge.
Norrie, A. (1993) *Crime, Reason and History*. London: Weidenfeld and Nicholson.
Rush, P., McVeigh, S. and Young, A. (eds) (forthcoming) *Criminal Legal Doctrine*. London: Dartmouth Press.
Stanley, C. (1996) *Urban Excess and the Law: Capital Culture and Desire*. London: Cavendish.
Stychin, F. C. (1995) *Law's Desire*. London: Routledge.
Yates, A. F. (1966) *The Art of Memory*. London: Routledge.

13

Queering Theory: An Essay on the Conceit of Revolution in Law

Larry Cata Backer

Introduction

Since the early part of this century, Americans in particular, have viewed the courts, and more generally this thing summarized as *law*, as the place where societal changes can be made most effectively. Law, and more generally, political institutions as the wielders of law, are viewed as the site from out of which will emerge social and cultural transformation of the most fundamental sort. Hence, it seems that the endless project of legal élites in the late twentieth century has been to perpetuate the myth of the power of law and its transformative potential. Law, it is argued, is a god who can be manipulated to impose a sort of endlessly paradisiacal state on humankind, or at least the white European world. We still yearn for the appearance of the Messiah.

Modern critical theory, and the strains of the emerging work of queer theory scholars, has not escaped this 'last temptation' of theory. The 'temptation' of revolutionary transformation in queer theory dotes overmuch on Biblical Messianism of the type that queer theorists so enthusiastically criticize as the basis of the oppression practiced by the dominant forces of heterosexualism. Yet what these strains of queer theory speak is a gospel of postmodernism. This particular gospel announces that *power* resides in all activity, including the enterprise of theory. It prefers to cloak its other message: that theory laced with Messianism may be a cloak for recasting, rather than casting out, that old nemesis – hegemony. Any theory of perfectionism ultimately carries with it a foundation for subordination. A queer theory which suggests that there is a permanent good state of things is mis-focused.

In this chapter, in the place of the pseudo-transformative project of critical theory, I offer a critical realism for our times. I suggest that, indeed, social change of a limited nature may be attained. The means by which such successful change may be accomplished I introduce here as the notion of subversive calumny. This project of subversive calumny is critical and realist. It insists that the slow, never-finished project of moulding current expression of culture must be consciously undertaken.

My purpose here is not to trash critical or queer theory. Critical theory is a powerful analytic tool. But it mis-serves when used as a substitute for traditional teleology. It serves better Lord Devlin's 'man in the Clapham omnibus' (Devlin, 1988, pp. 15, 25) as he seeks to interpret the possibilities within culture as expressed in the way he lives his personal and institutional lives. My only quarrel is with the millenarianism, the Christian-Hegelian notion of 'synthesis' and repose, which permeates some strains of queer theory.

Although I have chosen to situate discussion of the general problem of legal Messianism within queer theory, the lessons I draw can be generalized. Certainly, the Messianism of queer theory is shared with other critical approaches to theory. Strains of critical race theory, feminist theory, and perhaps even the ways in which we conceptualize social movements in other disciplines, notably intellectual history, are imbued with the sense of progress towards an absolute form of perfectibility. Theory must abandon its self-consciously utopian characteristics. It must cultivate a 'pragmatic' sense of the uses of current institutions for the achievement of the presently impossible. To do otherwise is to create gods out of their respective visions of perfection.

A ship of fools

What is emerging as queer theory, like critical race and feminist theory, is as varied as its practitioners, and as fractious (Delgado and Stefancic, 1993; Stychin, 1996a). Its object is the interrogation of the hetero-patriarchal culture in which we operate. Interrogation, though, sometimes can imply more. Valdes describes it as a perspective that will 'help legal theory and legal culture to appreciate the need to address, critique and reform social norms and conditions tied to, or produced by, the conflation of sex, gender, and sexual orientation (Valdes, 1995, p. 31). Stychin suggests that 'A queer sexuality seeks to destabilise the entrenched categories of identity and the essentialisation of those categories through a discourse of immutability. Instead, sexual identities might be conceived as multiplicitous, shifting, fluid, and fragmented' (1996a, p. 153). Queer legal activists 'must at once be aware of their role both inside and outside the law: to reform and subvert juridical heterosexism' (Rosenblum, 1994, p. 122). I mean here to query the process of transformative queerness. Queerness and its transformative potential are constrained by the reality of the human imperative to categorize. I begin with what will become an increasingly ironic rendition of a queer *revolutionary* call to arms (though any other would have served as well).

Heterosexualism sucks[1]

Heterosexualism is the background norm providing the reality of sexuality in our culture, the complex of power relations 'concerned with the sensations of the body, the quality of pleasures and the nature of impressions' (Foucault, 1978, p. 106). Its existence is dependent on differentiation from the 'other'. In that act of definition a hierarchy is created. This hierarchy is based on the normative superiority of the thing defined, the heterosexual.

Faced with the fact of heterosexualism as the background norm, the tendency is to seek to overturn the current cultural order and to substitute another version of a cultural order more agreeable to the advocate. The assumption is that this overturning will achieve not only justice, but repose as well (Arendt, 1958, p. 51; Harris, 1996, pp. 207, 217). The substitute culture will usher in the permanent new world cultural order. That's the rub – groups, dominant or subordinated, cannot resist the attempt or the dream of dismissing the rest of all possible worlds, in order to find that which results in the best of all possible (only) worlds.

The revolution so popular among critically inclined academics today is a manifestation of the extent to which critical theory remains *inside*. Shorn of its sermonizing, it is little more than a dominance game that a socio-cultural minority is incapable of winning. It is the dream of the imposition of a 'dictatorship of the (sexual) proletariat' on a slumbering culture that ought to know better, and once (re)educated, will, either freely or not, embrace the 'light' forever. Nevertheless, I suggest the future is not in revolution. The future requires an embrace of the enterprise of cultural calumny; a subversive assimilationist project whose goal is a modulation of values *within and not outside* our culture. This requires the embrace of law as a tool (Backer, 1993) and an object (Lobel, 1995; Spann, 1995).

Reluctantly, it is in this context of group norm-making, of culture (writ large) and discipline, of identity and contests for power, that queer theory participates. Reluctantly, because it prefers to speak with the authority of divine universal writ. Queer aims to burst the fetters chaining world queerdom, and liberate us all in some fashion. Post-liberation humankind will live in a world substantially different from that before its raising to grace. Thus, there is war in the heavens and war on earth. 'Social constructivism understands change in the law and society to be a process of rupture by which the orthodoxy struggles to cope with rebellious victim groups in an escalating conflict which inevitably ends either with suppression of the rebellion or with an overthrow of the old framework' (Spann, 1995, p. 641). In this spirit, Valdes argues that 'the common denominator that should delineate Queerness in legal culture and theory should not be minority sexual orientation as such, but a willful (political) consciousness devoted to the containment and reformation of Euro-centric hetero-patriarchy' (Valdes, 1995, p. 356).

Queer theory critiques the binary division of sexual identity into heterosexual and 'other.' The acceptance of this division limits the diversity of human sexuality and consolidates heterosexuality as the background norm. The inevitable conclusion is that the heteronormativity binary must be destroyed. Such destruction is possible and inherent in the instability of the constructs 'heterosexual' and 'other' (Halley, 1993). Here the language of 'religious rights' is used to equate the establishment of a state sexuality to the establishment of a state religion, 'to destabilize heteronormativity rather than to naturalize gay identities' (Valdes, 1995, p. 10). Implicit in the campaign is the notion that, assuming that hetero-normativity can be disestablished, the 'problem' will disappear once and for all. There is no sense that a state of disestablished heteronormativity will need defending (Valdes, 1995, p. 11). So, Adrienne Rich suggests the necessity of this object 'especially, by those individuals who feel they are, in their personal experience, the precursors of a new social relation between the sexes' (Rich, 1980, p. 637).

The strain of queer theory with which I concern myself here, therefore, seeks to attack the validity of categorical sexual identities, or at least the norm-giving category, heterosexual (Henriksson, 1995, pp. 108–9; Stychin, 1996b, pp. 181–6) As such, queer theory also emphasizes anti-assimilation; normalization within heterosexuality is rejected in favour of diversity (Eaton, 1994, pp. 172–3). 'Queers use legal descriptions of homosexuality to create contestation in the public sphere, to re-imagine community and to transform the political field by challenging community members' own identifications' (Bower, 1994, p. 1019).

But the solution does not require revolution, a revolutionary overthrowing of culture and the foundationalist perspective from which it springs. *Revolutionspeak*, ideological deconstruction, revolutionary social constructionism, are misguidedly utopian and ultimately ignored as mere theory. Revolutionary rhetoric is noise – it is at once incomprehensible and annoying to the dominant culture; it has no positive *cultural* effect (Backer, 1996a; compare Teubner, 1993, p. 71; Feldman, 1996a). 'Up to now, all revolutions have been made by moralizing dilettantes. They have always been in good faith and perished because of their dilettantism' (Koestler 1941; compare Schlag, 1996). But it is not only dilettantism that 'ruins' revolution.

In this sense, Eskridge is inaccurate in suggesting that dominant culture does not listen (1994, p. 636). Culture does not respond in the way the speaker expects (hopes). Our dominant heterosexualist culture has so refined the techniques of annexing the 'oppositional' discourse of its sexual minorities that it passes virtually unnoticed and unopposed (Brown, 1996). Such discourse is 'in every instance a function or extension of history, convention, and local practice' (Fish, 1984–5, p. 439). Moreover, revolution is hard to hear, even among its practitioners (Fuss, 1991, p. 6).

The political in revolution effectively seeks to change the identity of the dominant group, to reimpose a hierarchy of value that mimics the one that it ostensibly replaced. It is merely a change in the structure of domination, not its elimination. It is never a question of *whether* one will serve a master, but *which* (Devlin, 1988, p. 32). This applies to contests for dominance between subordinated and dominant groups, between subordinated groups (Ikemoto, 1993; Farber and Sherry, 1995), and also within subordinated groups (Butler, 1991).

Queer theory 'also serves to highlight an irresolvable tension between

... the deconstruction of categories of identity; and ... the political necessity of invoking (often in a fairly totalizing way) those same categories' (Stychin, 1996b, p. 182). Fuss rightly states that:

> What we need, Foucault writes in 'The Gay Science,' is 'a radical break, a change in orientation, objectives, and vocabulary.' While this writer remains suspicious of the faith Foucault places in epistemological 'breaks', since such breaks inevitably seem to reassert what they sought to supersede, the call for new orientations, new objectives, and especially new vocabularies is still admittedly a seductive one. (Fuss, 1991, p. 7)

Ironically, the revolutionspeak of queer theorists is its own best evidence of the ways in which revolution (as rhetoric and political goal) mimics the dominating force it so passionately wishes to replace with something else. Revolutionspeak is the ultimate essentializing force. It essentializes the discourse of the dominant, creating the construct 'oppressor', which can then be differentiated and replaced. In a sense, revolutionspeakers turn the tables on the owners of hegemonic power, but only by trading places. And yet, what applies to the techniques of dominance applies with equal force to subordinated groups. Critical theory has acquired the defects that it claims as an essential sin of the dominant group: the narrow hermeneutic vision of lawyers. It *includes* and *excludes* us all at some point and at some time. Revolutionspeak reduces culture, construction, and group essence to politics. This can be dangerous, especially for and between subordinated groups in the world of swirling and intersected identities within a system of hegemonic meta-culture (which subordinated groups disown for political convenience) in which we live (Farber and Sherry, 1995, p. 879).

Ultimately, what is involved is control over the mechanisms of what Foucault has described, in a very Euro-centric way, as truth, 'a system of ordered procedures for the production, regulation, distribution, circulation and operation of statements ... linked in a circular relation with systems of power which produce and sustain it, and to effects of power which it induces and which extend it' (Foucault, 1980, p. 133). Truth provides the filter through which culture itself can be reduced to process, to enforcement. Foucault notes that:

> Each society has its regime of truth, its 'general politics' of truth: That is the types of discourse which it accepts and makes function

> as true; the mechanisms and instances which enable one to distinguish true from false statements, the means by which each is sanctioned; the techniques and procedures accorded value in the acquisition of truth; the status of those who are charged with saying what counts as true. (Foucault, 1980, p. 131)

Revolution necessarily remains the captive of the 'group' and the strength of group feeling (ibn Khaldun, 1967). There is, as Pierre Schlag suggests in another context, the element of the romance novel in revolutionary academic rhetoric:

> The legal academic, similarly, wants to be supremely just, to experience a law that is the best it could ever be, to submit to a jurisprudence so majestic, so encompassing, that it will take him out of this world.... But, it will only happen as a result of achieving Herculean power and vanquishing countless jurisprudential enemies. (Schlag, 1996, p. 1818)

Revolution is perverse; it is ultimately little more than an extreme form of the traditional hegemonic enterprise of 'community'. Revolution has no place in the revaluation enterprise. And worse, it seeks stasis, permanence, cultural immobility within the norms it chooses. Once the optimum state is reached so will some sort of eternal cultural equilibrium. Critical theory mis-focuses by looking to the courts and legislature for the successful imposition of change in popular behaviour. There can be no victory 'against' culture, there are only small revolutions within culture. I here begin my exploration of why this must be so. The effort is precursory; its aim is to provoke discourse and advance the enterprise of queer theoretics from multiple perspectives.

Queering culture; culturing queers

To understand the misdirection of transformative queerness, we must move beyond identity/culture to something more complex and subtle. Interrogating the revolutionary/transformatory tendencies of queer theory can lead us to a more nuanced understanding of culture and the nature of change (not progress). But this enterprise requires an understanding of the relationship between culture (the principal focus of queer theory) and *popular* culture, the very real and very ephemeral manifestation of cultural choice. This is also very queer. '[Q]ueer has been characterised as a stance generated from a position of dissent and resistance to attempts at rigid categorization within both dominant culture and sexual subcultures. It inhabits the position of being both an identity category and a resistance to identity' (Stychin, 1996b, p. 181).

At any one time, there is no such thing as culture. There is only a faint manifestation of a portion of its possibility; popular culture. Popular culture is the way in which we replicate culture. In this sense, *culture* serves as a meta-system, immutable in its totality, yet preserving a certain indeterminacy and fluidity, a certain play in its expression. Culture acts as meta-system because it contains within it all possibilities, all combinations possible, given the set of basic assumptions that define a group as 'distinct'. Culture is the box within which its expression is implemented, and re-implemented, as popular culture, over and over again. 'Even granting that within any culture a concept such as personality homeostasis or self-realization has validity, the content of such concepts still vary in different times and places' (Marmor, 1971, p. 169). Beyond culture is outside; the inconceivable. 'That, after all, is what it means to be acculturated into a sexual system: The conventions of the system acquire the self-confirming inner truth of "nature". If one could simply think oneself out of one's acculturation, it wouldn't be acculturation in the first place. And I can't imagine de-acculturating myself any more than I can imagine de-sexualizing myself' (Halperin, 1990, p. 53). Within culture is an infinite variation. We can choose to persecute or ignore sexual nonconformists *within* our culture. Thus, *popular* culture is both a selective and collective evidence of culture *in practice*. The process of selectivity and collectivity provide useful points for interrogation and change. In this sense, I agree with David Halperin's suggestion that '[p]articular cultures are contingent' (*ibid*., 1990, p. 51).

If things were even this simple, it might be possible to speak of an authoritative and unitary form of interrogation and transformation, which critical theory advances. Rather, culture as popularly expressed in a single moment reflects the *hegemony* of a particular realization of the value judgements of those who (collectively) dominate the machinery of cultural practice. These value judgements of the collective are 'what defines the costs associated with the particular ends among which individuals can choose' (Ortiz, 1993a, p. 1021). Popular culture as collective prejudice (Gadamer, 1989, p. 306) is the fundamental nature of the interpretive community (Fish, 1980, pp. 303–4). But the notion of valuation does not imply a singular act of valuing. The expression of popular culture, always shifting, is made infinitely more complex because social rules do not invariably result in a unitary interpretation of conduct norms, even core norms. People don't always shift in unison, even people who belong to the same 'cultural' group. More perverse, perhaps, is the reality that there may be significant norm sharing between dominant and subordinate groups. The possibilities of sharing increase as the fractures grow. Dominant norms blend into those of subordinated groups on multiple levels and within and outside the realities of cultural colonization. And here lies the problem: the politics of struggle, like that of hegemony, militate strongly in favour of essentializing the 'other' and that other's culture. It's easy, clean, and invaluable in the struggle for dominance. That struggle is made even easier by essentializing a monolithic and unchanging culture from which the evils of that other always spring. The fact that an essentialized other does not exist is a detail that can be sorted out by the historians. Yet the battle also requires strong denunciation of the essentializing and subordinating culture of that 'other' because the politics of morality and dominance is not played evenly or fairly. Thus, political and legal hermeneutics tend to be treated as officially and institutionally catholic; when we debate we all pretend that groups and culture against which we struggle speak with a unified and singular voice. And all pretend that culture, but not popular culture, exists.

What then of dissent (difference) in this scheme; conduct that does not conform to cultural norms? Tolerance of difference is built into the system. Dissent helps to explain the survival power of our core cultural norms. Our dominant culture operates on a principle of incompetence: the acceptance of the notion that, as popular culture, core norms can never be completely effectuated. As a consequence, popular culture is equipped with the tools needed for the management of its own imperfection. Dissent is the expression of the failure to fully inculcate group norms within a targeted population. Toleration is the name we give to a necessary cultural safety valve; toleration advances political stability and permits social modulation within the parameters of underlying basic social (hetero)sexual conventions. Dissent is tolerated because, like the difference between venial and mortal sin, some cultural taboos are more important than others.

More importantly, social rules do not invariably result in a unitary interpretation of conduct norms, or even core norms. To the extent that ambiguity exists and will not interfere with core social norms, variation will be tolerated. But, beyond variation from interpretive ambiguity and *de minimis* violation of taboo, society will tolerate no deviation without punishment (Case, 1993). Dissent is subversive; it is deviance of a kind that might threaten to substitute an orthodoxy of deviance for that of the current standard. Dissent is guarded, it is analysed, and it is catalogued. Dissent is tolerated to the extent that it is judged not to be dangerous.

The interplay between tolerance and assimilation can occur because of the interpretive potential of our core socio-cultural structural conduct norms. Because these rules do not prescribe an optimal set of behaviours, they allow for a range of possibility within which the group can identify. Arguments for change that compromise culture, though known through the writing of academics and others, as a practical matter are excluded, denied, concealed. This limitation does not necessarily confine the choices we believe are available within the boundaries of dominant culture. We can choose to persecute or ignore gay men and lesbians living outwardly assimilated lives, we can prosecute them, we can concentrate on sexual deviance committed in 'public', we can normalize marriage between people of the same sex and recriminalize fornication. All of this we can do *within* our culture: all have been done and will be done again (Foucault, 1978; Davies, 1983; Brundage, 1987, pp. 521–30; Goldberg, 1992).

On the means to movement; subversive calumny

Popular culture is the antithesis of repose. This is a good thing. It situates the problem as well as the seeds for 'struggle' in the dynamism of cultural norms. Ironically, a cultural voicing of what is 'right', in the sense of socially shared creations (Ortiz, 1993b, p. 1834), is a function of *calumny*, the deliberate game of cultural miscognition that we all play.

The lesson of subversive calumny, of the true nature of image and modulation *within* culture, is its capacity for *irony and indeterminacy*. I introduce my notion of calumny as a subversive device through an analytical prism as pain, power and time. Pain, power and time comprise the core parameters within which cultural sex talk can be used to construct apocryphal images of the sexual *anti-norm*. I accept the Judeo-Christian implications of these parameters. What better and more perverse way to describe the socio-cultural operation of (sex) law than through the exemplar of Christ, or the life of the Hebrew patriarchs. Let's look at each in turn.

Pain

Pain is either endured or those on whom endurance is imposed must seek the revaluation of pain-bringing norms. Think about the hermeneutics of modulation Christologically. Every modulation requires its martyrs and saints, its crucifixion. It may well be that it takes the 'crucifixion' of Michael Hardwick, as recounted in *Bowers*,[2] to produce the normative world of the majority in a case like *Romer*.[3] He is risen! Modulation also requires its Lucifer, its Nero. Think about Jesse Helms in the United States and his crusade against all things 'homosexual' (Stychin, 1996a, pp. 49–51). Saints have been created by our courts. Consider, for example, the military exclusion cases in the United States[4] and Britain.[5] The painful insidiousness of archetype solidifies its object and prepares the way for resistance. Persecution sometimes seems to have a unifying and transformative effect (at least politically) on the persecuted (Bower, 1994, p. 1015). We see its internal political manifestations in the emergence of a visible gay and lesbian identity politics (D'Emilio, 1992). We understand its socio-cultural dimension as revaluation. But revaluation requires a reinterpretation of dominant norms. It does not *require* revolution – the destruction of culture, and the substitution of another. Revaluation is modulation *within* culture; it is interpretation and reinterpretation. It is resistance and rumour (Coombe, 1993, p. 412).

Power

Revaluation through modulation requires alternative narrative. And our culture likes stories, new as well as retold. In this sense, revaluation is *power*; power is evidenced through internalized narrative. '[R]ight, as the world goes, is only a question between equals in power, while the strong do what they can and the weak suffer as they must' (Thucydides, 1951, paragraph 90). That, really, is the central point of this article. A particular result in sodomy jurisprudence is infinitely easier to achieve within the narrative created by the courts; a tightening of the private is possible when the protagonist archetype is disgust. 'Representations ... have an active power; they make things happen, usually by painting the world in such a way that certain policies ... will appear justified. More importantly, perhaps, the very act of painting itself enacts the policy' (Ryan, 1990, p. 1774).

Narrative itself contains the core judgement. The judgement implicit in the way a narrative is constructed requires only a retelling in the particularities of law and legal constraint. How hard is it, after all, to suppress *predator*, *seducer*, *paedophile*, *whore*, *provocateur* (Backer, 1996b). Each archetype carries with it judgement. Modulating image carries with it the possibility of alternative judgement, and even of positive judgement within the broad limits of Western cultural constructs. We have, after all, survived the destruction and reconstruction of the cult of virginity with our cultural core intact. For narrative to modulate there must be stories, problematizing ancient archetypes and the creation of alternative characterizations. That requires the power of voice (McClosky and Zaller, 1984, p. 235) and the will to speak. 'In a world where the presence of power lies increasingly in the realm of the imaginary ... rumor may be understood as cultural guerrilla tactic – "political" in their significance, if not in their self-consciousness' (Coombe, 1993, p. 426).

Voice, then, becomes a prize more important than its underlying consequences. Voice is the measure of power. Those who seek to speak, seek also to exclude, to limit the possibility that archetypes will be redrawn. A significant tool of voice is government. Control of governmental voice is more important than control of norm breakers (Jacobs, 1996, p. 928). We all understand the stakes involved in controlling the machinery of imagery. The holders of power have an inherent advantage through their capacity to control 'not only the actions of those they dominate, but also ... the language through which those subjected comprehend their domination' (Terdiman, 1987, p. 813). Such miscognition is structurally necessary for the reproduction of the social order, which would become intolerably conflicted without it.

Governmental voice is norm setting. *That* has been the great discovery of the twentieth century. Likewise, British *politics* reflects a contest for control of the cultural power of the political machinery. Moran has shown us how the Wolfenden Committee constructed the 'homosexual' it then sought to regulate 'humanely' (Moran, 1995). American politics follows suit (Backer, 1993).

Time

Even the *correct* result, the best expression of culture, can only be a temporary articulation. It can last only so long as we can live and relive our cultural text the same way, that is, as long as we give the same value to that which goes into the translation of cultural rules into enforceable reality. Valuation of cultural imperatives, and the implementation of these imperatives, constantly change. The ideological dream of permanent revaluation and the attainment of stasis is a false dream, made more dangerous by the consequences of change. Certainly, this is the lesson traditionalists have learned over the course of the last 50 years as our popular culture has begun to revalue the nature and importance of sexual and gender roles, and that revaluation has permeated legislatures and courts. And this is the positive moral of this chapter. It is not just sexual nonconformists who face challenges to normalization within popular culture; sexual traditionalists have begun facing the same challenges. Traditionalists are far stronger, but the monopoly of imagery that they had, the monopoly that was taken for granted, has been lost. The contest for voice which has resulted is as much an indication of the challenges facing sexual nonconformists to normalize as it is an indication that dominant culture may no longer reflect popular culture.

Inconstancy and modulation

I want to emphasize a dilemma inherent in the critical realism of subversive calumny. The *possibility* of modulation does not imply any notion of permanency. Ironically, the impermanence of social or value changes in society brings me back to what I had started the chapter by trashing: revolutionspeak. I want to explore here the relationship between cultural impermanence and the possible utility of revolutionspeak as a tool of calumny.

To the myth of revolution and cultural repose I have posited modulation and revaluation as the tools of law- (and culture-) 'making' in our society. In the story-making of the courts, such modulation and revaluation require conformity and assimilation. A mountain of stories resonate within and between judicial and popular culture. The power of these stories is strengthened by their monopoly. It is maintained by the ability of the images themselves to silence sexual nonconformists. 'The images undermine their credibility whenever they are allowed to enter the dialogue' (Sears, 1995, p. 337). This is the *curse* of narrative, its judgement, its calumny.

But calumny and its judgement must be used as its own *blessing*. Calumny, as deconstructive hermeneutics, is the real instrument for the modulation of images, for problematizing ancient archetypes. That exercise requires the power of voice – and a sustained will to speak. For speech carries judgement within it. Voice is *law*, we pronounce it every day the way courts pronounce judgment in a more formal setting. Law is judgment imbedded in the stories litigants tell society, it is imbedded in stories courts tell as jurisprudence. Law is also imbedded in statute – the quite coercive stories legislatures tell society.

Within the power of story-telling is the power of voice. Voice is the real power of *law*. 'The role of the law in constituting persons by providing a forum for their conflicts over *who they shall be understood to be* is deeply material, even though it involves not physical force but the more subtle dynamics of representation' (Halley, 1993, p. 1729). Yet what courts listen to is what they want to hear, and what they want to hear is norm affirming. This requires placing the subject within an acceptable continuum of referents (Backer, 1996b). This is precisely what courts do when attempting either to control or 'liberate' sexual deviants. Either way, judicial decisions tend to be norm affirming; theirs is ultimately a political act (Backer, 1997). This is also what we do by other norm-affirming political and legal agendas. The most obvious of these is 'same-sex marriage'. There is much truth to Ettelbrick's arguments that a 'lesbigay' agenda stressing same-sex marriage has as its end the inevitable domestication of these groups (Ettelbrick, 1989). Yet, I would argue that this domestication is culturally inevitable, at least now, and at least for the moment.

But this does not mean that there is no place for a politics based on transformative aspirations. My sense is that while *revolution* is ultimately futile, a *politics of revolution* may not be. In reality, all social groups in our society engage in just such a politics. The ultimate benefit of this politics of revolution is not the attainment of the transformation that lies at the rhetorical heart of such politics, but the *power* of this politics to open up the assimilative potential of our culture socially, judicially and legislatively. 'The crucial point . . . is that discipline escapes the world of law and right – and then begins to colonize that world, replacing legal principles with principles of physical, psychological and moral normality'.

But here is precisely where the rhetoric of transformation may well have its place; as a goad (Lobel, 1995, p. 1333). The fact that discourse can be naturalized, that language is malleable, is strictly negative only if one fails to understand its positive potential. The same way in which language can be used to naturalize one particular form of linguistic hegemony, it can be used to legitimate any other. The process is both hopeful, and terrifying (Curran, 1994, p. 30). Hegemonic naturalization, after all, becomes 'bad' only when the group which you inhabit (or to which you are sympathetic) does not share in the hegemony. And then the question is not so much to abdicate hegemony, but to redefine it to include those you believe need not be excluded (that is, whose inclusion will not critically affect the hegemonic structure). I view positively a statement meant to disparage: 'Despite the American insistence that advocacy and adversariness promote truth, in reality they advance only salesmanship' (Quinn, 1995, p. 579).

On the incarnate word

When used negatively, storytelling is called calumny. My point is that it is used all the time. We unconsciously understand the painfulness and indeterminacy of narrative. We understand its power. We internalize its comedy and seriousness, and even give it divine inspiration. Christianity has recognized and celebrated the divinity of logos from the first; the *incarnate word* is pregnant with meaning. More importantly, we indulge our lust for its use for our own purposes. Those with a taste for the imposition of social ordering understand the rules of construction and reconstruction of image, especially through law. We know how it can be used negatively, as calumny, to more easily, more *naturally*, vilify sexual nonconformists, to quite literally run them out of town. With equal naturalness, calumny can be used to positive effect by those on whom it has been turned. Ultimately, the end is the word, and the word is with calumny, and the word is calumny – a judgemental narrative is our portion; revolution is our myth.

The consequence of my analysis of revolutionary transformation is an unhappy one, both for traditionalists hoping to hold on to that which is being lost, and for those who work for the change which may be coming.

There is no such thing as revolution or repose in these matters. There is no fruit from a divinely crafted tree that one can ingest, no revelation awaiting at Mount Sinai, no trumpet-blowing angels heralding the immediate coming of a new age, an age that will transform *law as system*, much less the popular culture that sustains it. The utopianism of modern critical theory, in this sense, exhibits a disconcerting modernist pretension. I question any presumption that we can control where our theorizing might go or what it might do (if, indeed, it 'goes' anywhere at all). Believing that our theorizing (or anything else we do) can revolutionize the world is modernist hubris. And so the great socio-cultural game continues, an endless dialectic of cynicism, hope and change in which law is *involved*, but in which jurisprudence, other than as apologia, is *excluded*.

Notes

1. I use the term heterosexualism in this chapter to denote a system in which cultural preference is given to the sexual proclivities of the majority of people. This definition (deliberately) does not imply consequences either for the social and political position of those who indulge in majority sexual conduct (men and women), nor does it invariably suggest the nature of the relationships between sexual majorities and minorities (Rich, 1980, pp. 637–40; Valdes, 1995, pp. 261–5).
2. *Bowers* v. *Hardwick*, 478 U.S. 186 (1986).
3. *Romer* v. *Evans*, 64 U.S.L.W. 4353 (20 May 1996) (State Constitutional provision preventing state and local governments from enacting legislation designed to protect the status of certain sexual minorities violated the federal constitution's Equal Protection Clause).
4. See for example *Meinhold* v. *U.S. Dept of Defense*, 34 F.3d 1469 (9th Cir. 1994); *Steffan* v. *Aspin*, 8 F.3d 57 (D.C. Cir. 1993), *rev'd en banc* 41 F.3d 677 (D.C. Cir. 1994); *Able* v. *U.S.*, 880 F.Supp. 968 (E.D.N.Y. 1995). For a discussion, see for example Stiehm (1992).
5. See *R.* v. *Ministry of Defence ex parte Smith*, [1996] 1 All England Reports 257. The appeal of administrative dismissal of three gays and one lesbian from the British military was dismissed. The facts present a very sympathetic picture of the people seeking reinstatement. Interestingly enough, the British military cases may now be captives of *European* norms. See 'Gay Dismissal Claim Adjourned', *Guardian*, 20 August 1996, p. 4 (Home Page) (noting that the litigants in several dismissal cases were seeking to have their cases referred to the European Court of Justice on the grounds that their dismissals violated the European Union's equal treatment rules). Ironically, the British House of Commons has only recently voted against an amendment to the Armed Forces Bill which would have lifted the ban on homosexuals in the military. See 'Hounded and Out', *Guardian* 13 May 1996, p. 14 (Features).

References

Arendt, H. (1958) *The Human Condition*. Chicago: Chicago University Press.

Backer, L. C. (1993) 'Exposing the perversions of toleration: the decriminalization of private sexual conduct, the Model Penal Code, and the oxymoron of liberal toleration', *University of Florida Law Review*, **45**, 755.

Backer, L. C. (1996a) 'By hook or by crook: the drive to conformity and assimilation in liberal and conservative poor relief theory', *Hastings Women's Law Journal*, **7**, 391.

Backer, L. C. (1996b) 'Essay: poor relief, welfare paralysis and assimilation', *Utah Law Review*, **1996**, 1.

Backer, L. C. (1997) *Inscribing Judicial Preferences into Our Basic Law: The European Court of Human Rights and the Project of Constitutional Interpretation in the Service of the Status Quo* (manuscript).

Becker, G. S. (1983) 'A theory of competition among pressure groups for political influence', *Quarterly Journal of Economics*, **98**, 371.

Bower, L. C. (1994) 'Queer acts and the politics of "direct address": rethinking law, culture and community', *Law and Society Review*, **28**, 1009.

Brown, W. (1996) 'In the "folds of our own discourse": the pleasures and freedoms of silence', *University of Chicago Law School Roundtable*, **3**, 185.

Brundage, J. A. (1987) *Law, Sex and Christian Society in Medieval Europe*. Chicago: Chicago University Press.

Butler, J. (1991) 'Imitation and gender insubordination', in D. Fuss (ed.), *Inside/Out: Lesbian Theories, Gay Theories*. London: Routledge.

Case, M. A. (1993) 'Couples and coupling in the public sphere: a comment on the legal history of litigating for lesbian and gay rights', *Vanderbilt Law Review*, **79**, 1643.

Coombe, R. J. (1993) 'Tactics of appropriation and the politics of recognition in late modern democracies', *Political Theory*, **21**, 411.

Curran, V. G. (1994) 'Deconstruction, structuralism, antisemitism and the law', *Boston College Law Review*, **36**, 1.

Davies, C. (1983) 'Religious boundaries and sexual morality', *Annual Review Social Science of Religion*, **6**, 45 (Fall).

Delgado, R. and Stefancic, J. (1993) 'Critical race theory: annotated bibliography', *Vanderbilt Law Review*, **79** , 461.

D'Emilio, J. (1992) *Making Trouble: Essays on Gay History, Politics and the University*. New York and London: Routledge.

Devlin, P. (1988) *The Enforcement of Morals*, in *Morality and the Law* (ed. R. M. Baird and S. E. Rosenbaum) (reprinted in edited form from Patrick Devlin, *The Enforcement of Morals* (1965)).

Eaton, M. (1994) 'Lesbians, gays and the struggle for equality rights: reversing the progressive hypothesis', *Dalhousie Law Journal*, **17**, 130.

Eskridge, W. N. Jr. (1994) 'Gaylegal narratives', *Stanford Law Review*, **46**, 607.

Ettelbrick, P. L. (1989) 'Since when is marriage a path to liberation?', *OUT/LOOK, National Gay and Lesbian Quarterly*, **6** (Fall).

Farber, D. A. and Sherry, S. (1995) 'Is the radical critique of merit anti-Semitic?', *California Law Review*, **83**, 853.

Feldman, S. M. (1996a) 'From modernism to postmodernism in American legal thought: the significance of the Warren Court', in B. Schwartz (ed.), *The Warren Court: A Retrospective*. New York: Oxford University Press.

Feldman, S. M. (1996b) 'The politics of postmodern jurisprudence', *Michigan Law Review*, **95**, 166.

Fish, S. (1980) 'Is there a text in this class?', in *Is There a Text in this Class?* Cambridge, MA: Harvard University Press.

Fish, S. (1984–5) 'Consequences', *Critical Inquiry*, **11**, 433.

Foucault, M. (1978) *The History of Sexuality*, Vol. 1, trans. R. Hurley. London: Allen Lane.

Foucault, M. (1980) 'Truth and power', in *Power/Knowledge: Selected Interviews and Other Writings*, ed. and trans. C. Gordon. Brighton: Harvester Wheatsheaf.

Fuss, D. (1991) 'Inside/out', in D. Fuss (ed.), *Inside/Out: Lesbian Theories, Gay Theories*. London: Routledge.

Gadamer, H. G. (1989) *Truth and Method*, trans. J. Weinsheimer and D. Marshall, 2d rev. edn. London: Sheed and Ward.

Goldberg, J. (1992) *Sodometries: Renaissance Texts, Modern Sexualities*. Stanford: Stanford University Press.

Halley, J. E. (1993) 'Reasoning about sodomy: act and identity in ad after Bowers v. Hardwick', *Vanderbilt Law Review*, **79**, 1721.

Halperin, D. M. (1990) *One Hundred Years of Homosexuality and Other Essays on Greek Love*. London: Routledge.

Harris, A. P. (1996) 'Forward: the unbearable lightness of identity', *Berkeley Women's Law Journal*, **11**, 207.

Henriksson, B. (1995) *Risk Factor Love: Homosexuality, Sexual Interaction and HIV Prevention*. Goteborg University, Dept. of Social Work, Goteborg, Sweden.

Ikemoto, L. C. (1993) 'Traces of the master narrative in the story of the African American/Korean American conflict: how we constructed "Los Angeles" ', *Southern California Law Review*, **66**, 1581.

Jacobs, A. M. (1996) 'Romer wasn't built in a day: the subtle transformation in judicial argument over gay rights', *Wisconsin Law Review*, **1996**, 893.

ibn Khaldun, Abd-ar-Rahman (1967) *The Muqaddimah: An Introduction to History*, trans. Franz Rosenthal. Princeton, NJ: Princeton University Press.

Koestler, A. (1941) *Darkness at Noon*, trans. D. Hardy. London: Cape.

Lobel, J. (1995) 'Losers, fools & prophets: justice as struggle', *Cornell Law Review*, **80**, 1331.

McClosky, H. and Zaller, J. (1984) *The American Ethos*. Cambridge, MA: Harvard University Press.

Marmor, J. (1971) ' "Normal" and "deviant" sexual behavior', *Journal of American Medical Association*, **217** (2), (12 July) 165.

Moran, L. J. (1995) 'The homosexualization of English law', in D. Herman and C. Stychin (eds), *Legal Inversions: Lesbians, Gay Men, and the Politics of Law*. Philadelphia: Temple University Press.

Ortiz, D. R. (1993a) 'Correspondence: saving the self?', *Michigan Law Review*, **91**, 1018.

Ortiz, D. R. (1993b) 'Creating controversy: essentialism and constructivism and the politics of gay identity', *Vanderbilt Law Review*, **79**, 1833.

Quinn, J. R. (1995) 'The lost language of the Irishgaymale: textualization in Ireland's law and literature (or the most hidden Ireland)', *Columbia Human Rights Law Review*, **26**, 553.

Rich, A. (1980) 'Compulsory heterosexuality and lesbian existence', *Signs*, **5**, 631.

Rosenblum, D. (1994) 'Queer intersectionality and the failure of recent lesbian and gay "victories" ', *Law & Sexuality*, **4**, 83.

Ryan, M. (1990) 'Social violence and political representation', *Vanderbilt Law Review*, **43**, 1771.

Schlag, P. (1996) 'This could be your culture – junk speech in a time of decadence', *Harvard Law Review*, **109**, 1801.

Sears, B. (1995) 'Rounding out the table: opening and impoverished poverty discourse to community voices', *Harvard Civil Rights and Civil Liberties Law Review*, **30**, 299.

Spann, G. A. (1995) *Race Against the Court: The Supreme Court and Minorities in Contemporary America*. New York: New York University Press.

Stiehm, J. H. (1992) 'Managing the military's exclusion policy: text and subtext', *University of Miami Law Review*, **46**, 685.

Stychin, C. F. (1996a) *Law's Desire: Sexuality and the Limits of Justice*. London: Routledge.

Stychin, C. F. (1996b) 'To take him "at his word": theorizing law, sexuality and the US military exclusion policy', *Social & Legal Studies*, **5**, 179.

Terdiman, R. (1987) 'Translator's introduction', *Hastings Law Journal*, **38**, 805.

Teubner, G. (1993) *Law as an Autopoietic System*. Oxford: Blackwell.

Thucydides (1951) *The Peloponnesian War* (411 BC), trans. Crowley. New York: Random House.

Valdes, F. (1995) 'Queers, sissies, dykes and tomboys: deconstructing the conflation of "sex," "gender," and "sexual orientation" in Euro-American law and society', *California Law Review*, **83**, 1.